Praise for Buck Owens

"It's hard to imagine what country music would have been like without Buck Owens. From 'Act Naturally' and 'I've Got a Tiger by the Tail' to 'Streets of Bakersfield,' Buck helped set the standards and pave the way in an industry that has been very good to many of us."

—*George Strait*

"In countless interviews over the years people have asked me to define country music. I just tell them to listen to Buck Owens and the Buckaroos doing 'Second Fiddle.' After all, a shuffle is worth a thousand words—and you can dance to it."

—*Emmylou Harris*

"Buck Owens was a stylist. His sounds have been copied for years. He was one of our best in country music."

—*George Jones*

"I don't know that Buck Owens knew how hip what he was doing was, even at the moment. It was that hip. But the players knew."

—*Dwight Yoakam*

"We took kind of the Buck Owens approach on *Workingman's Dead*. Some of the songs in there are direct tributes to that style of music, although they're not real obvious. And Don Rich's attitude was always so cool. His fiddle playing was great, too. He was one of those guys who just sounded good on anything he picked up."

—*Jerry Garcia*

"If somebody asked me to describe country music at its best, I would point them to the early records of Buck Owens."

—*Vince Gill*

"I think that alongside Fred and Ginger, Lennon and McCartney, Abbott and Costello, Lester and Earl, Elvis and Marilyn, they should clear off a place for Buck and Don because they, too, were a classic duo."

—*Marty Stuart*

"He was a great guy, just down to earth. I know he had money and fame and that voice that cut through barrooms and crummy car radios like no one else, but when we hung with him he seemed just like the guy I imagined all those years before when I first heard his records. He was one of us."

—*Chris Isaak*

"Buck Owens—rockin' big beat guitar and a big country smile."

—*John Fogerty*

"The Beatles were among his most ardent fans. Anytime Buck put out an album, we'd have to send it to the Beatles."

—*Ken Nelson, Capitol Records*

"Buck Owens, more than any other country artist of his time, brought the bandstand into the production of his records. The songwriting is very direct and poetic in its simplicity. The creative spark between Buck and Don Rich personifies what we call chemistry."

—*Rodney Crowell*

"Buck deserves to be remembered as one of the most important artists in all of music history."

—*Brad Paisley*

Buck 'Em!

Buck 'Em!

The Autobiography of Buck Owens

with
RANDY POE

Backbeat
Books

An Imprint of Hal Leonard Corporation

Published in 2013 by Backbeat Books
An Imprint of Hal Leonard Corporation
7777 West Bluemound Road
Milwaukee, WI 53213

Trade Book Division Editorial Offices
33 Plymouth St., Montclair, NJ 07042

Photos of Buck Owens on tour (insert two) appear courtesy of Rolene Brumley. Photo of Owens on the set of *Hee Haw* (insert three) appears courtesy of Gaylord Productions. All other photos are from the Buck Owens Private Foundation.

Printed in the United States of America

Library of Congress Cataloging-in-Publication Data
Owens, Buck, 1929-2006, author.
Buck 'em! : the autobiography of Buck Owens / with Randy Poe.
    pages cm
  Includes bibliographical references and index.
  ISBN 978-1-4803-3064-1
1. Owens, Buck, 1929-2006.   2. Country musicians–United States–Biography.
I. Poe, Randy, 1955– II. Title.
ML420.O945A3 2013
782.421642092–dc23
[B]

2013035097

www.backbeatbooks.com

"We worked eleven hours straight, six nights a week—now listen to this—with no intermission. You heard me right. *No* intermission. The music never stopped."

—*Buck Owens*

Contents

Foreword

IN A TIME WHEN COUNTRY AIRWAVES were awash in cosmopolitan string sections and large choral arrangements, a pair of silver sparkle Telecasters pierced through the foggy landscape like the high beams on a Cadillac. A crying pedal steel howled like a coyote. A drummer pounded away at a freight-train beat. And the artist behind this honky-tonk rebellion would go on to be one of the biggest stars in country music history.

Buck Owens was a great many things all at once: equal parts ace guitarist, television star, bandleader, businessman, and radio visionary, he would defy the classic "jack of all trades, master of none" saying and become master of everything he attempted—fascinating in his ability to always give people just what they were looking for, simply by being himself.

He would change the way country records were mixed, produced, written, and perceived. He would inspire everyone from ordinary everyday music fans to the Beatles. He would go on to play iconic shows at the White House and Carnegie Hall.

In the way that Chet Atkins crafted the Nashville Sound, Bill Monroe pioneered Kentucky Bluegrass, and Bob Wills was synonymous with Texas Swing, Buck Owens was destined to hold the deed to a dusty old California oil town that was the yin to Nashville's yang.

To this day it still baffles me that the "twangiest," "honky-tonkinest," "countryest" music made in the '60s was not made anywhere near Nashville, but in California by a Texan, actually. Buck Owens and his trusty Telecaster sidekick Don Rich would come to epitomize the Bakersfield

Sound, and change music forever—like some hillbilly Lone Ranger and Tonto out to restore justice and twang.

But there is so much more to Buck Owens than just this rhinestone-clad musical icon. He was a complicated guy, with intense dedication to his art and a tireless work ethic. He was a father, a husband (a few times, actually), and a truly loyal friend. He would outwit the record companies, invent a unique sound, and mentor countless younger artists like myself, Dwight Yoakam, and Garth Brooks. He not only perfected the honky-tonk Bakersfield Sound, he also built his very own state-of-the-art honky-tonk Crystal Palace, smack-dab in the middle of Bakersfield itself. And it was there that he would play out his twilight years with his fans coming to see him play his music in his hometown, instead of the other way around.

I thank God I got to know Buck Owens. From my earliest musical memory, which is "Tiger by the Tail" on my Papaw's turntable, to Saturday nights watching *Hee Haw*, I was a disciple. And getting to know the man behind the legend did not detract from the legend at all. He was a true inspiration. As you read this book, I hope you will get a similar feeling from getting acquainted with one of the twentieth century's most fascinating musical figures.

I miss Buck Owens. But his music and his story live on.

Brad Paisley

Preface

T O SAY THAT BUCK OWENS was a singularly unique figure in country music history would be light years beyond cliché. There have been four, maybe five, other artists in the history of the entire genre who have left as indelible a sonic imprint on so many millions of listeners' ears.

In addition, he and his band exploded *visually* onto the collective cultural scene. With a look of jet-age, honky-tonk hipness born from a fearless outsider's perspective, Buck responded to authority and convention with a steely-eyed hard shove back.

Yet there was still the necessary romantic innocence in Buck's longing drive to overcome the odds against any dream held—to somehow escape the doom of oppressively extreme existence that faced a red-dirt sharecropper's child almost from birth, during the Dust Bowl years of the Great Depression. He not only survived the daunting struggle of those meager beginnings to change his own life, he also went on to change the lives of almost every person who ever came into contact with him.

The last conversation I had with Buck was a three-and-a-half-hour marathon phone call on the Tuesday before he passed. It had nothing to do with the end of anything, but rather (ironically, given where you're reading this) it was about the future, and his plans to finally finish writing and publishing his memoirs. I had, in fact, made some calls to a literary agent I had been represented by in New York some years earlier, after a previous conversation with Buck about his planned autobiography. I had asked the agent to explore what interest the leading book publishers in New York might have in Buck's story, and I was happily relaying the resulting interest, which the agent had said was overwhelmingly enormous. Sadly, Buck wouldn't have the chance to see that last professional dream come to fruition.

What I didn't fully realize that day was the sheer volume of detailed recalling, in both longhand writing and recorded oration, Buck had already done. Though not yet having a completed structure or formal presentation, within that enormous tome of raw material was Buck's full life story, told in his own voice.

The stream of stories throughout this book captures, with an uncanny accuracy, the way I heard Buck speak whenever he told a story to someone—which is a large compliment to Randy Poe, who, from what I understand, had a mountain of audiotapes and handwritten pages to comb through, transcribe, edit, and present for us to read as Buck's own view of his life.

* * *

One time, in 1996, I was up visiting Buck, getting ready to perform with him at an event in Bakersfield. Usually, after not seeing each other for a period of time, Buck would tell me that he had been thinking about what I had done musically on my latest album, or he would offer advice on how I could maximize opportunities he thought I might be overlooking.

On this particular day, as we sat in an RV that acted as the backstage dressing area, Buck looked at me with an amused expression—as if he had finally sorted something perplexing out—and said, "Dwight, do you know what an anomaly is?"

Now Buck was acutely aware that, just like him, I was always somewhat suspect of where any given interaction in the entertainment business was really leading. I saw him smile slyly as the left-field nature of his question landed on me. It interrupted my usual untethered, ongoing stream of random thoughts, causing me to wonder where this odd breadcrumb trail might be heading.

I paused—looked across the motor home toward his always steady, present-tense bearing—and said, "Well I guess I could use it correctly in a sentence, if that's what you mean."

"No," he said laughing. "I mean its actual definition."

"Nah," I said. "If you're asking me for a precise, word-for-word reading of it from Webster's or the *Oxford English Dictionary*, I reckon not."

Becoming more excited and animated now that he had lured me in, Buck said, "Well, Dwight, an anomaly is a number that just keeps showing up inexplicably."

Then, with my complete bemused attention, he let the other shoe drop, saying, "I finally figured it out! That's what you are—an ANOMALY!"

"Yeah," I said, "I guess that's as close to right as any explanation for the 'what' or 'why' of me—and maybe you, too, now that I think about it. In fact, that is absolutely the explanation for the 'what' and 'why' of you. You're a big ol' anomaly, Buck!"

He reared back and bellowed with exasperation, "What!? Nooo! Not me! That's what *you* are. You're an anomaly, son."

"Okay," I said, as I grinned at him. "Okay, guilty as accused."

Still, if there ever was a clear example of an anomaly—something that "deviates from what is standard, normal, or expected" (which is the actual word-for-word definition of the term)—as far as country music is concerned, an anomaly surely did arrive in the form of Alvis Edgar "Buck" Owens Jr.

* * *

The simple honesty of Buck's own words recalling various stages of what became a spectacular journey—from its epiphanic prologue and stoically stated first chapter and throughout this entire chronicling of his life—draws back into sharp focus what was, I believe, the most profoundly powerful element of his personality and presence from the day we first met: his enormously charismatic directness. With Buck there was never, to quote the Yardbirds, any "Over Under Sideways Down" approach to anything. It was always straight ahead. As I grew to know him over the ensuing years, I learned to trust that innate quality in Buck's nature thoroughly, and I came to rely on it deeply at various times during our twenty-one years of friendship.

Buck's genius lay in his stellar gift for succinctness and simplicity. The artist he became and the musical sound he gave the world, indeed, was and is—simply fantastic!

Dwight Yoakam

Introduction

I F ALL OF THE NOVELISTS, screenwriters, playwrights, and poets in the world were given an infinite amount of time to convene in an effort to construct the best possible name for a country star, they would never come up with one so perfect as "Buck Owens."

That name—so simple—is the polar opposite of the man who bore it. On the surface, Buck seemed to practically glide through life—singing, writing songs, playing guitar, appearing on television, forming businesses, acquiring radio stations, and creating a country music empire in Bakersfield, California, that rivaled pretty much anything Nashville had to offer. The magic of Buck's brilliance was his ability to make it all look so effortless—though no one in the field of country music ever worked harder than Buck Owens.

As was the case with so many who experienced both the Depression and the Dust Bowl, his was a life that began in hardship. From the time he was a child, Buck worked at numerous jobs to literally help put food on the table. That work ethic carried over into every aspect of his life and career—a major factor in his later success.

Filled with ambition, drive, and determination, Buck decided early on, as he says in these pages, "to be somebody." It was a course of action from which he never wavered, and it was a course of action that led to many of the highs and lows not only in his life, but also in the lives of those around him.

Decades of almost nonstop personal appearances provided him with the adulation he craved as an artist, as well as the financial well-being that guaranteed those days when pieces of old linoleum were used to repair the holes in his shoes would never come again. But that constant workload also kept him away from a family in need of a more dedicated husband and father.

There are those who have claimed that Buck was emotionally remote. If he were still here to be able to discuss the matter, he might very well argue that the fact he had several wives proves just the opposite! On the other hand, he might simply say, "Mind your own damn business."

Buck was an extremely strong personality. Some remember him as being unduly harsh. Others say he was deeply caring. Sometimes it depended on the person. Sometimes it just depended on the day.

As with any man, it would be folly to presume that Buck Owens could ever be a model of perfection. But it is just as absurd to claim, as some have, that he was some sort of fatally flawed character. More than anything, Buck Owens was a driven man—one who created an incredible body of work that seems to defy both logic and possibility in terms of scope, ambition, and quality. In a life that spanned seventy-six years, he recorded more than sixty albums and scored an amazing twenty-one number one country singles—all but one of those between the years 1963 and 1972.

By the time his first number one hit, "Act Naturally," started climbing the charts, Buck had already created an exciting new kind of country music, which, due to his base of operations, many began calling the Bakersfield Sound. The dominant elements consisted of strong lead vocals, high harmonies, a Telecaster guitar or two, a driving drum beat on the up-tempo numbers (or a crying steel guitar on the ballads), and an intentionally trebly mix that made a Buck Owens record practically leap out of a car radio's speakers. "Act Naturally" was one of those up-tempo numbers, and Buck's record resonated so loudly that it prompted the Beatles—the biggest rock & roll band in the world—to record the song as well.

To put all of this in its proper perspective, at the height of their fame, Buck Owens and the Buckaroos—a collection of monumentally talented musicians fronted by lead guitarist Don Rich—were the five-man country music equivalent of the Fab Four. Buck and his band weren't just great musicians; they were *personalities*. The fans knew every Buckaroo by name: "Dangerous" Don Rich, "Dashing" Doyle Holly, "Tender" Tom Brumley, and "Wonderful" Willie Cantu—each member having an honorific adjective added to his name by the always market-savvy Buck.

Throughout the 1960s, Buck's records sold in the millions and his live concerts were constant sell-outs—a phrase that took on a much less flattering connotation as the end of the decade neared.

In 1969, Buck became cohost of the country comedy television show *Hee Haw.* The mere name itself seemed to poke fun at the very music and fan base Buck had worked so hard to create. The upside was that it made Buck Owens a household name practically overnight. Millions of television viewers who had never heard a Buck Owens record in their lives suddenly knew both his name and his sound.

The downside was that Buck—wearing his overalls backwards and playing straight man to Roy Clark and his cornpone punch lines—found it nearly impossible to retain his stature as the biggest country star in the world. It was as if John Lennon—even while the Beatles were making the most critically acclaimed recordings of their generation—had suddenly decided to take a side job playing the Cockney cohost of a BBC variety show. Almost as soon as Buck became a television star, his record sales began to drop.

In the mid-1970s, Capitol Records—the label for which Buck had provided those twenty number one hits—released him from his contract. Buck's career wasn't over, though—not by a long shot, although at the time the damage to his image appeared permanent. Critics and journalists of varying repute seemed to almost take glee in Buck's departure from the lofty heights of the country charts. He had long ago reached the top of the mountain, and now that his footing was on shaky ground there were more than a few who seemed all too eager to watch him fall.

Not that Buck hadn't brought plenty of his problems on himself. As he readily admitted, even as the corny comedy bits began encroaching upon the time originally allotted to the show's musical segments, the paycheck from *Hee Haw* was simply too tempting to turn down.

And then there was Nashville. Throughout Buck's career he fought Music City's attitude that "real" country stars had to live in Nashville, record in Nashville, use Nashville record producers, work with Nashville studio musicians, and sign with a Nashville music publisher.

Having his home base in Bakersfield, forming his own music publishing company, using his own band on his recordings, and ultimately having his own recording studio and producing his own records made Buck an outcast in the eyes of the Nashville music establishment. The fact that he had become country music's biggest star while breaking all of Nashville's rules only made matters worse.

Although he counted many Nashville-based artists among his friends, others there were jealous of his independence—and even more so of his entrepreneurship. While the typical country songwriter was signing with a Nashville-based publishing company, Buck was assigning the songs he wrote to his own publishing company (as he did those of Merle Haggard and many other California-based songwriters). While other country artists were willing to sign indentured-servitude-style seven-album deals with major labels, Buck was negotiating a deal requiring Capitol Records to give all of his masters *back*. Where a Nashville artist might have kept himself busy acquiring a fancy new bass boat, Buck was out shopping for radio stations. His ability to be both a creative artist and an astute businessman was nothing less than offensive to those in Nashville who felt that the twain should never meet. And the price he paid for doing things his own way resulted in the substantial delay of his induction into the Country Music Hall of Fame.

No matter where he ultimately ranks among the giants of country music, this much is most certainly true: Buck Owens was his own man. He was a proud American; he was a great musician; he was profoundly prolific, both as a songwriter and as a recording artist; he was a brilliant businessman; and he chose to follow his own path. During his lifetime, his friends, family, bandmates, and fans were the ones that mattered most to him. As for those who didn't care for his music, his lifestyle, his personality, or his decision to live out his dreams and career in Bakersfield, California, rather than Nashville, Tennessee, his response would be (or perhaps rhyme with) the title of his autobiography—*Buck 'Em!*

Randy Poe

Background

B UCK OWENS BEGAN WORKING on his autobiography in the latter half of the 1990s. Over the next few years, he talked into the microphone of a cassette tape machine for nearly one hundred hours, recording the story of his life. His final cassette entry took place in September of 2000.

Buck's original plan had been to eventually bring in a professional writer to work with the tapes, and with him in person, to create an official Buck Owens autobiography. Due to a number of issues, predominantly Buck's declining health over the last six years of his life, the book project never got beyond Buck's tapes.

Not long after the release of my book *Skydog: The Duane Allman Story*, I went to Bakersfield to meet with Buck's son Michael, his nephew Mel, and Jim Shaw—a longtime member of the Buckaroos who Buck referred to on one of his cassette tapes as "one of my very best friends, right up there with Don Rich."

The reason for the meeting with Michael, Mel, and Jim was to discuss the possibility of me writing Buck's authorized biography. However, when Jim took me into Buck's office and showed me the dozens of cassette tapes Owens had recorded, my "authorized biography" idea quickly turned into a totally different concept: to create Buck's *auto*biography, using his own words from his cassette recordings, just as he had originally intended.

To say there were some unexpected hurdles in putting this book together would be a vast understatement. First and foremost, Buck Owens could never be accused of thinking in a linear fashion. In other words, the first cassette tape didn't start with the story of his birth. That would come on Tape Twenty-One. The description of his famous 1966 Carnegie Hall concert was on Tape Twelve. He talked of his days on the TV show *Hee Haw*—which postdated the Carnegie Hall concert by three years—on Tape Five. No jigsaw puzzle ever created could hold a candle to the task of chronologically piecing together Buck's life story from his cassette tapes.

Incredibly, despite the seemingly random method in which Buck chose to relate the story of his life, there were very few pieces missing from the puzzle. In those cases where he failed to cover what I considered important ground, quotes were taken from various primarily unpublished interviews conducted around the same time Buck was recording his cassettes.

I will remain forever amazed by Buck's extraordinary memory—there are moments on the tapes where he describes long stretches on the road, naming specific venues that were played on specific nights. On one of my many subsequent trips to Bakersfield, while digging through boxes that had been in storage since the 1970s, I came across a ledger book listing every show Buck had played from 1962 to 1965. In every single case, Buck had remembered the cities, the venues, the years, and the days of the week correctly.

The writing I contributed to Buck's autobiography was minimal. In some instances, connective sentences were added for the sake of continuity. Also, throughout the text I infrequently corrected Buck's grammar. In the end, with only a handful of exceptions, the words in this book prior to the afterword are those of Buck Owens himself, telling the story of his incredible journey—from the back roads of rural Texas to the streets of Bakersfield.

Prologue

The Buck Owens Sound

I GOT SIGNED TO CAPITOL RECORDS IN 1957. By that time, I'd been playing in bars and honky-tonks for over a decade. When I signed that contract with Capitol, I thought, "Man, this is it! After all these years workin' my ass off in all those dark, smoky clubs and taverns, I've finally got it made." Well, it didn't take very long for me to find out just how wrong I was.

Things got off to a really bad start because my first few singles didn't even hit the *bottom* of the charts. On those early records, the producer had insisted on including all these damn background vocals—lots of guys and gals singing "oohs" and "aahs" under my stone country vocals. It sounded ridiculous. As a matter of fact, those singles came out sounding a whole lot like the kind of stuff they were recording in Nashville back in those days—and the last thing I wanted was for my records to sound like those pop-country things they were doing down there.

The next time I went into the studio, the producer let me do things my own way, which turned out to be a pretty good idea since we ended up having a little success with a song I wrote called "Second Fiddle." The record came and went pretty fast, but it made it to No. 24 on the charts—high enough for Capitol to want me to keep recording for 'em.

At the next session, I cut a song called "Under Your Spell Again." We had a Top Five hit with that one, and all of a sudden things were starting to look pretty good for ol' Buck.

When "Under Your Spell Again" hit the charts, I was living up around Tacoma, Washington. After those early singles had flopped, I'd left Bakersfield and gone up there to work at a radio station, and to play in a band with a fellow by the name of Dusty Rhodes. A few months after I moved to Washington, Dusty found the band a teenaged fiddle player named Donald Eugene Ulrich. Since nobody knew how to pronounce his last name right, I did him a favor and changed his name to Don Rich.

While "Under Your Spell Again" was still going strong, I got a call from Capitol to hurry up and come down and make another record. It was just before Christmas of 1959. I decided to take Don to the studio to play fiddle for me on the four songs I planned to cut.

Dusty Rhodes didn't play on my records, but he'd co-written one of the songs I was going to be doing on the session, so he volunteered to drive me and Don to Los Angeles in his '57 Cadillac.

It's over a thousand miles from Tacoma to LA, so we were doing anything we could to keep from being bored out of our minds. At some point after we'd crossed into California, I started singing "Above and Beyond"—one of the songs we were going to record. As I was singing the song, Dusty said, "Hey, Don, why don't you sing along with him?"

So there we were—riding along in this big ol' Cadillac—with me in the front seat playing the guitar, Don sitting in the back seat, and Dusty driving. I started to sing the song again, and Don started singing right along with me. I couldn't believe my ears. Our voices blended and matched perfectly. Somehow, he knew exactly the way I was going to sing every word. He came in at exactly the right times. If I slurred a word, he slurred the same word in harmony with me. He had the greatest ability to anticipate that I'd ever heard in my life. I swear to you, somehow he could tell—even that very first time we sang together—what I was going to sing and how I was going to sing it.

Now, a lot of folks talk about this thing called the Bakersfield Sound, and a lot of 'em seem to think they know exactly who and how and when it all started. The problem is, everybody's got their own definition of what the Bakersfield Sound is. Your definition might be different from mine, so I'm not going to try to tell you when the Bakersfield Sound started—but I can tell you *exactly* where and when the Buck

Owens Sound started. The Buck Owens Sound kicked in right before Christmas of 1959, in a 1957 Cadillac, on a long, lonely stretch of California highway. But I didn't create it alone. Don Rich was as much a part of that sound as I was.

When me and Don finished singing "Above and Beyond," I knew right then and there that I had found the sound I'd been searching for. I knew "Above and Beyond" was going to be a hit. I knew Don was going to be my musical partner for life. I knew that the two of us would be having hit records together for years to come. And believe me, we did. From 1960 to 1974, hardly a week went by that we weren't on the charts. And during that time, twenty of those singles went all the way to number one.

Then—in the blink of an eye—it was all over.

The Buck Owens Sound ended just the way it began—on a long, lonely stretch of California highway.

PART I

Call Me Buck

Chapter One

I WAS BORN ON AUGUST 12TH, 1929, at five o'clock in the morning. My mama said I was born with long black hair. She also told me that I was actually born in the back seat of a Ford Model A sedan. She said they cut the baby's umbilical cord—that baby being me—right there in the back seat of that Model A before they took me and mama into the hospital.

My father was Alvis Edgar Owens Sr. I was named after him. He was born May 23rd, 1909. My mother, Maicie, was born on December 4th, 1907.

My parents met at a church social, and they'd been dating for over a year when they decided they wanted to get married. My daddy went to my mother's dad and asked for his daughter's hand in marriage. He told my daddy that it was all right with him if that's what his daughter wanted, but that the wedding would have to wait until the crops were in. Once the crops had been harvested, my daddy and mother were ready to finally get married, but now her father said they'd have to wait until all the planting was done in the spring.

I guess my daddy got to thinking that this would turn out to be a really long courtship if her father had his way, so mama and daddy decided to run off and get married. Well, they didn't exactly run off very far. They drove over to their preacher's house with my mother's Uncle Edmund. He was one of the witnesses, and the other witness was the preacher's wife. They sat outside the preacher's house in my daddy's car while the preacher conducted the ceremony. Then, once the wedding was over, they drove over to my mother's parents' house and broke the news to 'em.

That was on the ninth of January 1926, which means my mother was eighteen and my daddy was sixteen on the day of their wedding. When I was a kid, I thought it was funny that my mother was older than my dad. But, as I got older, I found out it wasn't really all that uncommon.

My older sister was Mary Ethel Owens. She was born October 6th, 1927, in Sherman. My brother, Melvin Leo Owens, was born July 20th,

1931. By then we had moved to Van Alstyne, Texas. And then there was my sister Dorothy, who was born January 12th, 1934. Dorothy was born in Howe, Texas. We moved around a lot when I was a kid.

My earliest childhood memories start when I was around four or five years old. I can remember my mother holding me and my sister Dorothy up to a window to watch as the hearse went by that was carrying my mother's father. Dorothy and I were both just getting over bouts of pneumonia, so my mother had to miss her own father's funeral to take care of us. That was December 14th, 1934.

*   *   *

I can also remember being fascinated with the radio when I was real young. I wasn't old enough to understand how a radio worked, so I thought there were little people who got up inside of that thing and sang. Then when they'd get through singing, I thought they'd leave and go somewhere until it was time for 'em to sing inside the radio again. The only problem was I couldn't figure out why I didn't see 'em when they left. I'd try to hide so they couldn't see me, but I never could catch 'em leaving that box.

I don't remember the day I changed my name—but my daddy told me I did, so I know it's true. We had an ol' mule named Buck that we plowed with, and my daddy said that one day—when I was around three years old—I came in the house and said, "Call me Buck." My daddy said if anybody tried to call me Alvis or Junior or anything else, I just wouldn't answer. From that day on, they had to call me Buck—Buck Owens.

Chapter Two

THE FIRST MEMBER OF MY FAMILY TO ARRIVE in Texas was my granddaddy, Carl Lee Owens. He was born in Whistler, Alabama, in 1881. When I was a kid, I heard a couple of different stories about how he ended up living in Texas. One story was that he ran away from home when he was a teenager because his stepmama was so mean to him. The other story I was told—which is even worse—was that his daddy and stepmama were traveling through Texas when Carl Lee developed typhoid fever—so they just left him there. They talk about dysfunctional families today as if that's some sort of modern problem. Well, if either one of those stories about my granddaddy is true, I guess dysfunctional families have been around for a long time.

One other thing they told me about him is that there was another man in the area where he lived who had the same name—Carl Lee Owens. So, to keep his neighbors from getting the two of them confused, my granddaddy changed his name to Lee Carl Owens. I'm not really sure how much that helped people from getting them mixed up, but I guess that means I wasn't the first person in the family to change his name.

My grandmother on my daddy's side was Minnie Wattenbarger. She married Lee Carl in 1906, and my daddy was born three years later in Bonham, Texas.

My mother's parents were Michael Monroe Ellington and Mary Myrtle Curliss. They were living in Okolona, Arkansas, when my mother was born.

Like I said, my mother's dad was a farmer. My daddy was a farmer, too. He was a sharecropper, which means he farmed on land that was owned by somebody else. They used to call it "farming on the halves." The man who owned the land would provide the seeds. My daddy would farm part of the land. Other sharecroppers would farm other sections. When the crops came in, all of the sharecroppers would give half of everything to the landlord, and they'd get to keep half of what they'd grown. Farming on the halves meant splitting the profits. But some years, if the weather had been bad, there just wasn't a whole lot of profits to split.

We eventually moved on from Sherman to a bunch of other places in Texas. By the time I was eight years old, we'd lived in Sherman, Van Alstyne, Howe, Garland, Dallas, and Garland again. Like I said, we moved around a lot.

At one point we shared a house with a man and two boys. One of the boys was named James and the other one was named Duke. They had no mama there. The man went to work one day and the boys went to school. They'd left the fire going in the wood stove, and some of the burning wood fell out the front of the stove and onto the floor. The fire got put out before the house burned completely down, but it burned up everything of any value that we had.

I was in the first grade at the time, and I was going home from school that day to have a bite of lunch. When I passed by my uncle's house, he was out in the yard there, and he said, "Where ya goin' boy?"

I said, "I'm goin' home to get me some lunch."

He said, "Well, your house burned up. You better come in here and eat somethin'."

Now my uncle was quite a practical joker, so I thought he was kidding. I walked on down about another block to my house and, sure as hell, there wasn't anybody there. The house was still standing, but everything had burned up inside.

When the church folks found out about it, they came and brought us clothes—coats and other hand-me-downs. As it turned out, the stuff they gave us was better than what we'd had before the fire, so I ended up having mixed emotions about the whole situation.

Now, speaking of church folks, I must admit I haven't been too much of a churchgoer as an adult, but I went a lot when I was a kid. On Sundays, my mother was always looking for one of us kids to go to church with her, and for some reason it always ended up being me.

Just about everywhere we moved to, my mama would become the church's piano player. She was one of those good old piano pounders. She had a great left hand—the kind you need for playing gospel music. When she played those bass notes with her left hand, I used to think it sounded like thunder. You don't hear many of those kinds of gospel piano players any more, but they were really sought-after people back then—the ones with that thunder in their left hands.

When one of those preachers would get to preachin' about hell-fire and damnation on Sunday mornings, he'd cause me to end up having scary dreams on Sunday nights. I remember waking up many times, thinking that the ol' Devil was going to come right up through the floor and get me just because I'd done some little thing wrong.

Those good ol' "holy roller" preachers back when I was a kid— they could be really convincing people. Since my mama was the piano player, she made me sit right up front with her. When one those preachers would get to shouting and waving his arms around, I swear, I could feel the heat coming off of him. Being a kid, it was always a little frightening to sit through. But even though I knew I was going to end up having bad dreams, I'd go to church with my mama anyway—because I liked the music.

Chapter Three

THERE'S THIS JOKE ABOUT AN OLD MAN who lived right beside the railroad tracks. Every night at ten fifteen this great big freight train would run down through there and just shake the hell out of his house, making the loudest damn noise you ever heard. And every night the old man would sleep right through it. Then one night the train didn't run—and at ten fifteen on the dot, the old man jumped out of bed and said, "What the hell was that?"

I know how that old man felt because when we moved to Garland, Texas, we were living right by the railroad tracks. Those trains would go through there so close that they really would shake the whole house.

In 1936, my daddy took a job working at Dieterich's Dairy there in Garland. In fact, most of the time he worked two shifts a day. My younger sister Dorothy had been born a couple of years earlier, so by this time there were six of us in the family.

I used to play with Mr. Dieterich's son, Junior. The Dietrich family lived over in the better part of town. Sometimes Junior would come over to our house and he'd bring his Shetland pony. That's when I came to find out how mean those Shetland ponies are. They're meaner than hell. Junior's pony bit me and kicked me on several occasions—not hard enough to cause any serious damage, but it still hurt.

My brother Melvin was out in the yard with me one day when Junior Dieterich came over on his pony. Junior got off and said that the three of us would take turns riding. But then, anytime Junior felt like it, he'd say it was his turn to ride the pony again, even if it was Melvin's turn or my turn. That didn't seem right to me, so he and I got into it, and before long he was crying and riding his Shetland pony back home.

A little while later, Junior and his mother came over to our house, and Mrs. Dieterich wanted to know what had happened. I said, "Well, we got in this argument about whose turn it was to ride the pony. It was my brother's turn, but Junior said it was his turn again. When I told him, 'No, it's my brother's turn,' he got real mad at me and I got mad at him, and the next thing you know, we had a little fracas."

Mrs. Dieterich asked Junior, "Is that what happened?" Junior said, "It's my pony and I should be able to ride it anytime I want to."

Well, when my daddy came home and found out about it, he got real upset with me because it was his boss's son. He told me, "Son, it's Junior's pony, and you've got to respect that."

So that was my first experience—not only with selfishness—but also with people who had money and what they thought was a better life than we had. I realized early on that even though they were willing to come to my part of town, they still expected me to live by their rules.

Chapter Four

MY DADDY TOLD ME MANY TIMES, "When you have a job, you get there ahead of starting time. If there's something that needs to be done, you be the first to volunteer. Don't wait to be asked." He told me, "Have a smile on your face and—whatever your job is—do it expeditiously." Those were some of the greatest words of advice I ever got from him.

After he'd worked at Dieterich's Dairy in Garland for a while, my daddy decided to take a job he'd heard about at another dairy over in Dallas.

Back in those days, you didn't have a refrigerator—you had an icebox to keep things cold. Usually they looked like a wooden cabinet on the outside, and on the inside they had these hollow tin walls that had some kind of insulation in 'em. One section of the box held a big ol' block of ice—and that piece of ice would keep everything in the icebox cold for a few days. The iceman would come around pretty often to bring everybody in the neighborhood a new block of ice.

Well, the iceman in Garland had this pretty good-sized ice truck, so my daddy got him to take what belongings we had and help move us over to a house in Dallas that was just a few hundred feet from the Trinity River. I remember me and my brother and sisters rode on top of that ice truck to our new place.

The day after we moved to Dallas, my daddy went to the dairy where he was supposed to start his new job. We didn't have a car at that time. He had to walk all the way there. He came back later in the day and said the man at the dairy had told him the job wasn't available yet. Every day he'd walk to the dairy, and then he'd come back home with the same story.

This house we'd moved into had a fireplace, and that's what my mama used for our stove. She'd cook over the fireplace, making a pot of beans or whatever. Since my daddy's last job had been at Dieterich's Dairy, we'd always had plenty of milk and cheese. When we moved to Dallas, my mama had to make water gravy. First she'd make biscuits over the fireplace, then she'd mix flour and grease and water. So we'd have beans and we'd have biscuits with water gravy on 'em.

There was a pasture with a big silo on it not far from our house. A man would come over there every few days and bring a big load of silage. Since the job at the dairy in Dallas hadn't opened up yet, my daddy would help him unload the silage into the silo. For helping the man, daddy would get twenty-five cents and a pint of whiskey.

It was real cold when we lived in Dallas, so naturally all of us kids got sick. I guess riding all the way there on top of an ice truck probably didn't help matters much. I can still remember my mother mixing rock candy with a little bit of that whiskey to make cough syrup for all of us.

I also remember my mother and daddy having to go down by the Trinity River to cut up dead trees because that fireplace was the only heat we had in the house.

That stretch in Dallas was really rough. If we didn't already know we were poor before we moved there, we sure knew it once we'd lived in that pitiful house for a little while. Even though I was still a child, that's when I started thinking, "When I get big, I'm not going to have shoes with twine in 'em where the shoelaces are supposed to be. I'm not going to have to use pieces of old linoleum to plug the holes in the soles of my shoes. When I get big, I'm not going to be poor like this. I'm going to be somebody." I didn't know what I was going to do yet. I just knew I wasn't going to live the way I'd been living anymore once I had a chance to make something of myself.

*   *   *

As it turned out, the job in Dallas never materialized. After a few weeks of just making the occasional quarter and pint of whiskey from helping out at the silo, my daddy went to see Mr. Dieterich so he could tell him he'd like to have his old job back. Mr. Dieterich knew my daddy was a hard worker, so he told him to come on back to Garland.

Sure enough, the next day the iceman came again with his big truck, and we loaded up all of our stuff. My daddy went back to work for Dieterich's Dairy, and wouldn't you know it—we moved right back into the same house we'd moved out of a few weeks earlier. So, we all had to get used to those trains again, rattling the whole house every time they'd come through.

When I think back to that short time we lived in Dallas, I think about watching my daddy walking down the road to see if that job at the dairy had opened up yet. You know, he could've just kept on walking. A lot of men did in those days—just walked away from their families because times were so hard. But my daddy never did.

Chapter Five

THERE CAME A TIME WHEN I SAW THAT MY DADDY and my Uncle Vernon—my mother's brother—were making something at night out between the house and the railroad tracks. They'd gotten the rear axle off of an old automobile, and they'd started building a two-wheel trailer. They got some lumber and made the bed of that trailer about eight to ten feet long. Then they put these big sideboards on it about five feet high. It took 'em quite a while to build it because my daddy was still working two shifts a day at Dieterich's Dairy.

I didn't know it yet, but my folks had decided the time had come to get the hell out of Texas. It was November of 1937, and by that time a whole lot of people who'd lived in Texas, Oklahoma, Kansas, and some of those other states in the Midwest had already moved to California. Just a few years earlier, there had been all these massive dust storms in a lot of those states, so people couldn't farm the land any more. They called it the Dust Bowl. John Steinbeck wrote a novel about it called *The Grapes of Wrath*. Once the Dust Bowl folks settled out West, word began to spread back to my folks that there were jobs out in California—"the land of milk and honey." So, my parents and several other members of our family made up their minds to head that way.

I was only eight years old at the time, so of course I had no idea what was happening—but one day at about five in the morning they got us all up, put the mattresses on top of the car, and put everything else in the trailer. By this time we had a 1933 Ford four-door sedan—and if you've never seen one, you'd be surprised how small those '33 Ford sedans were.

There were my two sisters, Mary Ethel and Dorothy; my brother Melvin; and my cousin Jimmy, who was ten months old at the time. Plus, of course, my mother and my dad, and there was also my Uncle Vernon and my Aunt Lucille, and my grandmother on my mother's side—ten of us in this old Ford. We had this board that they put between the front seat and the back seat so everybody would have a place to sit.

So, we all struck out for California—ready to see that land of milk and honey. Even though I was only eight at the time, I can still remember very well how uncomfortable it was. In fact, it was awful.

That first day we only went about 80 miles. Because of the weight of all of us and everything we were carrying, the back end of the car and the front end of the trailer sat so low that the trailer hitch broke. We were in Weatherford, Texas when it happened, so we stayed there for a couple of nights at what they used to call an auto court—which was just a bunch of little ol' cabins—until my dad and Uncle Vernon could get the parts they needed to fix the trailer hitch.

After we left Weatherford, we didn't have enough money to stay at any more auto courts. In the evenings when it got dark, we'd just find a place to stop on the side of the road. Some of the folks would sleep in the car. For the rest of us, they'd put a couple of the mattresses down on the ground, and that's where we'd spend the night. Me and my brother—it was our job to go hunt up enough dead wood for 'em to build a fire and cook something for us to eat. We never ate in the mornings. We'd just get up, get loaded, and hit the road.

The trailer hitch broke one more time outside of Phoenix, and this time it was too far gone to try to fix again. But we had relatives in Mesa that we'd already planned to stay with for a night or two, so we left the trailer by the side of the road and headed to Aunt Nancy and Uncle Inmon's house. We got there around three or four o'clock in the morning. Aunt Nancy was actually my great aunt—my grandmother's sister on my mother's side.

When we'd first crossed into Arizona, we started seeing all these oranges and grapefruits and stuff growing on both sides of the road. They had those great big orchards out there, so when we got to Uncle Inmon's house, he said, "There's a man who owns an orchard near here who told me I could go over there and pick a little bit of his fruit anytime I wanted. Let's go over there and get some grapefruits and oranges and bring 'em back."

It was only a little after four in the morning but we were all hungry, so that's what they decided they'd do. So, Uncle Vernon, my daddy, Uncle Inmon, and Charles—one of Uncle Inmon's sons—all got in the car and went to get some fruit for everybody.

On their way there, they came across a big tow sack about half full of oranges, and they said, "Well, looky here! Somebody's left a sack of oranges right by the side of the road." So they figured, "Why go pick 'em when all we gotta do is take this tow sack?" They picked it up, put it in the car, and no sooner had they started off than this red light came on behind 'em.

The man who pulled 'em over was this guy who doubled as a deputy and a security man. It turned out he worked for a lot of the growers around there. They'd pay him for every arrest he made when he caught people stealing fruit. So he arrested my daddy and the rest of 'em and put 'em all in jail.

When the menfolk didn't come back to Aunt Nancy's house after a few hours, all the women were mystified. So, my mother and Aunt Lucille and my grandmother and Aunt Nancy walked into town and went straight to the police station to see if the police had heard anything about 'em. A guy at the police station said, "Yeah, we know all about 'em. We've got 'em back there in the jail."

Later that day they went up in front of the judge. That judge told 'em they were accused of stealing oranges, so they told him the whole story about the tow sack of oranges sitting out by the side of the road in plain view. There were no laws about entrapment in those days, but the judge didn't fine 'em or anything. When he realized what the deputy had done, the judge said, "Well, that's a pretty dirty trick," and he let 'em go with a warning not to take anything that didn't belong to 'em.

And that was our welcome to Arizona.

Chapter Six

WE'D ONLY BEEN STAYING WITH MY AUNT AND UNCLE for a few days when my daddy found out about a job at a dairy down in Winkelman, about a hundred miles southeast of Mesa. What was supposed to be a quick stopover in Arizona turned out to be a lot longer stay—by about a decade and a half or so. I guess my folks had decided there wasn't any need to rush to look for jobs in the land of milk and honey when there was work available in the state where we already were.

The bus us kids took to school was a Model A Ford with a flatbed attached on the back of it. The flatbed was covered by a canvas top. The bus would pick us up in Winkelman and take us to school in Hayden, which was several miles up the road.

That school bus is where I had my very first encounter with puppy love. This little girl's name was Nayda, and man, she was the cutest little thing. I was in the third grade at the time—I started liking women at a pretty early age and I never stopped.

One day I found a nickel on the playground right before we got on the bus to go home. Nayda lived out past where I lived, so she and I were on the same bus. On our way home that day, I said, "Will you be my girlfriend?" By the time I got off the bus, she was not only my girlfriend—she was also in possession of my nickel.

It was just the very next day that she said she didn't want to be my girlfriend anymore. She broke my heart because I didn't just lose my first girlfriend—I lost my nickel, too.

Chapter Seven

MY DADDY ALWAYS DID FARM WORK, either working the fields or working at a dairy farm, or both. He wasn't a sharecropper anymore once we moved to Arizona. By then, he worked what was called "by the piece," meaning he got paid by how many rows of maize he chopped, or by how many pounds of cotton he picked.

In the summer of 1939, my daddy took sick and went into the hospital. First he had appendicitis. Then, while he was recuperating from that, he got phlebitis in his right leg. Then he got pneumonia. It turned out he was in the hospital that whole summer.

Since he was in the hospital, the rest of the family had to work to make ends meet. I even had to work on my tenth birthday. I thought that was an absolute injustice at the time—having to hoe maize on my own birthday. But I did it because we were proud people. In those days, if you had to have some kind of financial assistance from the government, they called it going "on relief." My dad used to take pride in saying, "Well, at least we ain't on relief." My folks worked hard to support themselves so they could pay all the bills and feed all of us kids and keep a roof over our heads—not to mention having to pay for my daddy's long stay in the hospital.

The summer that my daddy was so sick, the rest of us would go to work close to sunup every day. We'd work until about three or four o'clock in the afternoon, and afterward we'd all hurry back to the house and get cleaned up the best we could. Then we went to the hospital every night to see daddy.

On Saturdays we'd work until noon, go get our weekly bath, and then head off to see daddy. Thinking about it now, I don't know how in the world we made it through that summer of 1939. It was hard—but we managed to survive it without ever once having to go on relief.

Chapter Eight

WHEN I WAS IN THE FOURTH GRADE I started out in one school district, went to two other districts, and then for about the last six weeks of the school year, we moved back to where the original school district was. As hard as it was to be constantly moving, the one good thing it did for me was it taught me how to deal with bullies.

Every time I went to a different school, the latest school's bully wanted me to know he was the boss. Changing schools all those times, I learned how to defend myself. Those bullies found out very quickly that I was going to fight for my right to be there, and defend my right to be who I was. It didn't take more than one fight per school for those bullies to tell their little henchmen, "You know, he's all right. We don't need to try to beat him up again because it didn't work out too good the first time."

I don't mean to sound like I'm bragging, but there's no denying that I was a smart kid. I was born that way because my folks were very intelligent. My daddy was very quick with numbers and my mother was great at reading. Wherever I was going to school, I was usually the teacher's pet because I used to do really well when the class would have spelling bees or math contests. Many times the teachers used to have me come up front and read whatever we were studying to the whole class. Maybe

I was always meant for show business because I enjoyed showing off a little even way back then.

I was good at those things because I could remember so well. I've been told I have a photographic memory, and maybe that's true. But there came a time when it all went away for a while.

We had this big old German shepherd named Racket. My daddy had named her Racket because she made so much noise all the time. Now in the summer, all of us kids would sleep outside in the yard. August in Arizona can get pretty hot, and although we had electricity, we sure as hell didn't have any air conditioning.

One August night, my mother and dad had gone to bed in the house while us kids were sleeping out on the lawn. After a while, Racket woke my daddy up with her whining. He yelled at her to be quiet, but she kept whining—and when he got up to go looking for her, he found her standing over me. I was lying there moaning, so he woke up my mother. By the time my mother reached me, I'd stopped moaning because I'd passed out. They told me later that Mama didn't know I was just unconscious—she thought I was dead.

Well, she went to hollering and screaming, just beside herself with grief. My daddy told her to bring him some cold water, and she was still bawling when she brought him the water. He started putting cold, wet rags on my head, but that didn't wake me up. Finally, my daddy took this real strong-smelling liniment and waved it under my nose. The whole time this was going on, my mother just kept wailing and crying. When that powerful liniment caused me to come to, my daddy asked what was the matter with me. I said, "What's the matter with me? Don't you mean, 'What's the matter with Mama?'"

I ended up being in the hospital for five or six weeks. I kept going in and out of consciousness. They never were able to tell my folks exactly what my illness was. In those days they just called it brain fever.

When I finally came around after a few days, I discovered I had lost my memory—or at least some mighty big pieces of it. Once I was well enough to get ready to go back to school, my mother said, "Let me see you spell your name."

I looked at her and said, "What does it start with?"

She said, "It starts with a B."

I said, "Okay. How do you make a B?"

Eventually, it came back to me, but I went through a couple of changes that were permanent. For instance, I couldn't hear as well as I could before I got sick. Also, before my illness, I had always been able to outrun my younger brother. I could just run off and leave him in a race, or outdo him in any kind of physical activity. But after I got out of the hospital—even years afterward—it was all I could do just to stay up with him, even though he was smaller and two years younger than me.

Decades later I had a CAT scan, and my doctors said they could see something that showed I'd once had a stroke. They didn't know when or how bad, but they could see that sometime in the past I'd definitely had a stroke. If that's when it happened, I can't imagine what would cause me to have a stroke at such a young age—but I've always been grateful old Racket was there to stand over me that night and whine loud enough to get my daddy out of bed.

Chapter Nine

MY FAMILY BEGAN MAKING TRIPS out to California in the early 1940s. All the kids would leave school about two weeks early, and we'd head west. We'd pick potatoes near Bakersfield. Then we'd go to Porterville and work the carrots. Then we worked the grapes up in Modesto. We'd work the tomatoes over in Tracy, and then go back to Modesto and pick peaches. Then we'd head back to Arizona where us kids would always be about two weeks late going back to school. I don't recall ever hearing anything negative about keeping a kid out of school to work. We weren't the only ones doing it, I'm sure.

My sisters and my brother and me worked in the fields right along with the grownups. We were in Modesto picking peaches when I found out that my brother Melvin was a little bit scrappier than I'd realized.

One thing you could never do to Melvin was mess with his cap. My daddy had gotten a job driving a truck at one point in Arizona, so he took to wearing a trucker's cap. He got one for Melvin, and my brother wore that thing all the time. My sisters and I knew not to mess with our brother's cap. It was his prized possession.

Unfortunately, there was one peach picker in Modesto who didn't know any better. Now, if you never saw a fruit-picking ladder, it looks like a regular ladder on one side, but on the other side it's got a pole with a spike at the bottom that sticks in the ground. It looks like a tripod with rungs on it, and you can move it a lot quicker than a regular ladder. This fellow, a big ol' friendly, red-headed boy—about six foot two, a couple of hundred pounds, and lots of muscle—was up on the fruit-picking ladder when my brother walked underneath him. Melvin was about ten years old at the time. As he walked under the ladder, this young, fun-loving boy reached down and just picked my brother's hat right off of his head, waved it around a little bit, then dropped it back down to him and said, "How you doin' there, bud?"

I didn't have a chance to warn that big ol' boy. The next thing that red-headed kid knew, he was being pulled off that fruit-picking ladder by a ten year old. By the time my brother was finished with him, that ol' boy had to go all the way over to where my daddy was picking peaches and apologize for what he'd done.

Melvin didn't cotton to anyone trying to take advantage of him. It didn't matter if they were a six foot two, two hundred-pounder and he was only five foot two and maybe a hundred pounds soaking wet. My brother was very serious about his hat.

That incident with Melvin probably seems so funny to me now because most of what went on out in the fields wasn't any fun at all. It was just backbreaking hard work. There wasn't much to laugh about out there in the hot sun all day.

* * *

Every place we'd go in California, we'd end up in a labor camp where they had these makeshift cabins. At the end of each row of cabins they'd have a bathroom with a toilet and a cold-water shower.

There was always music in the camps at night. In front of one cabin there might be some guy playing the banjo and another guy playing the guitar. Down the row a little bit there'd be a couple of guys playing fiddles. Then on down a little farther there'd be guys playing mando-lins. I really loved those mandolins.

They were folks just sitting on their front porches, playing for their own enjoyment. But every now and then, a whole bunch of 'em would get together. When that happened, everyone would come out of their cabins to listen, and we'd all have a good ol' time. It was truly wonder-ful music.

There wasn't just picking and singing in the camps, there was pick-ing and singing in the fields, too—it was just a different kind of pick-ing. You'd have blacks, Mexicans, and white folks stretched out over maybe fifty yards or more, and they'd all be singing. I don't remember hearing too many happy songs out in the fields. They'd sing songs that had lines like, "My good woman's gone and left me and she ain't comin' back." Here were these three very different groups of people, and every-body was singing songs about the same thing—about how the one they loved had left them. It was almost like a competition to see which group could come up with the saddest song. There was lots of pickin', but not much grinnin'.

Those songs being sung in the fields were something to pass the time. In the labor camps, though, everybody was looking to relieve the pressure of a long, hard day. Most of the songs they played and sang in the evening were happy, up-tempo songs. And when a crowd would gather around to watch and listen, it was exciting. I guess that was my first exposure to live music with an audience where people would tap their feet and clap their hands and even dance sometimes. It was sure a lot different than the music I'd heard in church.

There was just something about the music in those camps that af-fected me, and I would go visit with those musicians and worry 'em half to death, asking questions about how they played this and that. Those labor camps are where a lot of my musical background came from.

A lot of the folks who were born and raised in Arizona and Cali-fornia and had spent their whole lives there didn't like the fact that so many of us had moved out West from Oklahoma and Arkansas and Texas. They called us "Okies." One summer while we were in Califor-nia, I saw this store with a sign in the window that said, "No Okies

Allowed." Well, I wanted to buy some candy, so I went inside. The man behind the counter took one look at me and said, "Hey, boy! Didn't you see that 'No Okies' sign in the window?"

I looked him right in the eye and said, "I saw it alright, but I ain't no Okie. I'm a Texan!" He got a big kick out of that and told me I could shop in his store anytime I wanted to. But I still didn't like the idea of anybody being told they weren't allowed to go someplace just because of the way they were dressed, or because of where they were from.

Every time I had to deal with that kind of prejudice, I just kept telling myself the same thing I'd been telling myself since those days we'd lived in Dallas: "When I grow up, I'm not gonna be poor any more. I'm gonna be somebody."

Chapter Ten

BY THE TIME I WAS ELEVEN, we were living back around Mesa, Arizona, during the school year. My sisters and brother and me had to bring our lunch to school because we couldn't afford to pay for lunch in the school cafeteria. Well, I decided I'd had enough of that, so I went to the principal and found out if I'd do some extra work around the school, it would take care of paying for our lunches.

Every Saturday morning I'd go to the school and clean the desks, refill the inkwells, dust the erasers, and all that sort of stuff. Every couple of weeks I'd have to mow the grass. About the hottest I've ever been was mowing that big ol' schoolyard in the Arizona sun on a Saturday morning.

We got to stand in the lunch line and eat with the other kids in the school cafeteria all right, but I had to eat my lunch pretty fast because at twelve-fifteen, two or three times a week, I'd have to be out on the school grounds with this broomstick-sized pole that had a nail on the bottom of it. For the rest of the lunch hour, I'd be out there picking up all the papers and trash on the ground with that pole. I can't say I liked having to do all that extra work, but I was proud that my brother and sisters and me got to eat that cafeteria food every day.

A couple of years later, I got a paper route. The morning newspaper was the Arizona Republic and the afternoon paper was the Phoenix Gazette, so I was out there on my bike delivering papers twice a day. I had route 325, which was the longest paper route around. I guess one of the reasons I got the job was because none of the other paperboys wanted it.

Now, every boy who's ever had a paper route has stories they could tell you about being chased by dogs. The worst dog I had to deal with was this big ol' German shepherd. The folks back at the newspaper office in Phoenix got a lot of reports about me that weren't very good because of that damn dog.

Every day, about a hundred yards before I'd reach the house that had the German shepherd in the front yard, I'd get up as much speed as I could on my bike. When that dog would start running up the road to try to get me, I'd stick my legs up on the handlebars and coast by that house real fast, throwing that paper as hard as I could. Well, there's a certain way you have to throw a newspaper to keep it from coming apart—and a newspaper just ain't gonna be thrown the right way if you're flying down the road with your legs up on the handlebars of your bicycle. Going as fast as I'd be going past that house, the wind would catch that paper almost every time and just blow it all apart. If the paper blew apart in front of anybody else's house, I'd get off my bike and go put it back together. But I refused to get myself eaten up by that German shepherd, so I never did stop to put those folks' newspaper back together. I had that paper route for a couple of years, and that dog chased me every single day. I kept hoping his owners would move somewhere else, or at least cancel their subscription—but they never did.

I liked Sundays best because there was only one paper on Sunday, and because most Sundays my daddy would drive. I taught my brother how to throw the paper, too, so every Sunday we'd get in the back seat of the car. Melvin would throw papers out one side and I'd throw 'em out the other. Shoot! We'd be done with that paper route in thirty minutes.

My daddy always had the radio on when we were delivering the papers on Sundays. On December 7th, 1941, the music on the radio stopped in the middle of a song. Then this reporter came on and said the Japanese had attacked Pearl Harbor. Of course, I didn't know where that was, or what the ramifications would be, but I could tell it was something serious.

I'd find out just how serious it was three years later when my daddy got drafted at the age of thirty-five. I remember seeing him getting on a bus to go off to basic training with all these young men who were between about eighteen and twenty years old. I didn't know of anybody else my daddy's age who'd been drafted. None of my friends' daddies had been drafted, so it didn't make any sense to me.

They decided not to ship my daddy overseas, or even make him stay in the Army all that long, which was a big relief to my mama and us kids. He got his honorable discharge in April of '45, and a few months later the war was over.

*   *   *

My days delivering newspapers ended in 1942 when I found out there was an opening available at Western Union. Once I got the job, I'd ride my bike to the Western Union office every morning and wait. When a telegram would come in, my boss would tell me where to take it, and then I'd hop on my bike and be on my way. Delivering one or two telegrams at a time was a hell of a lot easier than throwing newspapers—and the best part was, I didn't have to deal with that damn German shepherd anymore.

Well, one day I went to the office and the boss gave me three telegrams to deliver. After I'd hopped on my bike and dropped off the first two, I saw he'd left me a note on the last one. It said, "When you hand this to Mrs. Wallace, you are to sing 'Happy Birthday' to her and smile."

I rode my bike to Mrs. Wallace's house and rang the doorbell. When she opened the door, I handed her the telegram and started singing "Happy Birthday," just like the note said. Well, I didn't make it past the second line of the song before Mrs. Wallace put her hand up to stop me. I quit singing and was just standing there with my mouth still open when she looked at me and said, 'Son, whatever you do, don't ever try to have a career as a singer." And then she slammed the door—while I stood there with my mouth still open.

Chapter Eleven

M Y AUNT LUCILLE AND UNCLE VERNON, they lived in an old trailer house in back of the house we lived in. Uncle Vernon was a guitar player, so occasionally he'd have some of his acquaintances congregate at our house to play music together. One of the fellows was a mandolin player. I guess he didn't practice much because he'd always leave his mandolin hanging on the wall of my uncle's trailer. Now, my aunt and uncle both worked all day, so when I'd get home from school, I'd sneak out back to their place. This was in the days before everybody always had their doors locked when they weren't at home. Well, since their door wasn't locked, I'd sneak into that old trailer, take that mandolin off the wall, and try to play it. I didn't really know how. I just started out by trying to put my fingers in the right places to make it sound pretty. It just about killed me when that guy decided not to leave his mandolin at my uncle's place anymore.

When I was still real young—before we moved to Arizona—I'd heard the Monroe Brothers on the radio. I thought Bill and Charlie Monroe were two of those little people I was telling you about earlier—the ones who snuck inside the radio when I wasn't looking. This was the same Bill Monroe who got famous later with his group, Bill Monroe and the Bluegrass Boys. When I heard the Monroe Brothers on the radio back in Texas, I didn't know what that instrument was that Bill was playing—and I didn't find out until I saw mandolins being played by those men in the camps that first summer we spent out in California. When I first saw one, I loved the way it looked. I loved the sound it made. And after that mandolin wasn't at my uncle's place any more, I knew I had to have one of my own.

I pestered my parents about it enough that they finally got me one for Christmas. I remember that Christmas so well because it was the first time we had our own Christmas tree. I also remember it because I couldn't take my hands off that mandolin. I decided to figure out how to play this song I'd heard on the radio called "Just Because"—and I was determined to learn it right away. While I was lying there in bed

Christmas night, picking out the notes to "Just Because," I heard my mother call out, "That sounds real good, son. Now put down that mandolin and go to sleep!"

I was thirteen years old that Christmas, and right away I pretty much lost interest in everything else but that mandolin—and girls, of course.

Sometime after that my daddy brought home a Regal guitar. It was a pretty cheap model. The further up the guitar you went, the further away the strings were from the fretboard. My mama knew how to play a little, so she showed me where to put my fingers to make a few chords. So did Uncle Vernon. After that, I just kinda taught myself for the most part. But mainly in those days I was trying to get better and better on the mandolin.

By the time they gave me that mandolin in December of '42, I'd already dropped out of school. It wasn't really all that unusual back then for kids to leave school before they graduated. World War II was still going on at that time, and I was really big for my age, so there were jobs available for somebody my size who was willing to work. I ended up leaving Western Union and working at a citrus shed. I also had a little night job that led to me meeting the first real love of my life.

Chapter Twelve

IN MESA THERE WAS A PLACE called the Mazona Roller Rink. You could go there and skate for two or three hours for a dime. It wasn't like today where you rent shoes with skates already on 'em. In those days you wore your own shoes and the guy at the roller rink—he was called a skate fixer—he'd attach these flat metal plates with wheels on 'em right onto your shoes. Then he'd tighten 'em up with what they called a skate key. The old gentleman who ran the roller rink would let me work for a couple of hours as a skate fixer, and then he'd let me skate for the rest of the evening for free.

Of course, when you're a skate fixer, you end up meeting a whole lot of people. One night I met a couple of pretty girls from Gilbert, a town about eight miles from Mesa. One of the girls was named Betty Campbell, who was thirteen, and the other was Betty's sister, Bonnie, who was a year older. I don't want to say Bonnie was cuter, but let's face it— Bonnie was probably the prettiest girl around in those days. But I took a liking to Betty at first, so she became my girlfriend. We went out a few times, but we'd always go as a group. Bonnie and Betty had an older brother named Charlie, and Charlie could drive the family car. So Bonnie and whoever her boyfriend was at the time, and Betty and me—we had transportation thanks to Charlie.

After a while, Bonnie and I started going together. When we were both fifteen, we started going steady.

Around that same time, I began sitting in with various bands, for free, in all the honky-tonks around Mesa that I could. Not every place would let me play because you were supposed to be twenty-one. I was still just a teenager, but a lot of the club owners said if I didn't leave the bandstand area, they would let me play there. When there was an intermission, I had to go outside. I had to be either on the bandstand, in the bathroom, or outside. But that didn't bother me. I just wanted to play music.

My mother and daddy weren't happy about me going to honky-tonks. In fact, they were terribly nervous about it. My daddy said—a number of times—that nothing good could come from hanging around in those places. My parents thought the only thing I'd learn there was how to get drunk. So they were worried, and I suppose I would've been, too, if I was them. But I wasn't going there to drink and dance and carry on. I was going there to play music, and to meet other people who played. Just like I'd done with those musicians in the labor camps in California, I was constantly asking questions—trying to learn how to play better.

One of the musicians I met was a guy named Theryl Ray Britten. Everybody called him Britt. He was about three years older than me. We started playing together, and we even managed to get ourselves our own radio show. The radio station was KTYL there in Mesa—1490 on the dial. It was one of the only two radio stations in town at the time. The other one was KARV. Both of those stations were 250 watts. Neither station carried very far, but it didn't really matter much since most folks in Mesa listened to all of those radio stations over in Phoenix anyway. Phoenix was only about fifteen miles away from Mesa, and those big Phoenix stations were a lot more powerful than a little 250-watter like KTYL.

I didn't sing yet back then. Hell, I didn't want anybody to hear me sing after I'd tried singing "Happy Birthday" to Mrs. Wallace. Britt played guitar and sang, and I played the mandolin. We were on the radio three days a week at three o'clock in the afternoon. We called it the *Buck and Britt Show*. It didn't last all that long, but we were just happy to be good enough to get on the radio. Plus, the radio show helped us to start getting gigs, especially after we added a trumpet player. Bonnie's sister Betty had a boyfriend who played the trumpet. He was what we called a flyboy, meaning he was in the Air Force.

Now that we were an actual band, we decided we were going to go find us a steady place to play, so we went over to a joint called the Romo Buffet there in Mesa. The guy who ran the place was named Sid Silver. Sid's talent was arm wrestling. He was fifty-six years old, and people would come in there to watch him arm wrestle these big ol' truck drivers. I was astounded to see this man in his fifties beating all of these strapping truck drivers who were half his age. Once they'd get beat, they'd always want to go double or nothing on a ten-cent glass of beer. I have no idea how he did it, but I never saw him lose.

Well, we made a deal with Sid to play for ten percent of what was in the cash register each night. It was an old-fashioned cash register that was kind of like an adding machine. At the end of the night, he'd hit "total," and say, "The cash register shows we took in eighty dollars, so here's your eight bucks."

There weren't a lot of places to go for entertainment in Mesa, so it wasn't very long before word spread that there was a band at the Romo Buffet. On Friday and Saturday nights, it would be just crammed full—a hundred people or more. The first time that place was packed out, I thought, "Boy, we're gonna make some money tonight!" But at the end of the night, that cash register said the total was $110. So, we ended up getting eleven dollars.

I went to Sid and said, "There must be something wrong with that cash register."

"Oh no," he said. "It works good!"

I kind of suspected ol' Sid was turning that cash register's little wheel back throughout the night, like somebody turning back the mileage on an odometer. And maybe he thought I was getting wise to him because eventually he decided that instead of paying us a percentage of the cash register, he'd just pay each of us three dollars a night, no matter how large or how small the crowd was.

We worked there six nights a week from nine in the evening until one in the morning. It might not have been much, but that was my first real paying job in the music business.

Chapter Thirteen

IT'S A DIFFERENT WORLD NOW, but back when I started going steady with Bonnie, us guys, if we were to have some sort of sexual encounter, we didn't do it with the girl we were going steady with. You weren't supposed to have sex with the girl you planned to marry—until you were married to her. There weren't any sex education classes back then. Talking about sex with your parents or teachers was out of the question. So, you kind of made up your own rules.

Well, I was a male human being and I liked girls. I always have. My problem was I liked 'em too much. In fact, I can safely say that at least ninety percent of the troubles I've had in my lifetime had to do with women—mainly because I was trying to have too many women at the same time.

Anyway, Bonnie caught me with other girls a few times. She didn't know how far I'd gone, but on one occasion she found out I'd been fooling around with this real pretty girl with long dark hair. Her name was

Virginia Whittler, and she was just crazy about me. I liked her a lot, but not in the same way I liked Bonnie.

I was old enough to drive by then, and I'd finally made enough money to buy a 1933 Ford Coupe. It was one of those three-window jobs with a long rumble seat—and I do mean long. That rumble seat had lots of room for *my* seat and the seat of whatever girl I had with me. Looking back on it now, instead of worrying about me spending so much time in those honky-tonks, my parents probably should've been worried about me spending so much time in my car.

One Sunday I told Bonnie some story I'd made up about what I had to do that day, but the truth was I'd made a date to take Virginia Whittler to a place called Canyon Lake.

My daddy was working for the gas company in Mesa at that time, so my folks were prosperous enough to have a telephone. The day after I took Virginia to Canyon Lake, the phone rang. I was home having lunch, so I answered the phone. It was Bonnie, and she sounded so upset that I took the afternoon off from my job at the citrus shed and drove over to her house in Gilbert to try to straighten things out.

Well, what had happened was Virginia Whittler went to Gilbert High School—the same school that Bonnie and her sister Betty went to. Believe it or not, Virginia had passed this note over to Betty, and it said, "I spent the afternoon with Buck yesterday. He sure is fun." Of course Betty showed the note to Bonnie, and it just kind of broke Bonnie's heart.

When I got to Bonnie's house, I could tell that she was really disturbed, so I got really disturbed. At first I tried to deny it, but when I realized that was going nowhere, I just said, "Nothing happened. We didn't do anything." All I could do was apologize and hope for the best.

The next year there was a junior prom where Bonnie went to school. Since I didn't go to high school, I was thinking, "Hey, I ain't never been to no junior prom, or any kind of prom for that matter. This is gonna be fun!"

When I asked Bonnie if she was going to invite me, she said, "I want you to go with me, but I can't invite you because there's a rule against taking somebody who's not in school." She said, "So, there's this guy I'm going to take named Lester Murphy."

I remember how hurt I was whenever I found out later that there wasn't really any rule against taking somebody who wasn't in school. When I confronted Bonnie about it, she said, "Well then, I guess you could've gone with Virginia Whittler!" She still hadn't forgotten about what had happened the year before. And over fifty years later, I still haven't forgotten the name Lester Murphy.

Chapter Fourteen

AFTER I'D BEEN PLAYING THE MANDOLIN and the guitar for a while, I found out I had what they call perfect pitch. My mama could play a note on the piano, and—without looking—I could name the note she'd just played. As time went by, I got to where—if an instrument had strings on it—I could figure out how to play it.

One of the instruments I started hearing a lot on the radio was the steel guitar. Bob Wills had one in his band. So did Hank Williams. It wasn't nearly as complicated as the steel guitars you see today that have a double neck and pedals, but it made a similar sound. There just weren't nearly as many strings, and you couldn't control the sustain the way you can with a modern steel guitar.

I guess I must have expressed an interest in wanting one so much that my daddy finally bought me one. Then he made me a little amplifier for it out of an old radio speaker.

So, the first three musical instruments I had were all given to me by my parents. As much as they didn't like me playing in those ol' honky-tonks around Mesa, they were still real supportive of the idea of me trying to become a good musician.

After the *Buck and Britt Show* ended, I met a guy named Mac MacAtee. Mac ran a Mobile gas station in downtown Mesa. He had this little bitty studio—about six feet by six feet—that he built there at the gas station. From three to four in the afternoon, Monday through Friday, he'd play records over these loudspeakers there at the gas station, and they would broadcast it over KTYL.

Mac decided that he wanted to form a band, so he let everybody know he was looking for musicians. He needed a steel guitar player, which I could play a little bit by then—good enough to play in his band anyway—so I applied for the job and got it. He named the band Mac's Skillet Lickers. He didn't sing. He didn't play an instrument. In fact, he didn't know a thing about music, except that he liked it and wanted to have a band.

He managed to get the band a thirty-minute show on KTYL. We would play for a half-hour three nights a week at 7:00 p.m., Monday, Wednesday, and Friday. I'll tell you how much we made for that—absolutely nothing. He told us when the show got sponsors, we'd get paid. The only problem was he didn't have much luck getting us very many sponsors. But just like with the *Buck and Britt Show*, we enjoyed being on the radio. It felt like the big-time to us.

We decided to rehearse on Tuesdays and Thursdays. I showed up for rehearsal one day and found out Mac was holding auditions for a girl singer for the group. Lo and behold, my girlfriend Bonnie was there.

I said, "Hi sweetheart. Are you here looking for me?"

She said, "No, Buck. I'm here because I want to be a singer on the radio show."

I was stunned. I said, "You want to be a singer on the show? Well, do you sing?"

She said, "Yes, Buck, I can sing."

And that was the first I knew about it. She'd never mentioned to me that she sang. But she sure did—and she was so good that she ended up being a permanent member of the group.

We got a few jobs around town that paid us about five bucks a piece. There are a couple of gigs that stand out in my mind. One was when Mac decided he was going to promote a show at this big hall that held four or five hundred people. Mac rented the hall and promoted the show on the radio. We all went there to play, really excited about this big event—and about thirty people showed up. The band was about one-fourth of the size of the audience, but we played for 'em anyway. At least they all had plenty of room to dance.

Another time with Mac's Skillet Lickers I had my first experience watching a fight break out while I was on the bandstand. We were playing at a joint in Elroy, Arizona. I'm telling you, it was a rough town back then. This place we were playing at had a stage—if you want to call it that—that was maybe half-a-foot off the dance floor. We were in the middle of a song when the fists started flying right there in front of us. Then all of a sudden beer bottles started flying, too. Well, I kept playing for about another minute or so, and then I realized somebody on the bandstand could get hurt—namely me.

So, the band and I started to head for safety when I heard the owner of the place start yelling, "Don't leave! Don't leave! Just keep playing!" That was the night I learned one of the main rules about playing in rowdy honky-tonks: If a fight breaks out, don't stop playing—just start playing louder.

Chapter Fifteen

B ONNIE AND I WENT TOGETHER FOR A LONG TIME—maybe two years—before we had any sort of "social touching." I mean she absolutely would not let me do anything, period. I could kiss her and hug her, but not anything more than that. By this time, we were both seventeen. I didn't know it yet, but Bonnie had been thinking, "Okay, Buck's eighteenth birthday's coming up on August 12th, so I just might give him what he's been wanting."

Like I said, back in those days we didn't have any kind of knowledge about sex or reproduction. But Bonnie had heard enough to know something about how there were supposed to be a certain number of days before and after a woman has her period when she's not supposed to be able to get pregnant. She very carefully counted the days, and my birthday fell in just the right spot. So, for my birthday present, I got to have Miss Bonnie.

To say that I was very happy with my present would be an understatement. But then, sure as the world, she got pregnant. Despite all of her careful counting, her math skills turned out not to be nearly as good as she thought they were.

About four months after we discovered Bonnie was pregnant, we got married. My daddy and Bonnie's mother and Bonnie and I went to the courthouse in Phoenix because that was the county seat.

To tell you the truth, we got married way too young. It was really tough on both of us. But we were real happy when our first son was born on May 23rd, 1948. His full name is Alan Edgar Owens, but we always called him Buddy.

Chapter Sixteen

WHEN IT COMES TO WOMEN, I've managed to stay in hot water way too much of the time. Some of it was my own fault. Okay, maybe most of it was—but the one time I nearly got killed over a woman, I was totally innocent. Okay, maybe not totally innocent—but still innocent enough.

I was nineteen, and I was playing guitar in a group with some guys over in Phoenix at a place on East Van Buren called the Round-Up. By then I'd moved on from the steel guitar to a Gibson L-7, which was an archtop acoustic guitar that I'd put a pick-up on and played through an amplifier so my guitar-playing could be heard above the noise of the honky-tonks I was playing in.

The job at the Round-Up was steady work for once—six nights a week at five bucks a night, plus tips. We had an old, empty cigar box that had the lid taped shut. The box had a hole cut in the lid just big enough for coins and bills to go in—but small enough so nobody could reach in there and steal our tip money. People would drop money in the box, and then they'd ask us to perform a particular song they wanted to hear. We'd play it if we knew it, and if we didn't know it, we'd just kind of fake it.

Across the street from the Round-Up there was a drugstore that had one of those old-fashioned soda fountains. Since my daddy had told me many times to always get to work early, every night I'd get to the club before anybody else. So, I got into the habit of going over to the drugstore around seven o'clock and having an ice cream malt. There was this beautiful young blonde Scandinavian-looking woman named Shirley who worked behind the soda fountain. I went over there six nights a week, so we got acquainted. As time went by, we got more and more acquainted.

Eventually we got together one night after I got off work. I swear to you, nothing happened between us. Now something probably would've happened, but that night she told me her husband was the piano player at another club about a mile from the Round-Up. Once I found out she was married, I never got together with her like that again. I'd still see her at the drugstore, but that was it. We liked each other, and we sure could've had a lot of fun together under different circumstances, but I didn't want her husband to catch us. Of course, I didn't want Bonnie to catch us either, but Bonnie and I lived over in Mesa, so I wasn't as worried about Bonnie finding out about me and Shirley as much as I was worried about Shirley's husband finding out.

Well, one night not long after our one little rendezvous, I was on the bandstand playing music when this nice-looking young man walked up to the stage and said, "I'd like to talk to you at intermission if you have a minute."

So, at intermission we went over and sat down at a table back in the corner there and he introduced himself. When he told me his last name, I started to get a little nervous because it was the same as Shirley's. He was wearing a nice suit, and when he unbuttoned his suit jacket, I saw what looked a whole lot like the butt of a pistol sticking out of his inside coat pocket. My mouth got so dry so quick, I couldn't hardly talk. I waved a waitress over and told her I needed a glass of water.

The man sat there with his suit coat unbuttoned. Then he leaned toward me and said, "You know a young lady named Shirley?"

I said, "Let's see. Shirley…Shirley," trying to act like I didn't know who he meant. About that time, the waitress brought me my water, and I started drinking it fast.

He said, "The girl who works at the soda fountain in the drugstore across the street."

I said, "Oh, *that* Shirley. Yes, I've seen her on many occasions because I go over there quite often to have a malt."

He said, "Well, that's my wife."

I said, "Really? Then I guess congratulations are in order because she sure seems like a nice young lady." My mouth went totally dry again, so I grabbed that glass of water and started drinking it faster and faster, trying to get my tongue unstuck from the roof of my mouth.

Then he said, "The story I've been told is that you've been foolin' around with her."

"That's just not true!" I told him. I said, "We're just acquaintances. I've only seen her at the drugstore."

He looked me right in the eye and told me, "That's not what *she* said."

I said, "I can't imagine why she'd say something like that." Drinking that water had finally loosened my tongue up real good. I started talking a mile a minute. I told him I was a married man with a young son. I told him I worked during the day and played music at night. I told him there wasn't enough hours in the day for me to have time to fool around with his wife or anybody else's, for that matter.

When I finally stopped talking, he said, "I want to tell you something. I brought a gun with me tonight. If I knew for sure that you'd been fooling around with my wife, I'd shoot your sorry ass right here, right now."

I started stuttering and sputtering, and I knew he could tell I was scared half to death. I said, "Mister, I never touched your wife. I don't know what you're talking about." Well, I knew exactly what he was talking about. She'd gone and told him that we'd been alone together, but apparently she'd sort of failed to tell him that we didn't do anything. I guess maybe she was mad at him and trying to make him jealous or something, but I sure as hell didn't see any reason to get myself shot over it.

I wasn't real sure if he believed me or not, but finally he stood up, buttoned his suit jacket, and walked out without saying another word.

I was still so scared—even after he left—that I took ill. I was shaking so bad and I was so sick to my stomach that I had to just grab my guitar and go home.

When he'd been sitting there with that gun in his coat pocket, I thought sure I was about to meet my maker. I guess the moral of the story is don't get too friendly with a married woman because you never know when their gun-toting husband might come see you. Either that, or don't get too friendly with a married woman unless you know for sure that her husband don't own a gun.

Chapter Seventeen

OUR SECOND SON, MICHAEL LYNN, was born on March 8th, 1950. I was playing guitar where I could find work around Mesa and Phoenix, but I also had to work day jobs to support the family now that there was four of us. When Bonnie said she thought we ought to move to Oakland, California, where her sister was living, she didn't have to say it twice. I was ready to go.

Well, we went to Oakland and moved in with her sister, but that didn't last too long. It turned out that finding work in Oakland was harder than finding work in Mesa or Phoenix. After about six weeks, we were on our way back to Arizona.

Once we were back in Mesa, I managed to get a job as a truck driver. That's how I came to meet Marty Robinson. He was a trucker, too, but he was also a singer who played in clubs around Phoenix under the name Marty Robbins. He even played steel guitar for me one time when I had a gig at the Astor Hotel in Phoenix. Just a couple of years after he sat in with me there at the Astor, he got signed to Columbia Records. I remember hearing his first hit on the radio. It was called "I'll Go On Alone." And he just kept having one hit after another for years after that.

My truck route included Bakersfield, so I'd end up out there for a day or two fairly often. Uncle Vernon and Aunt Lucille and my cousin Jimmy had moved to Bakersfield several years earlier, so I'd go to see them when I was out that way. On one of my trips, Uncle Vernon told me that there was a pretty good music scene going on in Bakersfield. He said they had a lot more clubs and honky-tonks than there were in Mesa, and that big country stars came to play in Bakersfield on a fairly regular basis.

That sounded pretty good to me, and when I got back home and told Bonnie about it, she said it sounded good to her, too. Our marriage had been pretty rocky for about as long as we'd been married, and I guess this was an opportunity for her to escape, so she just went ahead and moved out there with Buddy and Mike, and they moved in with Uncle Vernon and Aunt Lucille.

A few months later, in May of 1951, I moved to Bakersfield, too. I'd been moving from one town to another my whole life, but Bakersfield turned out to be the most important move I'd ever make.

PART II

Welcome to Bakersfield

Chapter Eighteen

M Y PARENTS MOVED OUT TO BAKERSFIELD THAT SAME YEAR, so pretty soon most of the folks who had made that original trip from Texas to Arizona ended up in the same town again. The only one who didn't eventually make the move was my older sister, Mary Ethel. She'd gotten married in Arizona, so she stayed there. My younger sister Dorothy had been a senior in high school when my parents moved to Bakersfield, so she lived with Mary Ethel until she graduated. Then she came on out and moved back in with our parents. A year later, Melvin came to Bakersfield, too. It was where we'd all planned on going back in 1937. It just took us a little longer to get there than we'd thought it would.

When I got to Bakersfield, I found out my Uncle Vernon had been absolutely right about the music scene that was going on. In fact, Bakersfield had been kind of a music hot bed, I guess you'd say, going back quite a few years before I arrived.

Bob Wills had been a regular at the Bakersfield dance halls back in the '40s. There'd also been a fiddler named Jimmy Thomason who played a big dance at the Beardsley Ballroom every week. He started playing there in '49, and I guess he would've played there forever if the place hadn't burned down in 1950. I think Jimmy might've been about the first resident of Bakersfield who actually got a record contract. He was signed to King Records, a label that put out a bunch of great blue-grass and country stuff in those days. None of Jimmy's records were chart hits or anything like that, but being a genuine recording artist sure made him a big deal around town. When television finally arrived in Bakersfield, he became a local TV star. He and his wife hosted a bunch of different country performers on *The Louise and Jimmy Thomason Show*.

There was another place in town called The Rainbow Gardens where everybody went to dance after the Beardsley Ballroom burned down. Outside of the city limits a little ways was a place called the

Pumpkin Center Barn Dance. A guy named Ebb Pilling ran the Pumpkin Center. He called himself Cousin Ebb, and he played the banjo in his own band there. Cousin Ebb booked a lot of bands at the Pumpkin, including the Maddox Brothers and Rose. Bonnie and I had seen the Maddox Brothers and Rose back in Mesa when we were teenagers. I remember another Bakersfield guy—Roy Nichols—was the guitar player the night me and Bonnie saw 'em. Rose and her brothers were the first act I ever got to see that wore really colorful Western-type outfits with rhinestones on 'em—the kind of things all of us country singers started wearing in the '60s.

All of these places I'm telling you about—the Beardsley Ballroom, the Rainbow Gardens, and the Pumpkin Center Barn Dance—were great big places with big ol' dance floors. Most of the music being played at those places during that era was Western Swing. I loved Western Swing. In fact, one of the earliest Western Swing bands was a Texas outfit called the Light Crust Dough Boys. I still remember listening to the Light Crust Dough Boys on the radio when I was real little.

The folks who were going out to those dance halls in Bakersfield were mainly people who had migrated to the area during the Dust Bowl years. So, they'd kind of brought their own music with 'em in a way by letting the owners of all those dance halls know what kind of music they wanted to hear. They wanted to hear Western Swing like they'd heard back home, and they were also partial to real down-home country acts like the Maddox Brothers and Rose.

Now those Western Swing groups had a lot of people in 'em. Bob Wills and the Texas Playboys had a dozen or so musicians in the band. With that many people, you could be pretty loud without having to have a bunch of electric instruments and amplifiers. But as time went on, the economics just sort of stopped making sense. Why would you want to have a huge dance hall and a dozen or more musicians to pay when you could have a lot less expensive place—a small club with a smaller, louder, band that played electric guitars? For the guy running a club, the overhead was less all the way around than at those big ol' dance halls.

So, in Bakersfield, things began to move in that direction. The first of those smaller clubs, to my knowledge, was the Rhythm Rancho out on Highway 99. Well, around the same time the Rhythm Rancho opened, a musician named Bill Woods moved to Bakersfield and started sitting in with the house band. Bill Woods was one of those guys who played a bunch of different instruments, so he could fill in just about anywhere he was needed.

As good a music town as Bakersfield had been up to right then, Bill Woods was the one who really brought everybody in the music scene together. Years later, folks would call Bill the "Godfather of the Bakersfield Sound," and I'd be the first to agree with that. He helped just about all of us who were trying to make a living playing music in Bakersfield.

After the Rhythm Rancho opened up, other honky-tonks came along. Three of the main ones were the Clover Club, the Sad Sack, and the Lucky Spot. Bill played 'em all at one time or another. He eventually formed his own group, but in those years he played in a bunch of other people's bands.

While Bill was playing in the house band at the Clover Club, he talked the bandleader into hiring a piano player named Herb Henson. In fact, Bill was the one who had talked Herb Henson into moving to town from Fresno because Bill was determined to make big things happen in Bakersfield. Well, Herb Henson didn't disappoint him. Just like Jimmy Thomason, he'd go on to have his own TV show called *Cousin Herb's Trading Post*. I ended up being on that show a lot. Bill Woods also brought a guy named Billy Mize in to play at the Clover Club. Later, Billy ended up being a regular on Herb's TV show. Bill Woods just worked tirelessly to promote Bakersfield music.

As popular as the Clover Club and the Sad Sack and the Lucky Spot were, the biggest and best of the bunch was a place called the Blackboard. When I got to town, Tex Butler was the regular act there. He had a couple of pickers in his band named Fuzzy Owen and Lewis Talley.

Now I know I've told you the names of a bunch of people, but all of those gentlemen—Bill Woods, Cousin Herb Henson, Billy Mize, Fuzzy Owen, and Lewis Talley—would end up being responsible for a lot of what happened to make Bakersfield an important music town. They were all real helpful to me, too, in the early part of my career.

Chapter Nineteen

IN 1951, I HAD A TEN-YEAR-OLD CHEVY. It was what I drove, and it was what I slept in. At the time, I guess I just had too much pride to move back in with my parents. I didn't think that was something a man who was almost twenty-two years old should do. There's a place called Central Park between Golden State Avenue and R Street in Bakersfield. I'd go park there at night, and nobody'd ever bother me.

About all I had to my name was my old car, my Gibson L-7, and maybe fifteen dollars. It wasn't long before that money ran out and I had to hock my guitar so I'd have enough money to be able to get me something to eat. I signed the pawn ticket that said I had a week or two to come get my guitar out of hock. At that point I just needed the money, so I figured I'd worry about the guitar later.

A couple of weeks after I'd taken my guitar to the pawnshop, I met a steel guitar player named Dusty Rhodes. He was the leader of this four-piece band that was playing at a place called the Round-Up. Of course, the last place I'd played called the Round-Up was that tavern in Phoenix where I'd just about got myself shot. So, I didn't particularly like the name of the joint, but I went out there anyway and borrowed a guitar from one of the guys in the band so I could show off some for Dusty. Now, the band was making forty dollars a night—ten dollars a piece. When Dusty heard me play, he decided that he and the rest of the band would take a cut in pay so they could add me to the group. I was always grateful to Dusty for that.

After Dusty told me I was hired, I went back to the pawnshop to get my guitar—but I was too late. The pawnshop owner had already sold it. Here I finally had me a job to play music in Bakersfield, and I didn't have a guitar to play it on. Well, when Billy Mize heard about my predicament, he loaned me one of his. I didn't have anything decent to wear onstage either, so Bill Woods's friend—a fiddle player named Oscar Whittington—loaned me a nice shirt. I found out real fast just how close-knit the whole Bakersfield music community really was. In fact,

Dusty even let me sleep on his couch after he found out I'd been sleeping in my car.

Chapter Twenty

ONCE I STARTED MAKING A LITTLE MONEY, I knew I couldn't keep borrowing Billy Mize's guitar anymore, so I started asking around to find out if anybody had one they wanted to sell. When I told Lewis Talley I was looking for a guitar, he said he'd just sold his old Fender Telecaster to a guy named Hank. I don't remember Hank's last name, but I found him and told him I really needed a guitar pretty bad. I guess Hank figured I needed it worse than he did because he agreed to sell me Lewis's old guitar for thirty dollars. Let me tell you, that was the best thirty dollars I ever spent in my life because the sound that Telecaster made was like a buzz saw. It could cut right through anything. I loved the way the neck felt when I played it, and I loved the way it sounded. The Fender Telecaster became my main guitar from then on. I've lost track of how many of 'em I've had over the years—but I've still got the one I bought from Hank in 1951.

When we'd take an intermission at the Round-Up—which wasn't very often—I'd just lean my guitar up against the wall. One night after I'd only had that Telecaster for three or four weeks, it was leaning against the wall at intermission when somebody bumped into it. Of course the guitar fell over, and on it's way down it hit one of the legs of the piano. When it hit that piano leg, a chip broke off of the little strip at the top of the guitar's neck. That little strip is called the nut. Well, the nut is supposed to have these six little grooves in it that the strings rest in—that's what holds the strings in place between the bridge of the guitar down at the bottom and the tuning pegs up at the top. When I picked my guitar up off the floor, I saw that one of the grooves had broken off.

I didn't know what I was going to do. I couldn't play it the way it was because one string was just dangling since there wasn't a little groove to hold it in place. I showed it to Jelly Sanders, our fiddle player, and he said, "Do you have a comb?" Back in those days we combed our hair, so I handed him my comb. He broke one of the teeth off of it, and then he carved a little groove into that tooth.

I said, "Well, it looks like it would work, but we don't have anything to glue it on with."

So, Jelly went to the bar and got some brandy. He put a little brandy on it, wedged it into place where the missing part of the nut was, and put the dangling string in that little groove he'd carved out.

Like I said, I've still got that guitar. I've changed the strings on it hundreds of times, and that little piece of comb is still there, still doing its job, still holding that string in place.

*   *   *

I'd played a lot of honky-tonks by the time I got to Bakersfield, and one thing I'd learned by then was that it was a lot more comfortable to be picking inside a nice cool place at night than it was working outside in the hot sun during the day. But as far as the clubs in Bakersfield were concerned, the Round-Up was really the bottom of the line. Any other club in town was a step up. If you were pickin' there, you were always looking to move on somewhere else as soon as you could—so I got to pickin' harder.

By the time I'd joined Dusty's band, Tex Butler had left the Black-board. The new act playing there was Bill Woods and His Orange Blossom Playboys. Bill had finally formed his own band, and they were really bringing in the crowds. In fact, the Blackboard had to add onto the building to accommodate the growing number of people that wanted to be able to get in and dance to the music Bill's band was making.

In September of '51, I got a call from Bill, asking me to come be the lead guitar player for the Orange Blossom Playboys at the Blackboard. I didn't want to leave Dusty, but I sure didn't want to stay at the Round-Up any longer. On top of that, Bill had made me an offer I couldn't possibly say no to. I was making eight dollars a night at the Round-Up, and Bill said he'd pay me twelve dollars and fifty cents a night to move over to the Blackboard. It sounds funny now, but Dusty couldn't get mad at me for taking a job that was going to be paying me four dollars and fifty cents a night more than I was making. Hell, you'd have to be crazy to turn down that kind of money.

Chapter Twenty-One

THE BLACKBOARD WAS AN OLD, RECTANGULAR, BUILDING that held about 500 people, and it had two spotlights that were always on. Those spotlights were bright yellow, and that was the extent of our lighting when we performed. But it wasn't so much about the building or the lighting as it was the music and the atmosphere.

When I joined Bill Woods and His Orange Blossom Playboys, we played from three in the afternoon to two in the morning. We worked eleven hours straight, six nights a week—now listen to this—with no intermission. You heard me right. *No* intermission. The music never stopped. But I was happy to have the job because it meant I was making a living playing music at the best joint in town—and I enjoyed being part of a band as good as the one Bill Woods had put together.

One of the most important things I learned from Bill was how to get people to dance. That was the whole idea, you see. The folks who came to the Blackboard were people who were ready to have a good time after a day of working in the oil fields or picking crops or some other kind of manual labor. These days I guess they'd be called blue-collar workers. We just saw 'em as hard-working men and women that came to the Blackboard to have a good time and forget about everything else. Those folks wanted to dance, and if they couldn't dance to the music you were playing, they'd just go someplace else.

I remember one of the things we used to do was a great ol' Bob Wills song called "The Kind of Love I Can't Forget." It was a medium tempo song with that Texas two-beat. It was the perfect song for getting people out of their seats and onto the dance floor.

These days, some people talk about what a rough joint the Blackboard used to be, but I remember those years really well—and I can tell you right now that there was probably no more than two or three fights a month. That ain't too bad. I can honestly say that in all the years I was there I never saw anybody get seriously hurt. About the worst I ever saw was when the cops were trying to handcuff a friend of mine. In fact, the guy was my barber. He was a big ol' strong guy, and it ended up taking six or seven of 'em to get the handcuffs on him. He just kept flinging those cops all over the dance floor. I don't think they would have got him cuffed at all if he hadn't finally just given in and let 'em. I guess people want to romanticize about how things were back then, but the Blackboard wasn't a bad place. I ended up working there from 1951 to 1958. It was like home to me.

Chapter Twenty-Two

IN THOSE EARLY DAYS AT THE BLACKBOARD, I wanted to be the world's best guitar player. I had no interest whatsoever in singing. Back then all the bands had a singer. I mean that's all he did. He didn't play an instrument—he just stood there and sang. Well, one day at the Blackboard, Bill Woods looked at me and said, "You're gonna have to sing a little bit to help us out until our singer gets back." Eventually I noticed that two or three months had gone by and that singer still hadn't come back.

One day I finally said, "Hell, Bill, I'm doin' all the singin' here. I just want to play the guitar."

In those days, there was this recording act called Speedy West and Jimmy Bryant. Jimmy was about the fastest guitar player alive. So when I told Bill I just wanted to play guitar, he said, "If I wanted a guitar player who doesn't sing, I'd hire Jimmy Bryant. Right now, I need a guitar player who can sing, so you're gonna do both."

Well, it didn't seem fair to me at all that I was suddenly stuck having to do two jobs, so I decided to have a little chat with Frank Zabaleta, one of the owners of the Blackboard.

Mr. Zabaleta was a Spanish Basque man, and he talked in broken English. He couldn't say "Buck." He always called me "Bach"—like the composer. Frank said, "You know, Bach, the waitresses like-a you zing.

The people like-a you zing." He hit himself on the chest a couple of times and said, "And *I* like-a you zing."

I said, "Well, thank you, sir."

He said, "So, you get-ta to be the zing-ah."

What he and Bill Woods had figured out was that they could have me play the guitar *and* have me sing, and Frank would be paying one less man. So, sensing an opportunity here, I said, "Okay, Mr. Zabaleta, I guess I could do that. What am I gonna get for it?"

He looked me right in the eye and said, "You gonna get-ta to keep-a you job!"

Well, I definitely wanted to keep my job, so I decided not to complain to Mr. Zabaleta any more about me having to be the damn singer.

Chapter Twenty-Three

IN THOSE DAYS, I wasn't looking to be the center of attention all the time. I guess you can tell I got over that problem.

Before Bill made me the lead singer, I'd been perfectly happy standing off to one side, playing my guitar. After I became both the guitar player and the singer in the band, Bill Woods still did most of the talking between songs—but as soon as I'd start singing, everybody would be staring at me.

Even though I was the lead singer, it was still Bill's band, so he didn't just tell me *what* to sing—he told me *how* to sing. When I'd first begun singing at the Blackboard, I'd sing in a key that was comfortable for me. But Bill would always say, "Why don't we move this up a key." So we'd move the song up half a step, and then he'd say, "Let's go up another half-step between verses." He was the one who caused me to sing songs near the very top of my range. By the time I started making records, I sang near the top of my range without even thinking about it. So even though I wasn't very happy about having to sing, I have Bill Woods to thank for making me sing, and for helping me develop my own vocal style.

There were a couple of other things that contributed to the way I sing: one thing was that the Blackboard didn't have any monitors. Monitors are these speakers that face you when you're on stage so you can hear all the musicians, and so you can hear yourself. Since there weren't any monitors at the Blackboard, I'm sure that's why I developed my hard-sounding vocal style. I was trying to hear myself so bad that I was always singing really loud.

The other thing about my singing style goes back to when I'd gotten real sick when I was a kid in Arizona. I told you about how I couldn't outrun my little brother anymore after that. Well, one of the other ways I was affected was that I couldn't hold a note out for very long. Physically, I just couldn't do it. So, when I sing, I kind of clip off the end of every phrase. I didn't start out doing it on purpose—I just didn't have a choice.

So, the way I sing came about because of Bill Woods making me sing in a higher register than I was comfortable with; having to sing really loud because there were no monitors at the Blackboard; and not being able to hold notes out very long because I'd been sick when I was a kid. That's a hell of a way to develop a singing style, ain't it?

* * *

Most nights, Bill Woods and His Orange Blossom Playboys were the entertainment at the Blackboard, but once a week we'd have a guest performer. Our band would be the opening act, and then we'd be the backup band for whoever the guest was that evening. We had all these great people come through: Lefty Frizzell, Rose Maddox, Skeets McDonald, Tommy Duncan, T. Texas Tyler, and a bunch more over the years.

One night the guest act was Joe Maphis and Rose Lee. Joe was a great guitar player—they called him the "King of the Strings"—and Rose Lee was his wife. So, Joe played guitar and they both sang. They'd been performers for several years on a radio show called the *Old Dominion Barn Dance* in Richmond, Virginia before they moved to Los Angeles in the early 1950s. As it turned out, their very first gig in California was at the Blackboard. Well, neither one of 'em had ever seen anything like it. They were used to playing on a radio show where the studio audience just sat there and listened. They'd never played in a joint where people were dancing and carrying on the way the crowds at the Blackboard did.

Joe told me years later he'd never played with a louder band than ours in his life, and that he'd never been in a club that was just filled from floor to ceiling with smoke. Back in those days, you could smoke indoors—and believe me, everybody did.

When Joe and Rose Lee finished their part of the show that night, they headed back to Los Angeles. On the way home, Joe wrote a great song called "Dim Lights, Thick Smoke (and Loud, Loud Music)." I always liked that song, and I liked it even more when Joe told me that the inspiration for it had been playing that night with our band at the Blackboard.

Chapter Twenty-Four

AFTER I'D BEEN AT THE BLACKBOARD for a couple of years, I'd gone through a lot of personal changes. Bonnie and I had finally gotten divorced in January of '53. We had tried to work things out, but I guess the last straw came when I was still playing at the Round-Up in '51.

Bonnie and I had gotten back together a few months after I'd moved to Bakersfield, but I was also seeing another woman on the side. There I was, in a town as small as Bakersfield was back then, trying to juggle these two women at the same time. I'd made enough money to be able to move Bonnie and the kids out of my aunt and uncle's house and put them up at the Park Motel—and, believe it or not, I'd put the other woman up at the Tower Motel there in town because I'd gotten her to come out from Arizona to visit me.

One day I was driving the other woman in my car when I saw Bonnie and the kids. As I drove by, I heard them yell at me, but I looked straight ahead and went right on down the road. The woman in the car with me said, "Were they yelling at you?"

I said, "Well, if they were, I don't know why, because I don't know 'em."

God, what crazy times. I'd just turned twenty-two years old, and I didn't have any sense when it came to women. I ain't got a whole lot now, but I didn't have *any* back then.

I thought I was getting away with having these two women at the same time until two or three days after Bonnie had spotted me and the other woman in my car. The band was rehearsing at the Round-Up when in the front door came the two of 'em, arm in arm. They walked right up to the stage and said, "We'd like to talk to you."

I said, "Yes, of course you would."

So, we went outside and they told me I could have one of 'em but not both of 'em. Bonnie said, "Which one of us do you want?"

I said, "Well, can I have some time to think about it?"

And they both said, "No!"

I guess it wouldn't have mattered what I said because I ended up with neither of 'em. Pretty soon, the one from Arizona had a baby and then went back to Tucson where her husband was. Yes, I was married to one woman and having an affair with another woman who had a husband back in Arizona. But it was her husband who'd gotten her pregnant. Like I said, I've always been pretty good with math, so I know it couldn't have been me. They tried to say I was the daddy for the longest time, but I didn't bat the ball on that one.

Bonnie and I would remain friends forever, and she would even go on the road with me for a little while at one point, but we just weren't meant to be married—at least not any longer than we were.

* * *

Since I'd moved to Bakersfield, I'd gone from living in my car to living at Dusty's place to living with Bonnie again to getting thrown out and having to swallow my pride and move back in with my parents until I could find a place of my own.

But as far as playing music was concerned, things were moving in the right direction. There was a singer named Bud Hobbs who'd made a bunch of records for the M-G-M label in the 1940s and early '50s. In the late '40s, he'd had a few hits. I remember one was called "Lazy Mary." Now, by the time I played on a recording session with Bud in June of 1953, he'd already had all the hits he was going to have. Of course, nobody knew that at the time. I was just excited about getting to be the guitar player on a recording session in Hollywood for the first time.

Bill Woods and Bud Hobbs knew each other, so when Bud asked Bill to put together some players for Bud's next session, Bill brought me in to play lead guitar. The other musicians were Ferlin Husky, Oscar Whittington (the guy who'd loaned me a shirt to wear when I'd gotten the job at the Round-Up), Ray Heath, Jack Trent, and a guy named Leonard Sipes.

Looking back on it now, that was quite a lineup of musicians. We recorded four songs with Bud Hobbs that day, and just a month later, Ferlin Husky—the bass player on the session—had a record hit the charts called "A Dear John Letter." It was a duet that he'd recorded with Jean Shepard for Capitol Records.

The funny thing is, Bonnie—*my* Bonnie—had recorded "A Dear John Letter" first. She and Fuzzy Owen had cut the song for a little Bakersfield label called Mar-Vel Records.

Not long after she'd moved to Bakersfield, Bonnie had gotten a job waiting tables at the Clover Club, and from time to time she'd go up on the bandstand and sing a song. Around Bakersfield she became known as "the Singing Waitress." She and Fuzzy became romantically involved after she and I split up, and "A Dear John Letter" was one of the records they recorded as a duet. Of course, their record was on a tiny label, so it didn't do anything. But when Jean Shepard and Ferlin Husky recorded it, it became a huge hit. It was number one on the country charts for weeks, and it started long careers for Ferlin and Jean both.

Leonard Sipes played rhythm guitar on that Bud Hobbs session. Just a couple of days later, he had his first session for Capitol as a recording artist. Bill Woods played piano on that session, and Ferlin Husky played lead guitar. Lewis Talley was the other guitar player, and Fuzzy Owen played bass. So, you can see that all of these Bakersfield guys were starting to kind of infiltrate the country records that were being made in Los Angeles, mainly for Capitol Records. Before his record was released, the folks at Capitol decided the name Leonard Sipes didn't have much of a showbiz ring to it, so his stage name became Tommy Collins.

Well, the Bud Hobbs record came out and nothing happened. Nothing much happened with Tommy Collins's first single either. Then one night a few months later, I was working at the Blackboard when Ferlin Husky called the club and asked to speak to me. When I got on the phone, Ferlin told me that Tommy Collins had another recording session coming up soon and that he wasn't going to be able to play lead guitar on it like he'd done before because he and Jean Shepard were going on the road.

So, on September 8th, 1953, I played lead guitar for Tommy Collins on four songs, including one called "You Better Not Do That." The man producing the record was Ken Nelson. It was my first time being a session guitar player for a Capitol recording artist, so that was the first time Ken got to hear me play. He told me he liked the lick I'd come up with that kicked off the record, and he said he might be calling on me again. Well, they paid me $41.25 to play on those four songs, so I made sure Ken Nelson had my phone number. When "You Better Not Do That" became a big hit, Ken started calling me a lot.

Chapter Twenty-Five

ONE NIGHT IN 1954, a guy named Terry Fell was the weekly guest artist at the Blackboard. Terry recorded for this label called X, which was a subsidiary of RCA. His biggest hit—in fact, it was his only hit—was a song called "Don't Drop It." The other side of the single was one he wrote called "Truck Drivin' Man." I doubt if too many people still remember "Don't Drop It," but "Truck Drivin' Man" ended up being recorded many times over the years by everybody from Dave Dudley to the Flying Burrito Brothers. I even cut it myself in 1964.

My friend Red Simpson, who played with me for a while at the Blackboard, would end up making a career out of singing truck-driving songs. He had a bunch of hits like "Roll Truck Roll" and "I'm a Truck," and a real good one called "Diesel Smoke, Dangerous Curves." But Terry Fell wrote and recorded one of the best of all those trucking songs—and it ended up being on the wrong side of the record.

Of course, Terry heard me singing and playing guitar when he was at the Blackboard that night. At the end of the evening, he asked me if I'd written any songs. He said if I had some original material, he thought he might be able to get me a deal on X Records. So, I decided I'd better get to work writing some songs.

Pretty soon I'd written "Down on the Corner of Love," "Right After the Dance," "The House Down the Block," and "It Don't Show on Me." The next time Terry Fell came back to the Blackboard, I sang him my four songs. Shortly after that he sent me a contract that said he'd be the publisher of those songs if he could get me on a major label. I called him up and said, "You've got a deal."

RCA gave him the go-ahead, so we went to down to LA to do the session. Lewis Talley played rhythm guitar; Fuzzy Owen was the steel player; and Jelly Sanders—the guy who had fixed my guitar with a tooth from my comb—played fiddle.

I thought the session went pretty good, but Terry called me up a few days later and said, "RCA decided that they're gonna use their X label just for rhythm & blues records from now on, so they're not gonna be puttin' out the songs you recorded." So, there went my big major label deal.

Not long after that, Terry asked me to come to his house. A man named Claude Caviness was there. Claude was a baker from Pico Rivera who had a little label on the side. Terry introduced me to him and said, "This man has a company called Pep Records. He'd like to have you as an artist. He wants to sign you for a year, and he wants you to record eight songs."

Well, I'd already recorded four, so I said, "One year, eight sides—I can do that."

Claude released a single of "Down on the Corner of Love" on his little Pep label. When I say he released the record, I'm kind of exaggerating. He didn't really have much in the way of distribution—in fact, I'm not sure he had a single distributor—so it wasn't in a lot of stores. But he got it to some radio stations, so even though it only had a little bit of regional success, it wasn't long before other people started to cover the song. A guy named James O'Gwynn recorded it for Mercury Records, and Red Sovine recorded it for Decca. It was also one of Bobby Bare's earliest records. So even though my version didn't do much, I took it as a good sign that those other guys had wanted to record it. None of 'em had a hit with the song, either, but it began to get my name out there a little bit as a songwriter.

Covering other people's records was a pretty common practice back then. A major star on a major label would hear something on a little independent label like Pep was, and then they'd go and record the same song on their major label and pretty much take the record away from you. Of course, Pep was never going to compete with those major labels anyhow.

Next, Pep released the other two songs I'd already recorded—"The House Down the Block" and "Right After the Dance." By this time, Lewis Talley and Fuzzy Owen had a little recording studio they'd put together in Bakersfield, so I went there and recorded four more songs over the course of a couple of sessions.

In the mid-'50s, Elvis Presley started having his first hits on Sun Records. Nobody'd ever heard anything like him. When Elvis first started recording for Sam Phillips there at Sun, they called his style of music rockabilly. I really liked what he was doing. I love country music, but I've never been a fan of just country and nothing else. I think guys like Elvis and Little Richard and Chuck Berry and Fats Domino had as much influence on my music as Bob Wills did.

A guy named Danny Dedman had sent me some lyrics he wanted me to put the music to. I fixed up the lyrics some and came up with a real up-tempo idea for the song. That one was called "Hot Dog." Then I wrote another fast one called "Rhythm and Booze." For that one I even managed to work in a line about "blue suede shoes," so it was pretty obvious I was trying to make an Elvis-sounding record.

If you listen to "Rhythm and Booze" real close, you can hear a guy moaning in the background. That was a disc jockey from Bakersfield named Red Butler. He worked at the only station in town that played my records. Ray Heath was the drummer on the session, but Red was so drunk, he decided he'd add some percussion of his own by beating on the bottom of a trashcan. I also had Roy Nichols playing lead guitar. I'm telling you, that day we made a real, honest-to-God rockabilly record.

But when Claude told me he was getting ready to put those two songs out as my next single, I got a little panicky. Here I'd just begun to make a name for myself around Bakersfield as a country artist, and I was about to have this rockabilly record come out. One thing that's always been true about die-hard country fans is that they don't want you to change. If you make a pop record, you might gain a pop audience, but you're going to lose a lot of your country fan base.

It's not like I had a whole lot of fans to upset yet, but I only had that one radio station in town that would play my records—and I knew for sure that once Red Butler sobered up, he'd hear "Hot Dog" and refuse to play it on his show. I was so worried that the radio station and the country fans around Bakersfield would turn their backs on me if they thought I'd gone all rockabilly on 'em, I told Claude I didn't want my name on the record. Of course, he'd already paid for the session, so he wasn't going to let the tapes just sit in the can. He said if I didn't want "Hot Dog" to come out under my own name, he'd just put another name on there. I don't remember how I came up with my pseudonym, but I told him to call the artist Corky Jones—and that's what he did. Corky Jones's career ended up being pretty short. That was his only record.

The next single that came out of those sessions had "Sweethearts in Heaven" on the A-side. The B-side was called "There Goes My Love." Wouldn't you know it—within a month of my record being released, George Morgan came out with "There Goes My Love" on Columbia Records. My single made a little bit of noise around California, but George Morgan's version went to number fifteen on the national country charts. And then, not long after that, Don Reno and Red Smiley came out with their version of "Sweethearts in Heaven" on Dot Records. Once again, I thought, "I've got some good material here that people like."

As things turned out, even "Hot Dog" ended up getting recorded by a guy named Pico Pete in 1956. So, I'd recorded eight songs I'd written, and half of 'em had been covered by other artists. I was starting to think if I couldn't make money as a recording artist myself, I might still make it in the music business as a songwriter.

Chapter Twenty-Six

RIGHT AROUND THE SAME TIME I'D AGREED to be signed to Pep Records, Tommy Collins had his first big hit with "You Better Not Do That." When he got invited to play on the *Grand Ole Opry*, he told me he wanted me to come with him to play that lead guitar part like I'd done it on the record. The *Grand Old Opry* took place every Saturday night at the Ryman Auditorium in Nashville, and was broadcast on WSM-AM. I figured we'd fly out there on a Friday and fly back on a Sunday, meaning I'd only miss a couple of nights at the Blackboard, so I agreed to go.

On top of that, I knew WSM was a 50,000-watt clear channel radio station that could be heard throughout just about the whole country at night, which was going to be a pretty big step up from KTYL's 250 watts in Mesa. And besides, I'd heard the *Grand Old Opry* on the radio ever since I was a kid, so I was excited about being on the show.

Then I came to find out that Ken Nelson was going to be taking the trip to Nashville with us—and Ken didn't fly. If he was going to New York or Nashville on business, he always took a train. Tommy had a '53 Buick sedan, so instead of taking the train and meeting us there, Ken said he'd ride with us. The problem was, Ken wouldn't let Tommy or me drive once it got dark. When we got ready to leave California for Nashville, Ken had the whole trip planned out. He knew how many miles we were going to go every day, and he knew which motels we were going to stay at every night. Instead of leaving on the Friday before the show, we left bright and early on a Monday morning, and we ended up getting to Nashville the following Friday night. You talk about slow—that was the slowest, most tiring trip I'd been on since I'd ridden on a board all the way from Garland, Texas to Mesa, Arizona. But we played games and came up with all kinds of ways to keep ourselves entertained during that trip.

Now Tommy—back when he was still Leonard Sipes—had moved to Bakersfield from Oklahoma in '52, so he'd been hearing me singing at the Blackboard for a couple of years by this time. But Ken Nelson only knew me as the guitar player on Tommy's record. During one of our conversations on that long trip to Nashville, Tommy started telling Ken that he ought to sign me to a record deal at Capitol. Tommy was telling him about what a good singer I was and all that kind of stuff, but I told 'em both I wasn't available because I had just signed with Pep Records. I'm sure Ken was wondering, "What the hell is Pep Records?" But Ken had a lot of class, so the subject was dropped, and we just kept riding on toward Nashville, stopping every day before it got dark outside.

Chapter Twenty-Seven

THE MUSIC SCENE REALLY STARTED to pick up steam in Bakersfield during the 1950s. Herb Henson's TV show, *Cousin Herb's Trading Post*, was on every weekday for forty-five minutes right before the local news. He'd have major country acts on his show when they came through town, along with local folks like me and Roy Nichols and Bonnie and Fuzzy Owen and Lewis Talley.

In the mid-'50s, Ferlin Husky and Jean Shepard were becoming big stars. After "A Dear John Letter," they'd each started having hits on their own. Tommy Collins had followed up "You Better Not Do That" with another hit I'd played guitar on called "Whatcha Gonna Do Now." And there were several of us from Bakersfield who were going down to LA pretty often to play on sessions for lots of other country singers who were signed to Capitol Records.

I guess one of the things that was pretty unique about the whole Bakersfield deal was that we all knew each other, and we were all kind of rooting for each other. I don't think anybody got jealous about the success that Ferlin and Jean and Tommy were having. I think we were all figuring that if they could do it, maybe we'd be next.

Mainly, we were having a good time making music and being able to make a living doing it. It seems like everybody played with everybody else at one time or another. If somebody had a dance coming up and needed a particular spot to be filled, one of us would step up and take it. I don't mean to sound like we were doing volunteer work. We were happy to take the gigs because we needed the money.

I remember one night back in '55, Roy Nichols, Cliff Crofford, Cousin Herb, Jelly Sanders, Fuzzy Owen, and I went up to the Green Mill Ballroom in Porterville. Roy Nichols was the main guitar player that night. They needed a rhythm guitar player, so that's what I did. We played the dance and everybody had lots of fun—especially Roy.

Roy had been known, on several occasions, to have several drinks. I mean he'd drink so much that he didn't know where he was or who he was. Well, after the dance, he managed to get in the back seat of my brand new '55 Chevy Bel Air. Cliff Crofford had ridden up to Porterville with me, so I was giving him a ride home—and now it was pretty clear that I was giving Roy a ride home, too.

Roy might've had too good a time every now and then, but that was okay with me. I'd admired him ever since Bonnie and I had seen him playing guitar for the Maddox Brothers and Rose back in Mesa. He even played guitar on my first recording session after I got signed to Capitol. A few years later he became the lead guitar player for another Bakersfield guy you might've heard of named Merle Haggard.

When we got to Roy's place, it was about two thirty in the morning. Now Roy wasn't very big. He probably didn't weigh an ounce over a hundred and forty pounds—but that night he was a hundred and forty pounds of dead weight.

Cliff and I tried to get him out of the back seat of my two-door Chevy, but he kept jerking away from us because he didn't know where he was or what he was doing. He just wanted to be left alone so he could sleep.

We eventually gave up and went to his apartment door and banged on it until his wife woke up and came out on the front lawn in her housecoat. She went out to the car and yelled at Roy four or five times, but he didn't even flinch. He just kept on snoring.

His wife turned to me and Cliff and said, "Maybe the three of us can get him out."

Well, we finally got him out of the car and onto this nice lawn in front of their apartment building. It was still thirty or forty feet to his apartment door, and I was thinking, "Man, this is going to be a real job to get him from here to there, up the stairs, and into his apartment."

In all this time, he hadn't woken up. Finally, his wife said, "Y'all just go on and leave him there."

I said, "Well, golly, I hate to do that."

She said, "Oh, it's alright. He's slept there before. When he gets cold enough, he'll wake up and come on in."

That's the way things were in Bakersfield back then. We all enjoyed playing music together, and we all had a good time.

Chapter Twenty-Eight

I N THE LATE SUMMER OF '53, I'd met a woman named Phyllis Irene Wall. Like a whole lot of folks in Bakersfield, she and her family were originally from Oklahoma.

We began dating shortly after we met. The next thing you know, I was spending the night at her place. We ended up living together for quite a while, and on March 7th, 1955, we finally got married and moved into this little rundown, two-bedroom house that I'd bought for next to nothing.

Phyllis was a widow with two children from her previous marriage. She had a daughter named Theresa and a son named Jacky. We'd only been married about five or six months when she got pregnant with our son, Johnny Dale. Johnny was born on May 9th, 1956. So now I was married again, this time with three children in the house—five of 'em when Buddy and Mike would come over.

Around the same time Phyllis and I got married, there was a big change at the Blackboard. In the years I'd known Bill Woods, he'd always been an innovator and an instigator—and a joker. I used to worry sometimes about us losing our job at the Blackboard. I'd say to Bill, "Are we doing alright here? What if we lose this club?" And every time I'd ask him, he'd always say the same thing: "Well, if we ever lose this lousy job, we'll probably be able to go somewhere else and get us a *good* one."

In March of '55, Bill really did find a job he thought was a good one. He and some investors opened a place called the Bill Woods Corral. Naturally, Bill wanted to take me and the rest of the band with him, but the owners of the Blackboard asked me to put together my own band and keep on playing there. I liked the idea of having my own band, so I got Lawrence Williams from Bill's band to stay on and be my piano player. The steel guitar player was Junior Stonebarger, and the drummer was Ray Heath. We called ourselves Buck Owens and His Schoolhouse Playboys.

So, as the years passed, I was still playing at the Blackboard, and I kept going down to Capitol Records in LA to be a studio musician for whoever Ken Nelson was producing. It had started with that Tommy Collins session, but I also ended up playing on records for Wanda Jackson, Gene Vincent, Wynn Stewart, Tommy Sands—lots of the artists that were signed to Capitol during those days. Ken would call me in because he liked my guitar playing and my musicianship. He knew he could turn to me to play the mandolin, piano, drums, or whatever he needed.

When Skeets McDonald came in to record "Hawaiian Sea Breeze," Ken asked me if I could play the ukulele. I said, "Well, sure I can!" So he sent me to the music store down the street to get a ukulele. Now, I'd never touched a ukulele in my life until that day, but I figured it only had four strings on it, so how hard could it be? I don't know if I even tuned it right, but by the time they were ready to roll tape, I had it figured out well enough to be able to pass for a ukulele player on Skeets's record.

I even played guitar—and other things—on Stan Freberg's comedy records. I remember Stan's sessions mainly because his famous Hollywood friends would come by just to hang out. Ken would always want to try to get four songs cut in three hours, but the rules changed if a big enough star stopped by to visit. One day I was there for a Stan Freberg session when Frank Sinatra showed up with Peter Lawford. Stan and Frank and Peter went off somewhere to talk, and six hours went by without any of us recording a note. I made $110 dollars that day for not playing on a Stan Freberg session.

Chapter Twenty-Nine

CLAUDE CAVINESS COULD SELL SOME records around Bakersfield and a few other parts of California, but he was never going to have what you'd call a real hit because, like I said, he didn't have any distribution for his label. The major labels got their records distributed all over the country—all over the world, really—but Claude was a one-man operation. So, he decided to go see Ken Nelson and take him a copy of "Down on the Corner of Love"—which I guess Claude felt was the best of the recordings I'd done on Pep.

Of course, I already knew Ken really well by that time, and I didn't want to lose what I had going as far as session work was concerned. I didn't want to make him angry by trying to get him to record me as an artist. But Claude made an appointment with Ken and took "Down on the Corner of Love" to the meeting. So, Ken listened to it and said, "Buck really has no style. He's an imitator. He sounds like three or four other singers. I don't want him for Capitol."

Then Terry Fell went and did the same damn thing. He met with Ken, and Ken told him, "I have no interest in Buck Owens as an artist at all. I like him as a guitar player and as an idea person, but I'm not interested in signing him to the label as a singer."

Years later, when folks would ask Ken how I came to be signed to Capitol Records, he'd say the reason he signed me was because I kept bugging him until he finally agreed to give me a record deal. The truth is, I never spoke to him about me recording for Capitol. Not once. I think Claude and Terry were the ones who kept bugging him. But they weren't the reason I ended up getting signed to the label.

In fact, I almost got signed to Columbia Records first. Johnny Bond and Joe Maphis were both on Columbia. They were at the Blackboard together one night, so I gave 'em a copy of that last single I'd made for Pep—the one that had "Sweethearts in Heaven" and "There Goes My Love" on it. Well, after they both had a chance to listen to it, they talked about it amongst themselves and decided to send it off to Don Law—the head of the country division there at Columbia. A few days later, he sent one of 'em a telegram that said, "Hold on to Buck Owens." The telegram said he was coming out to the West Coast the next month, and that he wanted to come to Bakersfield and sign me to Columbia Records.

I was real excited about the idea of being signed to a major label, of course. But that next month came and went without Mr. Law coming to the West Coast. He'd gotten tied up with other things, so I just stayed as patient as I could, waiting for the day he was going to come up to Bakersfield and do the deal.

Since I hadn't signed with Columbia yet, I was still a free agent. I knew I wouldn't be able to work as a studio musician for Capitol anymore once I was signed to their competition, but I figured until that great day came, I'd keep going down to LA any time Ken Nelson would call on me. And, of course, I didn't tell Ken anything about Don Law's telegram because I needed the money he was paying me to play on his sessions.

*   *   *

There were these two singers named Bobby Adamson and Woody Murray. They were from Farmersville, up close to Fresno. They performed a lot on *Cousin Herb's Trading Post*.

Since Bobby and Woody were both from Farmersville, Herb had named them the Farmer Boys. In fact, Herb is the one who introduced them to Ken Nelson. Ken liked what he heard, so he signed 'em to Capitol. They'd gone down to LA and recorded a few things, but nothing had taken off yet. So, when they were getting ready to do their next session, they came to my house.

Now, by this time, I had already been contacted by Ken's secretary. She had told me the date to be there at the studio with my guitars because I was going to be recording some stuff with Bobby and Woody. Well, when the Farmer Boys came over a few days before the session, they said they wanted to hear some of my songs. I played several things for 'em, and they picked out four they liked. Of course, that was fine with me. I figured it would be a good thing to just keep getting songs cut like I'd been doing for the last couple of years.

On the day of the session, I went down to Capitol. When I arrived at the studio, Ken Nelson just got all over me. He accused me of what he called "slugging" his artists with songs. He told me he had already given the Farmer Boys the songs that he wanted 'em to record, and that he didn't like it one bit when other people—meaning me—came along and offered 'em other songs and then talked 'em into singin' 'em.

I said, "Now, Ken, that's not exactly the way it happened. They didn't tell me you had already sent 'em songs. They didn't tell me anything. They just said they wanted to hear some of my songs, so I let 'em hear some of my songs." I tried to explain to him that that's the way it'd happened, but he just wasn't in the mood to listen. He was absolutely infuriated with me.

So, we got to recording, and when we finished the first song, Ken asked over the talkback, "Who wrote the song and who's the publisher?" Well, of course he already knew I wrote the song.

One of the Farmer Boys said, "Buck Owens wrote the song. We don't know who the publisher is."

Ken said to me, "Buck, who's the publisher?"

I said, "Ken, I don't really have a publisher."

We recorded the next song and Ken said, "Who wrote the song and who's the publisher?"

One of the Farmer Boys said, "Buck wrote it."

Ken said, "Yeah, okay. Well, who's the publisher, Buck?"

I said, "Well, same deal as the other song, Ken. I was gonna ask for your guidance on that."

Ken said, "Let's take a little break. Buck, can I see you for a minute?"

I went into the control room, and I didn't know what was going to happen. He said, "You know, you've been kicking around here as a session guy long enough. I think maybe we'd like to have you on Capitol Records."

When he told me that, I knew I had to come clean with him about Columbia Records. I told him the whole story about Johnny Bond and Joe Maphis sending one of my Pep records to Don Law. When I mentioned Don Law's name, Ken got even more adamant about wanting to sign me. He said, "But Capitol should be your home. We know you. You know us."

I said, "I know, but Don Law said he was coming out to the West Coast himself to have me sign the contract with Columbia."

Now that really set Ken off. He asked me when Mr. Law was coming out, and I told him that he was supposed to have come out the month before, but he'd been delayed. Ken said, "Well, I'm ready to sign you right now."

I got to thinking that I might be missing out on a golden opportunity here. It was past the date when Don Law had said he was going to sign me to Columbia, and now all of a sudden I had a chance to be on Capitol—a label I was already familiar with. I really didn't know what to do, so I told Ken I needed to think it over.

He said, "OK, I understand. I'll be happy to give you some time to think about it."

I went back out to the studio and we cut the other two songs, which, of course, I had written. We had to go through the whole, "Who wrote it and who's the publisher" routine a couple of more times. When I told him two more times that I didn't have a publisher and that I'd like to get his advice, he finally said over the talkback that he thought I should sign them to a company called Central Songs. I said okay because that's what he suggested. It would be years before I would find out Ken Nelson was one of the owners of Central Songs. I knew about Cliffie Stone, who ran the company, but I didn't know Ken had a piece of it, too. In fact, anytime anyone would accuse Ken of having an interest in Central Songs, he would always deny it. When some artists finally got proof that Ken really was a co-owner, they complained that it was illegal. I don't know if it was or not, but I sure don't think it was right. The main thing I learned from that experience was to eventually set up my own publishing company.

Anyway, when we finished the Farmer Boys session that day, Ken said, "Just a second, Buck. I need you to come with me." We went up to the twelfth floor where his office was, and he pushed this contract in front of me.

I thought, "My goodness." I said, "Now, Ken, remember—I told you I wanted some time to think it over."

Ken said, "Well, it's been almost two hours! How long does it take you to think something over?"

He pointed to the contract and said, "Read it and sign it."

I looked at the date on the contract and it said, "March 1, 1957." I told Ken it wasn't March yet, but he just said, "Read it and sign it" again.

It was only seven pages long, but it was on legal-sized paper with little bitty writing. It said stuff about the party of the first part and the party of the second part, and I finally said to myself, "What the hell— you gotta take a chance somewhere."

After all, the headquarters for Capitol Records was in LA, so I would be just a couple of hours away. I thought it would probably be better than trying to record for a label based in Nashville—and of course anything was a step up from Pep Records—so I signed the contract.

Chapter Thirty

AFTER THE FARMER BOYS SESSION, I went back up to Bakersfield—back to the Blackboard, playing every night as the leader of Buck Owens and His Schoolhouse Playboys.

Believe me, I was ready to get that call to come on down to LA to do my first session for my new label. But before that phone call came, I got one from Frank Zabaleta, telling me that Bill Woods was coming back. And he wasn't coming back to play in my band. He was coming back to the Blackboard to be the leader of Bill Woods and His Orange Blossom Playboys again.

So, there I was, all ready to become a big country star. I even had the recording contract to prove it—and now I was being told that they were going to take down the big sign with my name on it and replace it with one that had Bill's name on it. And, just like in the old days, I'd be back to singing and playing guitar for Bill Woods in Bill Woods's band.

A lot of other guys would've probably refused to take a step down like that, but I guess I'm not like a lot of other guys. I wasn't making any money from Capitol yet, so I had to work. Besides, Bill was too likeable to say no to. And since I was the singer and the guitar player in both bands, nothing much really changed except a couple of the players and the name on the sign.

Chapter Thirty-One

ON SUNDAYS AT THE BLACKBOARD, we'd have a jam session from three in the afternoon until seven in the evening. Then the rest of the band would take a break while me and a piano player named Ernie Kelly would play pop standards—things like "Sweet Georgia Brown"—for a couple of hours. Then the whole band would come back and we'd play from nine 'til two. So, even on Sundays, I was doing that whole eleven-hour stretch on the bandstand.

During one of those Sunday afternoon jam sessions, Wynn Stewart came in, and he brought a guy named Harlan Howard with him. This was long before Wynn started having hits like "Wishful Thinking" and "It's Such a Pretty World Today," and it was also long before Harlan started writing big songs like "Pick Me Up on Your Way Down" and "Heartaches by the Number." Well, Harlan and I hit it off right away. We started writing songs together on weekends. He'd come to Bakersfield and stay at my place—which was a pretty good trick since we didn't have a whole lot of room to start with. One weekend we wrote a song called "Sweet Thing," and it was so good, I told Harlan I was going to record it.

I'd already been signed to Capitol for almost six months when Ken Nelson finally called me and told me to come down to LA to do my first recording session as an artist—and just like I'd promised Harlan, "Sweet Thing" was one of the four songs I cut that day. The guitar players were me and Roy Nichols and another great Bakersfield picker named Gene Moles. Jelly Sanders played bass, and Glen Ayers was the drummer.

There were also some background singers on that session. Some of 'em sang on some of the songs with me, and some of 'em were added on later. All of 'em were a bad idea as far as I was concerned, but Ken Nelson was producing the session, so he was the one in charge.

*   *   *

In October, my first Capitol single came out. The A-side of the record was a song called "Come Back." I was still working at the Blackboard as a member of Bill Woods's band, but I figured that once "Come Back" became a big hit, I'd be moving on to bigger and better things. Well, as the weeks went by, I kept playing at the Blackboard, and I kept waiting for that single to hurry up and hit the charts.

In *Billboard* magazine, when a record sells a bunch of copies and gets a lot of radio airplay, they put a little bullet next to the title on the charts. That bullet means the record's doing so well that it's probably going to go higher in the charts the next week. Let me tell you something: if "Come Back" would've had one of those little bullets next to it, it would've been pointing *down*. But my first single for Capitol never had a chance to have a bullet next to it because it never touched the charts at all.

Now, Capitol Records had a lot of clout. They couldn't make *Billboard* put a record on the charts, of course, but they could usually get the magazine to at least review their new releases. Well, *Billboard* finally got around to writing a nice little thing about how my record was "spinnable wax for country jocks," but they waited until January of 1958 to finally say if it was any good. By that time, there probably wasn't a radio station outside of Bakersfield that hadn't already thrown the thing in the trash.

To tell you the truth, when that first record came out, I wasn't really sure if it had much of a chance. I thought it was a good song, but I'd been pretty unhappy with the way the record sounded. Everybody played real good, but I hated all those background vocals Ken Nelson had included on it. He'd used a group that was trying to sound like the Jordanaires, a gospel group that sang on a lot of Elvis's early records. They sounded pretty good backing up Elvis, but it just didn't make any sense to have that kind of sound on my record.

In Nashville, the producers down there were doing that kind of syrupy thing with background singers, and even string sections, because they were always trying to get a lot of their country artists to cross over onto the pop charts. It almost never happened, but they kept trying. I guess Ken thought my record might be like one of those pop-country Nashville records if he "popped it up" a little bit. The problem was, with all of that extra stuff going on, it just didn't sound like me.

So, the year had come and gone without me having my first big hit record. I sang "Come Back" every night at the Blackboard, but I was singing it as one of Bill Woods's Orange Blossom Playboys. All I could do was wait for the next single to come out and hope for the best.

Chapter Thirty-Two

ABOUT THE SAME TIME *Billboard* finally got around to reviewing my first single after it was already dead, I got a call from my old friend Dusty Rhodes—the guy who'd hired me to be in his band at the Round-Up when I'd first moved to Bakersfield. He called to tell me he had a good thing going on up around Tacoma, Washington, and that I needed to get in on it. I was so disappointed my record hadn't been a hit that I was willing to listen to what he had to say.

He told me there was a man up there named Ed O'Hearn who'd bought a little radio station called KAYE. And when I say little, I mean you could barely pick the station up outside the shadow of the radio tower. It was a tiny AM station in a tiny place called Puyallup. Dusty told me that Mr. O'Hearn had come up with a way that we could become co-owners of the station with him. Our jobs would be selling ad time and being disc jockeys. The deal was that part of the money we brought in selling ads would go toward paying for our share of the station.

Then Dusty told me he had a band, and that his band had a dance going on at Spanaway Lake every week in South Tacoma. They also had a steady gig at a place called the Britannia. It sounded to me like I could be making more money up in Puyallup than I was making at the Blackboard, so I decided I'd better give it some thought.

Well, I didn't have to think very long. In April of '58, Capitol put out my second single. It was "Sweet Thing"—the song I'd written with

Harlan. Ken Nelson had insisted on background vocals for that one, too. This time there was just one guy—a bass singer—singing "Doo-wah" over and over during every verse of the song—and he was singing as loud as I was. Then a whole group of background singers showed up during the bridge, and they were drowning me out, too. They were more like *fore*ground singers. So, the same thing happened to "Sweet Thing" that had happened to "Come Back." When it was clear that record wasn't going to make the charts either, I turned in my resignation at the Blackboard. Then me and Phyllis and the kids packed up everything and headed for Puyallup.

Chapter Thirty-Three

THE RADIO JOB KEPT ME BUSY ALL DAY. I'd go to work at eight o'clock in the morning, Monday through Friday. I'd spend the mornings and early afternoons trying to get the local businesses in the area to advertise on the radio station. Then, after making my sales calls, I'd hurry in to the radio station where I was a disc jockey from three to six in the afternoon.

Man, it was a lot of fun to be a disc jockey in those days. There was no music director, no program director—there was nobody around to tell you what to play or when to play it. Nobody talked about demographics or ratings or any of that shit that's completely taken over radio today. I could play my favorite records the whole shift. I spun records I liked that I thought the listeners would like, too. There were no rules, and I loved it.

I didn't get paid anything to be a disc jockey. I made money from the radio station because I'd get to keep a percentage of all the ads I sold. And like I said, another percentage of the ad sales money was going toward me owning a piece of the station.

But even though I didn't get paid to play records, I got to advertise our band's activities while I was on the air—just like with the radio shows I'd been on back in Mesa. During my three-hour shift on KAYE,

I'd announce that we were playing at the Britannia Tavern Monday through Friday, that we'd be playing a big dance at Spanaway Lake on Saturday, and so forth. A lot of times the band would work on Sundays, too, playing at McChord Air Force Base or at Fort Lewis.

So, every day after my disc jockey shift was over at six, I'd go home, shower, eat supper, and then head to downtown Tacoma to play music at the Britannia, which was about ten miles away from Puyallup. I'd play there until 1:30 in the morning. When we'd finish playing, I'd go home, go to bed, and then be back selling ad time at eight o'clock the next morning.

I was suddenly making five to six hundred dollars a week working at the radio station during the day, and playing clubs and dances around Tacoma at night and on weekends. Just a few weeks before, I'd been pulling down $82.50 a week playing at the Blackboard, and now I was making the most money I'd ever made in my life—and not a penny of it was from being an artist on Capitol Records.

Chapter Thirty-Four

ONE DAY DURING MY DEEJAY SHIFT at the radio station, Dusty ran in all excited and half out of breath. He told me, "I got us a fiddle player!"

I said, "What the hell do you mean you got us a fiddle player? You didn't talk to me about hiring no fiddle player!"

I was upset because I knew it was going to cost us. The more people there are in the band, the less each member makes. Hell, Dusty knew that because he and his group all had to take a cut in pay back when they'd added me to the band at the Round-Up when I first moved to Bakersfield.

Dusty said, "Well, we gotta let him play with us on Saturday because I already hired him."

As soon as he played with us that first Saturday, I knew that we did *indeed* need a fiddle player, so I have to give Dusty all the credit for that. I guess Dusty Rhodes was always a little more willing to take a cut in pay than I was, but after I heard this teen-aged kid playin' the fiddle,

LEFT: Mary Ethel Owens with her younger brother, Alvis Edgar Owens Jr. Sherman, Texas, 1930.

BELOW: (*Left to right*) Melvin and Dorothy Owens with their older brother, now known as "Buck." Mesa, Arizona.

ABOVE: Buck's parents, Maicie Azel and Alvis Edgar Owens Sr.

RIGHT: (*Left to right*) Buck Owens and Theryl Ray Britten. Mesa, Arizona. "I didn't sing yet back then. . . . Britt played guitar and sang, and I played the mandolin. We were on the radio three days a week at three o'clock in the afternoon."

ABOVE: Mac MacAtee, leader of Mac's Skillet Lickers, behind the microphone. Standing next to Mac (*left to right*) is Bonnie Campbell (soon to be Buck's first wife), Buck, and Virginia Logan. (Others unknown.) "[Mac] didn't sing. He didn't play an instrument. In fact, he didn't know a thing about music, except that he liked it and wanted to have a band."

LEFT: Standing, Buck and his mother, Maicie. Seated, Buck's grandmother, Mary Myrtle Ellington, holding Buck's oldest son, Buddy.

Bill Woods and His Orange Blossom Playboys at the Blackboard. (*Left to right*) Ray Heath, Buck, Oscar Whittington, Bill Woods, and Lawrence Williams. "I was making eight dollars a night at the Round-Up, and Bill said he'd pay me twelve dollars and fifty cents a night to move over to the Blackboard. . . . Hell, you'd have to be crazy to turn down that kind of money."

Like the sign says, Buck Owens and His Schoolhouse Playboys. (*Left to right*) Buck, Lawrence Williams, Junior Stonebarger, and Ray Heath.

On the set of *Cousin Herb's Trading Post*. (*Left to right*) Lewis Talley, Fuzzy Owen, Bonnie Owens, Roy Nichols, Al Brumley Jr., and Herb Henson.

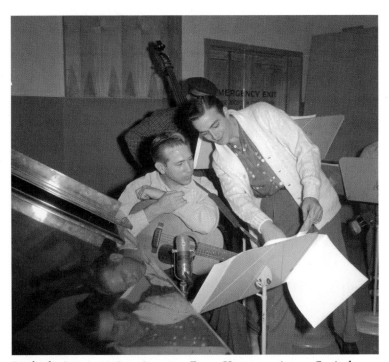

Buck playing acoustic guitar on a Faron Young session at Capitol Studios. "I kept going down to Capitol Records in LA to be a studio musician for whoever Ken Nelson was producing. . . . He knew he could turn to me to play the mandolin, piano, drums, or whatever he needed."

ABOVE: Buck on the steps of the Ryman Auditorium, home of the *Grand Ole Opry*. "Tommy Collins had his first big hit with 'You Better Not Do That.' When he got invited to play on the *Grand Ole Opry*, he told me he wanted me to come with him to play that lead guitar part like I'd done it on the record."

RIGHT: Buck with a fan during the era when Buck Owens and His Schoolhouse Playboys ruled the roost at the Blackboard.

LEFT: Buck on Halloween, "trick-or-treating" with (*left to right*) Michael, Buck's nephew B.J. Spence, and Buddy.

BELOW: (*Left to right*) Buck Owens and Tommy Collins. Bakersfield, California, 1956.

(*Left to right*) Don Markham, Don Rich, Rollie Weber and Barbara Vogel (behind Don), Gail Harris, Harvie Johnson, Loretta Lynn, Buck, and Dusty Rhodes (partially obscured by Buck). "The name of our band was the Bar-K Gang, so we called the TV show the *Bar-K Jamboree*. We didn't get paid anything, of course, but it was a big step up from not getting paid to be on the radio."

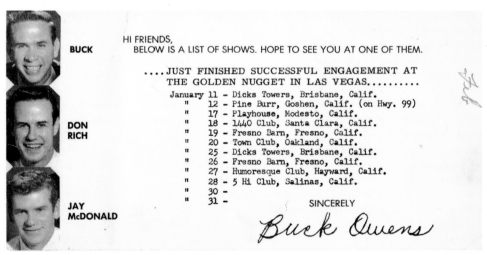

BUCK

DON RICH

JAY McDONALD

HI FRIENDS,
BELOW IS A LIST OF SHOWS. HOPE TO SEE YOU AT ONE OF THEM.

....JUST FINISHED SUCCESSFUL ENGAGEMENT AT
THE GOLDEN NUGGET IN LAS VEGAS.........

January 11 - Dicks Towers, Brisbane, Calif.
"   12 - Pine Burr, Goshen, Calif. (on Hwy. 99)
"   17 - Playhouse, Modesto, Calif.
"   18 - 1440 Club, Santa Clara, Calif.
"   19 - Fresno Barn, Fresno, Calif.
"   20 - Town Club, Oakland, Calif.
"   25 - Dicks Towers, Brisbane, Calif.
"   26 - Fresno Barn, Fresno, Calif.
"   27 - Humoresque Club, Hayward, Calif.
"   28 - 5 Hi Club, Salinas, Calif.
"   30 -
"   31 -   SINCERELY

Buck Owens

"I already had Don. The next person I added was a steel player named Jay McDonald. Jay could mimic the way Ralph Mooney played, so he was just the person I needed to help make what we played onstage sound like my records sounded."

even *I* was ready to take a cut in pay—and let me tell you, buddy, that was the only time!

The fiddle player's name was Donald Eugene Ulrich. I thought that sounded like a pretty fancy name for a country fiddle player. On top of that, nobody knew how to pronounce his last name right. I felt like he needed a stage name that everybody would be able to remember, so I told him we were going to introduce him from the bandstand as Don Rich. He just said, "OK, Chief."

I guess since I'd decided to change his name, he decided to change mine. From that day on, the only name he ever called me was "Chief."

So, I took a little cut in pay to add Don to the band. Meanwhile, the reason I hadn't been making anything from Capitol was because my records weren't selling enough for me to earn any royalties.

When you make a record deal, you're actually paying for everything yourself. The label covers the costs for you, but you have to recoup all their expenses out of your record sales. For instance, they charge you for studio time, so that's one of the things that goes against your artist royalties. In those old contracts, they even withheld a percentage of what they owed you for what they called "breakage." If they owed you a hundred dollars, they'd only pay you ninety because ten percent automatically came off the top to make up for any records that got broken in shipping. It didn't matter if two records broke out of two hundred thousand. They'd still take ten percent off for breakage. Record company rules were arcane and draconian. And to tell you the truth, they didn't really change all that much as the years went by.

So, you had to sell a hell of a lot of records just to earn back the cost of the studio rental time, the musicians, the unwanted background singers, the breakage, and everything else the label charged against your account. Can you believe that? Capitol owned the recording studio, but they still charged their artists to record there.

The way my recording career was going up to that point, I figured I was never going to make any money as long as I was on Capitol, so I decided the time had come to just cut my losses.

After I'd been in Washington for a few months, I sat down and wrote Ken Nelson a letter. It said, "Dear Ken, I can't do the kind of music you want me to. I'd like to do my type of music. If you want, let me do my music. If you don't want my kind of music, let me go someplace else. I don't want to hold you up." It wasn't exactly the Gettysburg Address, but I did my best to get my point across.

When Ken got my letter, he turned it over and wrote on the other side, "Dear Buck, We still want you. We believe you have talent. We're sticking with you."

So, Capitol was sticking with me—and since I was under contract, I was stuck with them. But we seemed to have come to an understanding. Ken was going to let me do things my way at my next session.

I took a few days off from my various jobs and went back down to LA in October of 1958. Like we always tried to do, we cut four songs in three hours. One of the four we did that day was called "Second Fiddle"—and we did it exactly the way I wanted to do it. No background vocals at all. Just me and the band. Ralph Mooney played steel guitar, Jelly Sanders played fiddle, and the piano player was George French Jr. We had Al Williams on bass, and the drummer was Pee Wee Adams. I thought everything sounded real good, but out of those four, I thought the two that had the best chance of being hits were "Second Fiddle" and "Walk the Floor."

Wouldn't you know it? My next single was one of the other two songs, "I'll Take a Chance on Loving You." Capitol had put that one on the A-side and "Walk the Floor" on the flipside. I'd won the battle of making my records the way I wanted them to sound, but Capitol was still in charge of deciding what they were going to release and how they were going to release 'em. The record made a little more noise than the others had. Just like the first two, it didn't hit the *Billboard* charts—but it did get some airplay around the country, so at least things were headed in the right direction. Plus, I won a little moral victory when several deejays turned the record over and started playing "Walk the Floor" instead of the side Capitol had picked to be the hit. But moral victories don't pay the bills, so I just kept doing what I was doing—selling radio ads, being a disc jockey, and playing music with Dusty and Don and the guys at night and on weekends.

*   *   *

There was a bunch of honky-tonks in the same section of Tacoma, and a lot of 'em put on talent contests. We had one going at the Britannia. One night this young gal came in wearing a cowgirl outfit. It was all blue, except for these white fringes that ran down the sleeves. She was wearing white cowboy boots that she had the bottom of her pants tucked into, and she had on a white cowboy hat. She was one of seven or eight people who were in the contest that night. The rest of 'em were just wearing regular clothes, so this young lady kind of stood out. When she signed in—like all the folks entering the contest had to do—I saw her name was Loretta Lynn.

She was cute as a button, and she was already a really good singer even way back then. Well, the contest winner was decided by the audience, and Loretta took the prize that night, which was a gold-plated watch in a real fancy case. I found out later that after she won the talent contest at the Britannia, she went on down the street to the Circle Inn, and she won the talent contest over there, too. It turned out the prize they were giving out was the same kind of watch she'd won at the Britannia.

Sometime after that, she told me that she'd won both contests that night, and that neither one of those watches ran. I promised her I'd make sure she got one that worked, and I guess I didn't do it because the last time I saw her, she was still teasing me about it, asking me when she was going to get that watch.

Chapter Thirty-Five

IN ADDITION TO EVERYTHING ELSE I HAD GOING ON, the band started doing a live radio show on Saturday afternoons. The KAYE radio studio was way too small for us to be able to do the show from there, so we did it in the studio of a Tacoma television station called KTNT. We didn't have hardly any real production facilities, of course, so what we did was to hook up a phone line between KAYE and KTNT so folks could hear us on the radio.

Now, the general manager of the television station was a man named Max Bice. One day we were there for our Saturday afternoon show when

Dusty Rhodes saw Max coming down the hall. Dusty said, "Hey there Mr. Bice, you'll be missin' a great opportunity here if you don't put us on your television station."

I couldn't believe Dusty would come right out and say something like that, but hell, he just acted like us being on TV was a foregone conclusion.

Lo and behold, Mr. Bice said, "Well, let's talk about that."

So, we talked about it for a little while right then and there, and by the time we got done talking, Mr. Bice had decided to air the show on his station, simultaneous with the radio broadcast. We ended up being on KTNT for the better part of a year. The name of our band was the Bar-K Gang, so we called the TV show the *Bar-K Jamboree*. We didn't get paid anything, of course, but it was a big step up from not getting paid to be on the radio.

When we'd be on the air, I'd say to the audience, "If you're watching us on TV, turn your radio on to KAYE, 1450 on your dial. If you're listening to us on the radio, turn your TV on to KTNT—because when you listen to us over both at the same time, you'll be hearin' us in stereo!"

Back in the late '50s, the word "stereo" was still pretty new. All I thought it meant was that the sound came out of two speakers instead of one. What the hell did I know? Besides, saying you could hear us in stereo sounded good—it sounded important. And the funny thing is, I'd say it every week, and I never had anybody correct me. I guess nobody who listened to the show knew the difference between mono and stereo, either.

Chapter Thirty-Six

DON RICH HAD A VERY PROTECTIVE MOTHER. Her name was Annie. She and Don's father, Bill Ulrich, had adopted Don when he was a baby. No one ever talked about the fact that Don had been adopted. At that time, I wouldn't have known about it myself if one of his aunts hadn't mentioned it to me.

When Don first joined the band, he was just a junior in high school—around sixteen or seventeen years old. He had a driver's license, and he knew how to drive a car, but Annie wouldn't let him drive by himself.

In order for us to present a halfway decent television show on Saturdays, we would rehearse on Friday afternoons. So, after my deejay shift on Fridays, I'd go to Don's high school in Olympia—thirty miles away—and wait outside for him to come out. Then I'd drive the thirty miles back so we could rehearse for Saturday's show. Every Friday for about a year I'd pick him up and take him back home. His mother was so protective that she never once let him make that drive to the rehearsal by himself.

Since we had a nice big television studio to perform the *Bar-K Jamboree* in, Mr. Bice decided we should do the show in front of a live audience. On Saturdays, Annie would always come to the show and sit in the audience, so at least I didn't have to pick Don up and take him home on Saturdays, too.

Don was in the band mainly because he was such a good fiddle player. But we had a lot of time to fill on the show every week, so occasionally I'd have him sing one of the popular country songs of the day. And when he sang, let me tell you, the young ladies in the audience noticed him in a big way.

Don was a really good-looking guy. He was about six feet tall, and he had a perpetual smile and a beautiful personality. At that point in his life, even though he was in his late teens, Don hadn't started dating yet. I think Don's mother came to the *Bar-K Jamboree* every week so she could whisk her boy out of there as soon as the show was over—keeping him away from the girls for as long as she could.

Well, Don's mother could come watch him when he was on the TV show every Saturday, but she couldn't follow him everywhere. One of the places she didn't come to was a place we played called Steve's Gay Nineties. They had three can-can girls there—those dancers who wear garter belts on their thighs and kick their legs up real high. One night, the youngest of those three can-can girls got a-hold of Don, in a manner of speaking. When Don found out how much fun he'd been missing, he started paying attention to the opposite sex for the first time in his life. Well, when his mother somehow got word of what was going on, she wasn't happy about it at all. She was afraid some girl was going to get a-hold of him permanently, and then she would lose all that control she held over him.

* * *

The lineup of the Bar-K Gang changed a lot during the years I was in Washington, but I remember who the members were the first time Don went with us on a job that required spending the night away from home. It was a Sunday night in Spokane—at the time, our band was me and Dusty, Ty Willard, Rollie Webber, Harvie Johnson, and Don.

We didn't get paid much for the Spokane gig, so we'd rented just two motel rooms—the kind that were joined together with a door in the middle. Since me and Dusty were the leaders of the band, the two of us slept in one room, and the other four guys were in the room next to ours. These were little rooms, and there were just two beds in each.

So, I was trying to go to sleep when I suddenly heard this great big ruckus going on in the other room. The walls were paper thin, so I yelled, "What the hell are you guys doing in there?"

Well, the noise in the other room kept getting louder until it reached the point where those boys had kept me awake just a little too long. I jumped out of bed, mad as a hornet. I swung open that door between the two rooms, and there was Don, lying on one of the beds, but with his back up against the wall. He was just lying there real still, and his eyes were wide as saucers.

I said, "All right, what the hell is going on in here?"

Don said, "Ty and Rollie and Harvie told me they're gonna draw straws to see which one's gonna get to sleep with me—and they said the winner is gonna get my cherry." Of course, I knew they were just messing with him, but I kept a straight face.

I just looked at the other guys and said, "Whoever draws the short straw is sleeping on the floor tonight." When I went back into my room, Dusty asked me what had been going on next door. When I told him, we both started laughing, but we had to laugh as quiet as we could because neither one of us wanted poor ol' Don to hear us through that thin wall.

Later Don told me, "Until we went to Spokane, I'd never gone no-where with a bunch of musicians before. I didn't know what musicians did when they went out on the road—but I sure as hell knew I didn't want 'em doin' it to me."

Chapter Thirty-Seven

IN MARCH OF '59, Capitol released my fourth single. The A-side was "Second Fiddle." I couldn't believe it. The label had finally done something right. And sure enough, "Second Fiddle" shot up the *Billboard* charts. It only made it to number twenty-four—and it didn't stay there for very long—but I could finally say I'd had a record of mine make it into the Top Twenty-Five on the country charts. I'd already written a song that had made the charts for somebody else—back when George Morgan had scored a hit with "There Goes My Love"—but now I had a chart record of my own, with me as the artist.

I was twenty-nine years old. Between my singles on Pep and my other releases on Capitol, I'd watched seven singles come out and I'd watched 'em all die. It felt mighty good to finally have a little bit of proof that there was a national audience for the kind of music I was making.

"Second Fiddle" had hit the charts in May of '59, and by the next month, I was back in Capitol Studios again. I was still a deejay, still playing clubs every night, and still doing the TV show on weekends, but some way or another I'd managed to find the time to write some new songs.

One of my new ones that I wrote with Dusty Rhodes was called "Under Your Spell Again." I'd heard this R&B song about a guy putting a spell on a woman. It might've been "I Put a Spell on You" by Screamin' Jay Hawkins, or it could've been "Castin' My Spell" by Johnny Otis, but I honestly don't remember. I just remember I decided to turn the idea around the other way—where the guy singing is the one who's under the woman's spell.

"Under Your Spell Again" came out that July, and I couldn't have been more excited about it. Well, the single had been out about three weeks or so when this package came in to the radio station from Columbia Records, and lo and behold, there in the package was a brand new record by Ray Price—"Under Your Spell Again." When "Second Fiddle" had come out, a lot of people had said it sounded like a Ray Price record. All of a sudden it looked like Ray Price wanted to make a record that sounded like me.

Back in those days, it was a pretty common practice for several different artists to record the same song—like when George Jones recorded "Why Baby Why." As soon as George's record came out and started going up the charts, Red Sovine and Webb Pierce ran in the studio and cut the same song as a duet, and their version started going up the charts, too. George's record made it into the Top Five, but Red and Webb's version went all the way to number one, and it stayed there for a while.

When I saw that Ray Price single, I thought, "My Lord, what a chance we had," because I figured Ray Price—being a much bigger star than me at the time—would be the one to end up with the hit. Well, it just so happened that he never did catch up with me—but he came close. My record got to number four on the country charts, and his got to number five.

I ended up kind of having mixed emotions about the whole deal—I would've liked to had the only hit version of the song at the time, instead of having to race a big star like Ray Price up the charts. On the other hand, since I co-wrote the song, I got paid songwriter royalties for my record and Ray's record both, so I really couldn't bring myself to complain about it all that much.

Chapter Thirty-Eight

NOW THAT I'D HAD A TOP TWENTY-FIVE record with "Second Fiddle," and then a number four hit with "Under Your Spell Again," the folks at Capitol started to believe in what I was doing. They began to understand that my music was straight country—no choirs and no string sections. The only instrument from the orchestra that I wanted on my records was a violin—as long as the person playing it knew how to make it sound like a fiddle.

"Under Your Spell Again" had hit the charts in October of '59, and I mean to tell you that thing *stayed* on the charts. It was still going strong when Ken Nelson called me and told me to come back down to Los Angeles in December to cut some more tunes.

When me and Don Rich and Dusty Rhodes took off in Dusty's '57 Cadillac to make the trip from Tacoma to LA in December, "Under Your Spell Again" was *still* in the Top Ten. It ended up staying on the charts for over five months—but it didn't hang around nearly as long as the next one did.

This was the trip I was telling you about in the Prologue—the one where Dusty had encouraged Don to sing along with me while I was practicing "Above and Beyond" in the car on the way down to LA. That's when I discovered that Don could sing such perfect harmony with me. Here he'd been playing fiddle in our band for months without ever letting me know that he had such a talent for singing harmony. He also hadn't told me he was a guitar player. But that's just the way Don was. He wasn't the kind of guy who would promote himself or brag about his talents. He just wanted to play music.

My old friend Harlan Howard had written "Above and Beyond," and my old friend Wynn Stewart had been the first to record it. His single had come out earlier that year, and I'd heard it on a radio station out of Seattle. I thought it was another really good song by Harlan—but I had an idea of how to make a different kind of record than the one Wynn had made. And I didn't feel bad about covering Wynn's record because his version had already come and gone without hitting the charts at all.

"Above and Beyond" had a great chorus, so I decided I'd kick off the song with that chorus, and then go into the first verse. Wynn had waited until after the first verse of "Above and Beyond" to sing the chorus—which, of course, is the way Harlan had intended for the song to be sung. But I'd started "Under Your Spell Again" with the chorus, and it worked out pretty good for that song, so I figured it would work for this song, too. I also thought the song needed to be a little more up-tempo than the way Wynn had done it, so I decided to speed it up some when I recorded it.

Don played fiddle at that session. It was the first of many that he and I would do together for years to come. The great Ralph Mooney was the steel player. Ralph played on a ton of records, including several of my early ones, and lots of Wynn Stewart's. He played on some of Merle Haggard's records, too, and even ended up being in Merle's band for a while—so Ralph was important to several of us on the Bakersfield scene.

Since Don had never sung with me before our drive down from Tacoma a couple of days earlier, I decided I'd better overdub my own harmony vocals on "Above and Beyond," which is what I'd done on "Under Your Spell Again." The time would come when I would let Don record most of the harmony vocals, but right then I was worried that he might get too nervous about singing when that red light came on in the studio, and that we'd have to keep doing more and more takes. So, I did 'em myself just to save time as much as anything else. I actually did my own harmony vocals on quite a few of my records after that—because the results were going to be exactly the same anyhow. When I go back and listen to a lot of my records from the '60s and early '70s, I can't even tell which ones are me singing harmony with myself and which ones are Don. That's how similar our voices could be.

On that same session, we did "Excuse Me (I Think I've Got a Heartache)," one that Harlan and I had written together. Harlan told me he got the idea from something a disc jockey named "Texas" Bill Strength had said. Harlan and Wynn Stewart had gone to visit Bill, and the three of 'em were sitting on the couch in the living room drinking beers when they saw Bill's wife start carrying stuff out of the house. She'd just walk right past 'em without saying a word. One time she was carrying a bunch of her clothes out to the car. The next time she went through, she was carrying a lamp. The next thing they knew, she was walking through the living room carrying a TV set! Finally, Bill just sighed and told Harlan and Wynn, "Go ahead and finish your beers guys, but you'll have to excuse me—I think I've got a heartache."

Well, Harlan and Wynn didn't know what to do, so they decided it'd be best just to sort of slip on out the door. As they were walking to the car, Harlan said, "My God, that was dramatic as hell! Here's this guy losing this gorgeous woman. They're breaking up, and he says, 'Excuse me, I think I've got a heartache.' The whole thing was like a country song—and he even provided the title."

Like I always tried to do, we got four songs recorded in three hours that day, including one Dusty co-wrote with me called "'Til These Dreams Come True."

After we finished at Capitol Studios, we headed back up to Washington for what turned out to be the last time. We just didn't know it yet.

Chapter Thirty-Nine

WHEN WE GOT BACK TO WASHINGTON, I went back to doing all of my various jobs. But now when the band performed, instead of just being the fiddle player, Don was singing harmony with me on a lot of the songs we did.

We had Loretta Lynn as a guest on the *Bar-K Jamboree* there at KTNT. I remember Loretta told me she was nervous because it was the first time she'd ever been on television. I found out later that she got her first record deal because the owner of the little label she got signed to had seen her performing on the show. Now that I think about it, since being on my TV show got her a record deal I guess I shouldn't feel so bad about not replacing that watch.

In February of 1960, Capitol put out my next single, "Above and Beyond," with "'Til These Dreams Come True" on the B-side. I was happy the song I wrote with Dusty had made the B-side because I knew he'd be making money off the record, too, if it sold well—and believe me, it sold really well.

When "Above and Beyond" started flying up the charts, I decided that I'd better move back to Bakersfield because it looked like I was finally going to have a real career. I sold Dusty my interest in the radio station and the other little ventures he and I had together. Then I went to Don and asked him to come with me, but he said his mother was set on him going to college up there. So, we shook hands and I thought, "Well, that's probably the last time I'll see him."

That was in June of 1960. I couldn't imagine losing Don because he had already become such an important part of my sound. But I didn't want to stop him from getting an education, and I knew I wasn't going to be able to talk him out of doing something his mother wanted him to do.

Meanwhile, I'd been so busy working and paying attention to my career that it had put a real strain on my marriage to Phyllis. By the time I'd decided to move back to Bakersfield, Phyllis had decided she'd put up with me long enough, so she was more than happy to drive me to the airport so she could watch me get on that plane and fly away.

After I'd been back in Bakersfield about four months, I got this letter from Don, written on notebook paper in pencil. It said, "Dear Chief, I don't like this college stuff. It ain't going to work out for me. I've decided I want to make music my life. In the months that you've been gone I've been playing with lots of other people, but they don't do it the way I like it. I like it the way we did it when you were here. So if you have a job for me, I'd like to come to work for you."

In the letter, when he asked me for a job, he'd spelled it j-o-b-b. At the end of the letter he wrote, "I got to go get that damn cat out of the kitchen or mama's going to kill me when she comes in." He'd spelled cat c-a-t-t, so it was pretty easy for me to see that Don Rich wasn't going to have much of a college career.

I decided I'd better offer him a "j-o-b-b."

PART III

"Act Naturally"

Chapter Forty

NOT LONG AFTER I MOVED BACK TO BAKERSFIELD, the money started coming in from Capitol Records for my artist royalties on my singles, and from Central Songs for my songwriter royalties for "Under Your Spell Again," as well as the other songs I'd written that Central Songs had the publishing on.

In those days, record labels and music publishers paid you only two to four times a year. A lot of 'em are still that way. In the '50s and '60s, they'd pay you sixty days or even ninety days after each quarter or half-year, depending on what your contract said. If your contract called for you to be paid twice a year, that meant the label could collect money in January, but they didn't have to pay you any of it until September or October. That way, they could hang onto your money for eight or nine months. And then there was that "breakage" I was telling you about. Any kind of way they could keep your money, they would. But "Under Your Spell Again" sold a lot of records and got a lot of radio airplay, so I was finally making real money—more than I'd been making up in Washington anyway.

A few years earlier, in 1957, I'd gotten a handle on what music publishing was all about, so Harlan Howard and I had formed a company called Blue Book Music. I was still signed to Central Songs, but I managed to work out a deal with 'em that would allow me to put some of my songs in their company and some of 'em in Blue Book Music. Before I left Washington to head back to Bakersfield, Harlan had gotten married and moved to Nashville. He called me from Nashville to tell me he was getting ready to sign with a company down there called Tree Music, so he wanted to know if I'd like to buy his share of Blue Book. I was happy to do it because I'd already figured out that a publishing company with good songs in it was a real smart thing to invest in.

Since I'd finally started making money as a recording artist and a songwriter and a music publisher, I got interested in some other little business ventures. There was a place a few miles outside of Fresno called the Big Fresno Barn. The house band there was Dave Stogner and the Western Rhythmaires, but the folks who owned it would let me rent the place out on Saturdays from time to time, so I'd book it and promote the shows and get sixty percent of the take. Sometimes I'd play there myself, and sometimes I'd book other acts to play there. Two of the biggest acts I remember booking were Hank Snow and Bob Wills. There weren't a lot of country radio shows to advertise something like that, so a lot of my promotion was just word of mouth. But if you started telling people around town that Hank Snow or Bob Wills was going to be playing at the Barn, they'd fill that place up.

I got bit by the business bug when I realized that I could make a lot more money if I owned my own publishing company instead of giving half of everything away to somebody else's publishing company. And then, when I got to own a piece of that radio station up in Puyallup, I found out that being involved in those kinds of things just didn't seem very complicated to me. My first love has always been writing songs and playing music, but I learned way back then that I also had a good head for business, so I didn't see any reason not to take advantage of it.

A lot of singers and songwriters are afraid to pay attention to their own business because they're worried it'll take away from their being able to write songs or something. I never understood that. Maybe it's just never been a problem for me because I was already working all day and playing music at night from the time I was a teenager. Having my own music publishing company didn't cause me to write less songs. It made me want to write more songs so I'd have 'em to put in the company—and that's exactly what I did.

Chapter Forty-One

NO MATTER HOW GOOD I AM when it comes to business, I'm the first to admit that I've had more than my share of problems when it comes to women. Phyllis and I had split up in Washington, but we managed to iron things out after a while. Pretty soon the two of us and the three kids were back under the same roof in a little house on Withee

Street in Bakersfield. And not long after that, we added another one to the household for a while.

I really wanted Don to come to Bakersfield, but I needed to make sure he was serious. So, after I got his letter about wanting a "j-o-b-b," I called him and said, "Don, a good education is a very important thing for you to have."

Now, I'd known Don for a couple of years by then, and I knew he was about as laid back as you could get. He wasn't what you'd call an ambitious kind of guy. He was one of those guys who didn't want to have arguments or any sort of conflict in his life. But when I called him and suggested that he should consider staying in school, he made it real clear to me that he didn't care what his mother wanted—he wanted to be in Bakersfield making music with me. Of course, I didn't really want to try to talk him out of coming to Bakersfield in the first place, but the way he was carrying on it wouldn't have mattered what I said. So I made him an offer. "Don, I can pay you seventy-five dollars a week, and you can come live here at my house until you've got enough money to get your own place."

We had that phone conversation in October of 1960, and he told me he'd be heading my way in December. Don was determined to come to Bakersfield, but he still needed a couple of months to figure out how he was going to break the news to his mother.

Chapter Forty-Two

A LOT OF THOSE FOLKS THAT WRITE about the history of country music have said that the '60s was my decade, and I'd have to agree with 'em. When 1960 rolled around, "Under Your Spell Again" was still on the charts. Then "Above and Beyond" came out. It went to number three, so that was my biggest hit yet. I'm telling you, it seemed like that thing stayed on the charts forever. The single had come out in February while I was still living in Washington, and it was still on the charts when "(Excuse Me) I Think I've Got A Heartache" came out that September.

In those days, *Billboard* magazine called the kind of music we made "country and western." In late October of 1960, the magazine published what they called their "Annual C&W Disk Jockey Poll." Jim Reeves won for "Favorite Male Artist," and Kitty Wells got "Favorite Female Artist." Felice and Boudleaux Bryant won as "Favorite Songwriters." Harlan Howard came in second in that category. I was happy to see that Harlan was so high up on the songwriters' list, and I was happy to see that Harlan's wife, Jan, was named "Most Promising Female Artist." But I was even happier to see that right there next to the picture of Jan was a picture of me. They'd picked Buck Owens as "Most Promising Male Artist" of 1960.

*　*　*

Don was still wrapping things up in Washington when I went back down to LA to record four more songs at the beginning of December. Ralph Mooney played steel guitar for me again, and Jelly Sanders was my fiddle player. That session included "Foolin' Around," which was another one I'd written with Harlan.

About the time I got back up to Bakersfield, I got a call from Don Rich's mama saying she wanted to talk to Donny. That's what she called him—"Donny." I told her he hadn't shown up yet. She said, "Well, they shoulda been there by now."

I said, "They? What do you mean 'they'?"

She said, "Shotgun Red is riding down there with him because I didn't want him to make that long trip by himself."

Now, Shotgun Red was one of the musicians who'd played with us for a while in the Bar-K Gang. He was a real good singer and an even better steel guitar player, and I guess he was in on Don's little plan to fool his mama.

I told her, "Well, if I hear from him, I'll let you know."

That was on a Tuesday, and Don and Shotgun didn't show up until that Friday. When they got there, I asked 'em where the hell they'd been. So, Don 'fessed up. He had a girlfriend named Marlane Schindler, so he'd gone and spent three or four days with her there in Washington before he and Shotgun finally headed down to Bakersfield. I knew his mama didn't want him to be hanging around with Marlane because she didn't like any female to be around her Donny. But the problem for me was—by that Friday morning—Don's mama had called me at least twenty-five times. She was so worried that she'd started to get me worried, too. So I told Don he was going to have to call his mother and tell her where the hell he'd been all that time.

I'm sure he must've made up a real whopper. He called his mama and told her some tale about why they'd been so late showing up at my place, but that he was here now and everything was fine.

Well, once Don got settled in, we started touring together right way. I was making money, but not the kind of money I needed to take a band out on the road. So Don and I just took a couple of acoustic guitars and his fiddle, and we drove my Ford from one job to the next. I didn't even take my Telecaster. But all of those joints where Don and I played had a house band, and they'd back us up just like Bill Woods and His Orange Blossom Playboys used to do when we'd have guest artists at the Blackboard.

* * *

One thing I knew, going all the way back to when it was just Don and me, was that I needed to develop a fan base. So, I was always as polite as I could be when people would come up and ask for my autograph, no matter how tired I was after a show. Nobody'd ever asked for my autograph when I was playing at the Blackboard, but now that I was a recording artist with my songs getting played a lot on the radio, there were plenty of young ladies asking for my autograph, or asking to have their picture taken with me. I've never forgotten this one night in 1961 when me and Don were just getting ready to go onstage. These two young ladies came running up to me and one of 'em said, "Buck! Buck! Can we have a picture with you?"

I said, "Well, sure you can."

Then the other girl said, "Great! Do you have a camera?"

I've probably had at least a thousand people come up and ask me for my autograph when they didn't have a pen or a piece of paper for me to sign it on—but that was the only time I ever had anybody ask to have their picture taken with me when they didn't even have a camera.

* * *

Ever since those early hits I wrote—the ones that Don and I would play at those clubs in the early '60s—I've always written songs that were intentionally simple. I wanted the lyrics and the music to be something my fans could relate to. I've written a lot of ballads like "Second Fiddle," but I've also written a whole lot of up-tempo songs that have that driving beat to 'em so people can dance if they want to.

I've never had any interest in writing real complicated melodies that would be hard to sing along with, or that would get in the way of the words. I've always tried to write the kind of songs that other bands could learn to play, just like I learned to play all those Bob Wills songs at the Blackboard.

A lot of folks have asked me which instrument I use when I write songs. The truth is, I've written a bunch of 'em without anything—just in my head. Mainly, though, I've used either a guitar or a piano. For the most part, those up-tempo songs I was writing, mainly in the '50s and '60s, were guitar-driven songs. Some of the best ballads I ever wrote were ones I came up with sitting at the piano.

As far as the creative part is concerned, I learned a long time ago that I couldn't sit down and manufacture a song. What I mean is, I couldn't sit down and say, "OK, today I'm going to write a song about a steamboat." I tried early on to write that way, and I'd labor over that song sometimes hours, sometimes days, sometimes months. I'd put all this time and effort into it—and when I was all finished, I'd have the worst damn song about a steamboat you ever heard.

I finally figured out that's not the way to write a song. At least it's sure not the way I write 'em. I just hear a phrase in a conversation or read something that I think would make a great title. Then, once I have that little germ of an idea, I sit down and put myself in a position for something good to happen. For me, a good song has always come fast. I might try to nurture it along a little bit, but if it doesn't come together pretty much right away, I have to let it go and move on.

In all the years I've been writing songs, if I've been in a happy mood, I've written a happy song. Looking back now, I guess during the '60s I was in a happy mood most of the time because my happy songs from those years outnumber my sad songs by a mile—and I wasn't necessarily sad when I was writing the sad ones.

Chapter Forty-Three

I N JANUARY OF '61, Capitol put out my next single, "Foolin' Around." That same month, they also put out my very first album. That album included everything I'd recorded for Capitol except those first four songs I'd done—the ones with all those awful background vocals on 'em. I was relieved they hadn't included those, but for some reason, they hadn't included "Foolin' Around," either. But, at the time, I was too busy to worry about why Capitol would make a dumb decision like that because Don and I were constantly on the road or in the recording studio.

One smart thing the label did was to let me make some records with Rose Maddox. Like I told you earlier, I'd seen the Maddox Brothers and Rose when I was a teenager in Mesa—and then later we'd backed Rose up when she'd performed at the Blackboard as a guest artist in the late '50s. By that time, she wasn't performing with her brothers anymore. But before Rose went solo, she and her brothers were known as the "Most Colorful Hillbilly Band in America"—and they were, too. Their outfits were colorful and they were colorful entertainers. In fact, they did a song called "Sally Let Your Bangs Hang Down" that was what you might call a little *off*-color. There was a line in that one about seein' Sally changin' clothes. The crowds just ate that stuff up.

If anybody was poorer growing up than the Owens family, it was the Maddox family. They were from Alabama, and they moved out West even before the Dust Bowl days. They came out to California and picked crops from dawn to dusk, and then they slept on the ground at night. There weren't any labor camps yet when the Maddox family moved out here. But the kids could all play and sing, so they formed a band and became really popular in the '40s and early '50s. People called their kind of music "country boogie," but it was really about as close to rock & roll as you could get. When the Maddox Brothers and Rose did up-tempo songs like "George's Playhouse Boogie," it sounded like rock & roll did just a few years later.

The band broke up in the mid-'50s, but I got to know Rose pretty well during the Blackboard days. So, me and Rose went to Capitol

Studios on January 16th, 1961 and cut four songs—"Loose Talk," "Mental Cruelty," and a couple of others. Ralph Mooney played steel guitar on that session, and Don Rich played fiddle.

I want to stop right here and tell you why it's so important that I mention that Don was on that session: From the day we recorded those two songs with Rose Maddox in January of 1961, Don played on every single record I made up to the middle of July of 1974. During all those years, he was always there with me. I had a lot of musicians come through my band and play on my records, but Don was the only person who was there for all of 'em, right up to the end of his life.

Chapter Forty-Four

JUST LIKE MY LAST THREE RECORDS HAD DONE, "Foolin' Around" started going up the charts. The single was getting a whole lot of airplay on country radio, so I knew a lot of people were requesting it and buying it. When it reached number two on the *Billboard* country and western singles chart, I got to thinking I just might have my very first number one record. For a couple of weeks, while mine was sitting at number two, my old truck-driving buddy Marty Robbins had a song called "Don't Worry" sitting at the top. Then along came Faron Young with "Hello Walls," one of those songs Willie Nelson wrote back years before he became a big superstar, which turned out to be the second biggest country record of that whole year.

So, Faron's record replaced Marty's record at the top of the charts, and it stayed there. My record sat in that second spot for eight weeks—and "Hello Walls" never budged. I thought that was mighty thoughtless of ol' Faron—especially since I'd played on so many records of his when I was a session musician for Capitol. I'm just kidding, of course, but I guess I did turn things around on him—he didn't have another number one record the whole rest of the decade, and a lot of the time I was the one to blame for that.

In those days, there was another music trade magazine called *Cash Box*. *Cash Box* had a country and western chart, too, but to tell you the truth, *Billboard* was the one that mattered the most. But I began to respect *Cash Box* a whole lot more when it listed "Foolin' Around" at the top spot for one week. So, technically I guess you could say that "Foolin' Around" was my first number one record. But *Billboard* was the trade everyone considered to be the real deal when it came to being on the charts. And a couple of years later I'd find out just what it meant to have a number one record on the *Billboard* charts. It turned out to be an absolute life-changer for me.

"Foolin' Around" hung around on the charts for exactly half a year. Meanwhile, me and Don kept making records and going from town to town, playing clubs with whoever the house band was every place we'd go to.

In March we went in the studio and recorded a whole album's worth of songs by Harlan Howard. Of course we'd already cut "Foolin' Around," which he co-wrote with me, so we cut eleven more in just two days. By then Harlan had written some really big hits like "Pick Me Up on Your Way Down" and "Heartaches by the Number," so we included those. One of the things that was special about those sessions was Don playing lead guitar on "The Keeper of the Key."

When he'd been in the band with me back in Washington, Don only played the fiddle. And, up until he played guitar on "The Keeper of the Key," the fiddle had been all he'd ever played for me in the studio. But I guess he secretly wanted to be my lead guitar player all along. Don just wasn't the kind of guy who'd ever say, "Hey Chief, let me be your lead guitar player." He just waited for me to figure it out for myself.

Chapter Forty-Five

B Y 1961, Johnny Cash had already had a bunch of hit records. Like Elvis, he'd started out on Sun in the '50s, and then a few years later he got signed to a major label. Johnny'd had so many hits by '61 that he'd put together his own package show.

A package show was when several artists toured and played on the same bill together. You'd have four or five acts that would go onstage one after the other, and then after intermission, the headliner would come on. When you had several artists on the same bill—with a real popular act as the main attraction—you could fill much bigger halls than you could if you were touring by yourself. You didn't make a whole lot of money if you were one of the opening acts, but it gave you a lot of exposure. Most of the people at the show were there to see the headliner, but if they liked what they heard, they'd start buying your records, too.

One day I got a call from Johnny Cash's manager, Stu Carnall. He said, "Johnny and I have been hearing your records on the radio a lot. You wanna be the opening act for the Johnny Cash Show?"

I said, "You bet we do."

So, me and Don went on tour with Johnny for a couple of weeks. We finished up our leg of the tour in Portland, and then Johnny was going to go do a TV show or something in LA. Since Don and I needed a ride back to Bakersfield, Johnny's guitar player, Luther Perkins, said we could ride in his camper with him. He didn't mind having us along because that meant he had a couple of extra drivers.

It's about 850 miles from Portland to Bakersfield. We'd left right after the Portland show, so we were dog-tired. Luther drove some and I drove some, and then Don drove the last six or seven hours.

So, we drug in around early afternoon the next day. When we went in the house, Phyllis told Don that his girlfriend Marlane had called, and that she seemed pretty upset. Don called her back, and when he got off the phone, he came to me and said, "Chief, I've gotta go to Washington. I'm gonna go get Marlane and we're gonna go get married."

I said, "Well, that's great, Don, but you've gotta stay here and get a good night's sleep before you start up there."

He said, "Oh Chief, I'm all right. I couldn't sleep now anyway."

I tried hard, but I couldn't talk him out of it. He had a '58 Plymouth Fury, so he didn't even unpack. He just threw his suitcase in that Plymouth Fury and headed right back in the same direction we'd just come from.

Thank God, he got there safely, picked up Marlane, and then they came back to our house. Then a couple of days later they headed off to Las Vegas and got married.

By then, me and Phyllis had moved from our little house on Withee Street to a slightly larger place on Quantico Avenue. After Don and Marlane got married, they moved in with us for a little while, and then eventually got their own place.

Not long after Don and Marlane had eloped, Capitol put out two of my duets with Rose Maddox. We'd recorded four songs, so the folks at Capitol chose to put "Mental Cruelty" on one side of the single, and "Loose Talk" on the other. Well, wouldn't you know it—both sides of the record became hits. "Mental Cruelty" went to number eight, and "Loose Talk," the B-side of the record, went to number four.

If the guys at the label had been able to know a hit when they heard it—which was supposed to be their job—they would've realized that they were about to throw away a whole lot of money. What I'm saying is, if "Mental Cruelty" and "Loose Talk" had come out as two separate singles, with those other two songs we'd recorded on the flip sides, the label would've sold twice as many records. But at least the fans were happy because they got to buy two hits on one record.

When you put a couple of country singers together and they make a record that becomes a hit, you rush them back into the studio to try to capture that magic again, right? Or at least, in our case, you put out the other two sides you have in the can. Well, that's what I would've done. It took the guys at Capitol a couple of years to figure that out.

But between the time Rose and me recorded those first four songs together in '61, and then finally recorded four more together in March of '63, I'd decided to put together a real band. I already had Don. The next person I added was a steel player named Jay McDonald. Jay could mimic the way Ralph Mooney played, so he was just the person I needed to help make what we played onstage sound like my records sounded. He was also one of those mechanically inclined people, which was good to have when we were out there on the road. Now that there were three of us, I bought a Chevy truck and put a camper on it so we'd have enough space for everybody in the band, and for all of our equipment.

Next, I got a drummer. His name was Wayne Stone, but everybody called him Moose. He was a wild and wooly guy—which is probably where the name "Moose" came from. Moose was a handsome, talented, happy-go-lucky drummer. And it's a good thing he was a good drummer because he was a handful.

Moose came into the picture because he hung out at the Fresno Barn. Don and Jay and I would go out on the road during the week, but we'd always try to be back in Bakersfield every other weekend so we'd be able to go up and play at the Barn. It was only about a hundred miles from Bakersfield to Fresno, so it was a pretty easy trip for us to make a couple of times a month. Just about every time we played there, Moose would sit in with us on drums. Eventually he'd go out on the road with us, and he even ended up playing on several of my records. But in those early Fresno Barn days—when he was just our every-other-weekend drummer—Moose always managed to make things interesting.

Well, he showed up for work one night and had on these great big ol' sunglasses. Now I was always very careful about our image. We always dressed alike in some kind of uniform. As time went by, those uniforms got flashier and flashier, but in those early days we'd dress alike, even if it just meant we were all wearing black pants, white shirts, and string ties. The point is, we were supposed to be dressed the same, and nobody was supposed to be wearing a pair of damn sunglasses onstage.

I'd seen him wearing 'em when he came into the Barn that night, but I figured he'd get rid of 'em before we hit the bandstand. After we kicked off the first song, I turned and saw that he still had those sunglasses on. I moved back a little ways so he could hear me, and I said, "Moose, take those sunglasses off!"

He looked at me and nodded his head and smiled, so I knew he'd heard me. About a minute later, I looked back at him and he was still wearing those things. I sort of slipped back toward him again and said, "Moose, take off those damn sunglasses now!"

He just kept smiling and playing his drums. Of course, I had to sing, so I kept having to move back to the front of the stage where the microphone was. The next time I had a chance to take a look behind me, I eased over to him and said, "Moose, if I turn around again and you don't have those sunglasses off, I'm gonna come right over those drums and I'm gonna take those goddamn sunglasses off of you myself."

Well, while I was still looking at him, he kept playing the drums with one hand, and he used his other hand to raise those sunglasses up—and I'm telling you, he had two of the most horrible-looking black eyes I'd ever seen in my life. Hell, they weren't even just black. They were purple and yellow and green, too. I said, "OK, keep 'em on. Keep 'em on!"

Turns out the night before, Moose had been up at the Cozy Inn there in Fresno. They had this little game at the Cozy Inn where you could sit at the bar and pitch a dime at this bowl that was back behind the bar, about five or six feet away. If your dime stayed in the bowl, your beer was free. If it didn't go in, you had to pay thirty cents for a fifteen-cent beer.

So, Moose was there at the bar, watching this guy pitch dimes. Every time the guy would miss, Moose would say, "No, that's not how you do it. You gotta pitch it up higher." Now Moose was a good-natured drunk, but he could eventually get on your nerves. This guy would pitch a dime and miss, and Moose would keep saying, "That's not how you pitch a dime in the bowl. You gotta pitch it up *higher.*" I guess Moose sort of misjudged how well his instructions were being received because—without saying a word—the guy just turned around and caught Moose with a sucker punch right in the middle of his face. The guy hit him so hard, he gave Moose two black eyes with a single punch—and that's why Moose was the only member of my band who ever got to wear sunglasses onstage.

One night a few months later, I walked into the Fresno Barn and saw this guitar player I knew named Chuck Seagraves. He came up to me and said, "Well, Buck, I'm your drummer tonight."

I said, "You're my drummer? How's that?"

Chuck said, "Moose can't be here this evening."

Now, Chuck was a hell of a guitar player, but it turned out his drumming sounded exactly like a guitar player trying to play the drums. We managed to make it through the show, and afterward I asked Chuck to explain to me where the hell Moose was. It turns out that Moose had been drinking and driving the night before, and he'd sideswiped a car. And instead of him stopping, he just took off. Somebody had seen him do it and got his license plate number before he got out of sight. So, a couple of hours later, the cops showed up at Moose's little apartment. When he came to the door, the cops told him they were looking for Wayne Stone. Moose told 'em, "He's not here right now."

One of the cops said, "When do you expect him?"

Moose said, "Well, I don't know. He just sorta comes and goes."

So, Moose hadn't shown up at the Barn that Saturday because he was in hiding. Sure enough, after a while, the cops finally gave up on trying to find him, so his plan had worked. Moose could be a real innovator when he had to.

When Moose went out on tour with us, I discovered just how bad his drinking was. I probably should've figured that out already, but he'd never gotten drunk or out of hand during all those weekends he'd played with us at the Barn.

Well, we were in Lubbock, Texas, on the very first tour we'd ever taken a drummer along with us. Now, if you've heard my records, you know we always had a heavy beat going. It's one of the main things that made my records sound so different than what was coming out of Nashville.

That night in Lubbock, that heavy beat was going strong until about halfway through the show. Pretty soon I noticed that the beat kept getting lighter and lighter. It sounded like Moose was using brushes instead of drumsticks. Then it got to where I could barely hear the drums at all.

When I finally got a chance, I turned around and looked—and Moose was sitting at his drum kit, absolutely sound asleep. He was still playing, right in time, never missing a beat—but his eyes were closed, he was kind of slouched over to one side, and his sticks were barely touching his drums.

I sidled back next to him and said, "Moose! Moose!"

Well, he finally woke up, and he played just fine for the rest of the show. But I've got to tell you, in my entire career, the only time I've ever seen a guy playing the drums in his sleep was that night in Lubbock, Texas.

And then there was Mexico. Any time we had days off, when we were playing down close to the border, we'd go across to Mexico. If we were playing around San Diego, we'd go down to Tijuana. If we were in Arizona, we'd cross over into Nogales. When we were playing in the southern part of New Mexico, we'd head down to Juarez. If we were playing Del Rio, Texas, we'd cross over and go to Ciudad Acuña. If we were anywhere near that border, we'd find a way to end up in Mexico.

It was fun and carefree down there back then. I think I've made it pretty clear by now that I've always liked girls. I liked them and they liked me—so, it was a very natural place for me to want to go.

But we'd never drive the camper across into Mexico. We'd always catch a cab, and then when we were ready to come back, we'd take a cab back to where we'd parked the camper.

It was no secret that some of the guys—especially Moose—would take diet pills to keep awake when they were driving the camper. Well, diet pills were one thing—but I knew those pills with the little crosses on 'em were illegal. I'd always say, "Don't take anything over there that's not legal, and don't bring anything back that's not totally legal, either."

We had this rule that I'd do all the talking to the border guards going each way. One thing I'd been told by some other country singers who'd gone down there was to never say you were a musician when you were coming back into the States. I knew that if a border guard asked me my occupation, I was always supposed to say, "I'm an entertainer." For some reason, I guess entertainers were considered to be kind of classy, but musicians were just automatically thought to be unsavory characters.

Well, Moose had gone and gotten pretty drunk when we made this one trip to Juarez, and it was around midnight when we got ready to head back up to New Mexico. As we were getting ready to cross into the US, the border guard looked at me and said, "Where are you from?"

I told him, "Bakersfield, California."

He asked me, "What's your occupation?"

I said, "I'm an entertainer."

So, the cab was getting ready to drive us on across, but the border guard kept talking. He looked at Don and started asking him the same questions. Don answered the same way I had. He told him he was an entertainer from Bakersfield. Then the border guard started questioning Jay—and by then, of course, I'd realized that border guard was going to give his little quiz to everybody in the taxi. So, Jay told him where he was from, and then he told him that he was an entertainer—just like me and Don had done.

And that just left Moose. The border guard asked him where he was from, and Moose said, "Yeah, man, I'm from Fresno, California."

I was starting to get a little nervous because Moose was clearly drunk, and the way he was talking to the border guard sounded kind of disrespectful. Sure enough, the border guard asked Moose, "What's your occupation?"

Moose said, "I'm a musician, man. I'm a drummer."

Well, that did it. It was bad enough that he'd said he was a musician—but saying he was a drummer was like tossing grease on the fire. That border guard told us all to get out of the cab and come with him. He led us into this little building, and for some reason he made us take off our shoes. Then he told us to empty our pockets and put everything on the counter in front of us.

We were all standing next to each other. Moose was at one end and I was at the other end. When Moose laid down his wallet and coins and everything, this little white pill with a cross on it started rolling down the counter. It slowly rolled past Don, then on past Jay, and as it was rolling past me, I just reached out and picked it up. The border guard saw me do it, but for some reason he didn't say a word. He didn't say, "What's that?" or "Let me see it," or anything. He just had each of us show him our I.D. Then he told us we could put our shoes back on and leave.

I was mighty relieved when that guard told us we could go. I guess we just caught him on a night when he didn't feel like hauling the whole band in for having one little illegal pill between the four of us.

Chapter Forty-Six

IN MAY OF '61, I recorded four more songs, including another one Harlan and I wrote called "Under the Influence of Love," and one of mine called "Nobody's Fool but Yours." The musicians included Ralph Mooney on steel, Don on fiddle, and Moose on drums. That meant I now had me and two members of my own band playing on my recordings, which—believe it or not—was one of those things Nashville really frowned on.

Down there, they had this small group of guys playing on just about every session. It didn't matter who the artist was, the piano player was going to be either Floyd Cramer or Owen Bradley. The guitar player was going to be Chet Atkins or Grady Martin, or both. The bass player was likely to be Bob Moore, and the fiddle player was usually Tommy Jackson. The steel player was either Jerry Byrd or Buddy Emmons.

Now don't get me wrong—all of those guys were really good at what they did. It's just that when you've got the same handful of folks playing on records by a bunch of different recording artists—and when you've only got a couple of record producers in town—then all of those records by all those different artists just start to blend together and sound the same. When those acts would go out on the road, they had to take a bunch of completely different musicians with 'em because the guys who'd played on their record were too busy playing on somebody else's record to be able to tour with 'em.

I wanted to have my own guys playing on my records so the audience would hear the same band they'd heard when one of my records was playing on their radio. And when people heard a Buck Owens record, I wanted it to stand out from all of those records they were hearing that'd been cut down in Nashville.

Apparently the country fans liked the way I was doing things because "Under the Influence of Love" was another number two hit for me in the fall of '61. This time around it was Leroy Van Dyke who got in my way—his latest record hit number one the same week my record reached number two. Remember when I said Faron Young's "Hello

Walls" was the second biggest hit of the year? Well, Leroy Van Dyke's "Walk On By" turned out to be the biggest country record of 1961. It was also the biggest country record of 1962, so my record never really had a chance of reaching the top.

Chapter Forty-Seven

THE DAY AFTER "UNDER THE INFLUENCE OF LOVE" hit number two, I went back into the studio and recorded five songs in one session. Like I said, Capitol always wanted us to get four songs cut in three hours, but I managed to get five in—probably because a few of 'em were songs I'd been doing for years. I reached back to some of the real early songs I'd written, including "Down on the Corner of Love" and "House Down the Block." Both of those were ones I'd recorded when I was still signed to Pep Records. I'd also written a song with Tommy Collins back in the mid-'50s called "You're for Me" that I cut that day.

We ended the year with one last session in December. Wanda Jackson, who had been Tommy Collins's girlfriend back in the '50s, had become both a country star and a pop star by the early '60s. She'd had a big pop record in 1960 with "Let's Have a Party," but she also had country hits with songs like "Right or Wrong" and "In the Middle of a Heartache." She was a multi-talented lady, so when she told me she'd written a song called "Kickin' Our Hearts Around" for me, I gave it a listen and cut it during that recording session on December 6th, 1961.

Chapter Forty-Eight

WHEN 1962 ROLLED AROUND, I went into what they call a "sophomore slump"—which seemed pretty funny to me since I'd never even made it to my sophomore year in high school.

In February, "Nobody's Fool but Yours" came out as my next single. It made it to only number eleven on the charts, which was a bit of a disappointment since I'd had five Top Five hits in a row before that.

In July, Capitol released "Save the Last Dance for Me," which was an old Drifters song I really liked that I'd recorded three months earlier. Lo and behold, that one stalled out at number eleven, too.

At the beginning of October, my third album was released. It was called *You're For Me*, and it included that song, "Under the Influence of Love," "Nobody's Fool but Yours," and nine others. I remember *Billboard* picked it as one of their "Spotlight Albums of the Week." In their little one-paragraph review they called me the "'Big B' of c. & w. music." I can't imagine why that nickname didn't catch on.

I was glad *Billboard* liked my album, but I was starting to get concerned because my last two singles hadn't done as well as I'd hoped. Luckily, Wanda Jackson's song started to turn things around for me. Capitol put out "Kickin' Our Hearts Around," and in late October it hit the charts, eventually making its way up to number eight. So, I managed to end the year with a single that hit the Top Ten.

That whole year was pretty much a blur because so much of it was spent on the road with me and Don and Jay and Moose—and whoever our bass player was at the moment—playing one-nighter after one-nighter. We'd recorded something like three-dozen songs in '61, but we'd only managed to squeeze in one recording session in all of '62.

*   *   *

Now, when I say we spent a lot of time on the road, I don't want you to think having all that success on the charts meant we'd graduated to plush theatres and high-end nightclubs. Let me hit on a few of the "highlights" for you:

In 1962, we did forty-five shows between January and March, mostly playing honky-tonks. Then we slowed down a little bit and only did thirteen shows that April, playing joints from California to Virginia to North Carolina to Florida. The first week of May, we played the Rainbow Ranch in Orlando; Jennings' Red Barn in Macon, Georgia; the Armory in Lynchburg, Virginia; Midway Hall in Calverton, Virginia; the Armory in Winchester, Virginia; and then back to Midway Hall in

Calverton again. That's six shows in six nights—from Florida to Georgia to Virginia.

Toward the end of the month, we swung down to Texas. We played the Maverick Club in Corpus Christi on the 24th. Then it was on to the Esquire Ballroom in Houston. The next night we were on the *Big D Jamboree*, a live radio show that was held every Saturday night at the Dallas Sportatorium. Sunday night was the Rhythm Hall in Midland—and then we had a day off to drive to our next gig at the VFW Hall in Artesia, New Mexico.

After the VFW Hall in Artesia, we had five more nights in a row coming up. We were going to be heading back to Texas, and then on to Oklahoma. On top of everything else, my camper was in the shop, so we had borrowed Cousin Herb's camper. The big difference between his camper and mine was that mine had a window you could crawl through between the camper and the cab of the truck. His didn't have a window, so if you were back in the camper, you were completely cut off from the guys up front.

Well, I was dog tired, so as we were getting ready to leave Midland and make the 200-mile drive to Artesia, I said to the guys, "I'll kill the first one of you that tries to wake me up." I could be gentle that way sometimes.

So, the four of them got in the cab of the truck, and I climbed into the camper and went to sleep. When I woke up, the camper was parked, so I figured we had to be in Artesia. Well, I climbed out of the back, tucked in the tail of my short-sleeved shirt, walked across the street to this little cafeteria, and had dinner. I was surprised when I got in there because I didn't see Don and the guys. But I didn't think anything about it at the time. I just ate my dinner, paid the bill, and walked back outside. The sun was starting to go down when I stepped outside, but I could see well enough to tell that the camper was gone. I went back inside the cafeteria to make sure I was in Artesia. The waitress said I was, which I was happy to hear. When I asked her where the VFW Hall was, she said it was about a mile away—which I wasn't happy to hear at all.

Remember, this was 1962. There weren't cell phones back in those days. So, the waitress gave me directions how to get there, and I just started walking. I was mad as hell, of course, and when I got about fifty feet away from the VFW Hall, I could see the guys opening the back of the camper to take the instruments out. That's when I heard Don say, "Oh shit!" because he'd just realized I wasn't still in the camper.

Then Moose turned around and saw me coming. He looked at Don and said, "'Oh shit' is right! He's heading this way and he doesn't look very happy to see us."

And it was about right then that I remembered I'd told 'em that I'd kill the first one who tried to wake me up. Well, I was embarrassed and they were embarrassed, so none of us said anything about it. We just went in, set up, and played the show. But I've got to tell you, after sundown it gets pretty cold in Artesia, New Mexico—especially when you have to walk a mile in a short-sleeved shirt.

Luckily, that was the only unfortunate incident we encountered on the road in May. In June, we did six nights in a row in California, and then five more nights in a row—going from Madison, Wisconsin, to Jefferson City, Missouri, to Camdenton, Missouri, to Aurora, Illinois, to Anderson, Indiana.

We played at the opening of a tire store in Sacramento, and the opening of a furniture store in Modesto. We played at places with names like the Little Black Book Club, the Dream Bowl, the Bamboo Club, the Tumbleweed Club, Okie's Round-Up, the Howdy Club, the Hi-Ho Corral, the Bell Avenue Corral, Stringbuster's Lounge—you name it, we played there. Between July and December we traveled all over the Western half of America, playing over a hundred more shows. Every single month of 1962, we were on the road more than we were home.

And that's when Don really started focusing on his guitar playing. Going all the way back to those days up in Washington, when we'd have some time to kill waiting to go onstage or getting ready to do the TV show, Don would always be sitting around wherever we were, picking on my Telecaster. He would ask me to show him how I did this or that on some of those Capitol recordings I'd played on when I was a session musician, and I was always glad to share my knowledge and my guitar-playing technique with him.

The most amazing thing about Don's picking up the guitar was how quickly he learned to play my style so well. By late '62, he was playing the lead guitar onstage, and very little fiddle. I don't even think we had a conversation about it. It just happened.

What he did was, he learned my playing style, and then he took it up a notch or two. I spent a while teaching him how to play certain things, and before long he completely surpassed me. Pretty soon I was learning from him. Eventually he was playing licks I couldn't even play.

In so many ways, it was almost like Don and I were joined together at the hip. He played guitar like me and sang like me. The tones, the attack of the voices, were almost exact.

Now and then, out of total, desperate boredom during those long tours that year—and many years to follow—I'd play little musical games with him on stage. I would slur a word, or maybe hold a note a little longer. Sometimes I would even change keys in the middle of a song with no warning. Don was never surprised by any of my antics. He was always alert. No matter what I did, he almost never missed a note—either singing or playing. It was like he could read my mind.

Chapter Forty-Nine

FOR A COUPLE OF YEARS, starting in late '61, that was the lineup: me, Don, Jay, and Moose. Bob Moore was usually my bass player in the studio, but I just couldn't find a bass player to tour with me that would hang around very long. I went through several, and I was looking for another one when Merle Haggard came into the picture.

The first time I met Merle, somebody brought him over to my house. Me and Don and the guys were getting ready to go out on a three-week tour, and I'd been told that Merle could play the bass. I liked him right away. At one point, Merle and the fellow who'd brought him got down on the floor and started doing one-armed pushups. Do you know how hard that is? Well, I was so impressed that I hired him right then and there. I figured if he could do one-armed pushups, he was bound to be able to play the bass.

So, Merle joined the band for a short while, and while he was with us, we just had nothing but fun. With Don, Jay, Moose, Merle, and me, we had a real good-sounding group. Merle was already a really good singer, so I remember he sang some, too, on that little tour.

We did about ten dates in Texas, and then we headed up to Michigan. Well, Moose was driving the camper as we came into Michigan. I was sitting in the middle. Merle was sitting next to the door. Don and Jay were sleeping in the back. We were traveling along this two-lane highway that was real hilly and curvy. But the scenery was nice, with beautiful trees on both sides of the highway.

Everything was going along real smooth, and then Moose got to talking about Elizabeth Taylor. He was saying how good-looking she was, and I was agreeing with him. Well, he got so excited talking about Liz Taylor that he wandered across the double line in the middle of the highway just about three hundred feet or so from an oncoming state trooper, who promptly turned around and stopped us.

He told us to all get out and had us line up against the camper, which he then proceeded to search. Well, he went in the back and found a couple of Don's twenty-two rifles in there. Don loved to target shoot when he had a chance while we were on the road, so he always brought those two rifles along. Now, I never saw Don get too uptight about anything, ever. When that officer started talking about confiscating those rifles, Don just looked at him real calm-like and said, "I can't let you have my guns." It was as simple as that. If Don had gotten all upset and started carrying on, who knows what that state trooper would've done? But instead, he just said, "In that case, put 'em out of sight until you get out of my state."

That trooper didn't know Don Rich from Adam. Hell, he didn't know who any of us were. But Don was so calm and spoke with such authority that the trooper must've figured Don was somebody he didn't want to mess with.

When he got done with Don, he moved on to me. Now, in those days, we didn't get paid with checks. In fact, we wouldn't take checks. When we played a show, we got paid in cash—and I was the one who held onto the cash until we got back home. Here we'd been on the road for around two weeks, and we'd been getting paid about five hundred dollars a night. Every bit of that money was in the pockets of my jeans. So, while we were all lined up outside the camper, the trooper said to me, "What you got in those pockets, boy?"

I said, "Money."

He said, "Money! Let me see it."

I began to pull that money out of my front pockets, and then out of my back pockets. I just kept reaching in there, pulling more and more money out until the officer said, "Okay. Just stay right there. Don't nobody move."

He went back to his patrol car and got on the radio to see if there'd been any robberies reported. When he came back, he looked real disappointed. I guess he figured he was just about out of reasons to haul us all in.

But he still hadn't checked the cab of the camper yet, so he leaned in there and opened the glove compartment, and there was nothing in it but a bottle of those little white pills with crosses on 'em that Moose took to stay awake. I don't know if he'd brought 'em back from another one of our trips to Mexico or what—but I knew he sure didn't have a prescription for 'em.

The trooper held up that bottle of pills and looked at Merle. Now, I guess most people know that Merle spent some serious time in San Quentin. He'd only been out a year or two at that point, so he was doing his best to look as innocent as possible when that trooper looked at him and said, "What's this?"

Merle said, "That's Moose's medicine, officer."

The trooper said, "Moose medicine? I never heard of such a thing. Okay, just put it back in the glove compartment, everybody get in the vehicle, and get out of my sight."

It was all we could do to keep from busting out laughing. As soon as we got back in the camper, we were all laughing so hard we were almost crying. I'm sure nobody was more relieved than Merle when that state trooper turned his car around and drove away.

Merle was only with us about three weeks. Years later he'd tell people he only stayed with me for three weeks because he couldn't afford to work for me any longer than that.

That's okay. I can't get mad at Merle for that little insult because he made a contribution to the band that I've always been grateful to him for—and I'm not talking about his bass playing, either. Before Merle came along, we were introduced every night as just "Buck Owens and his band." It was during that short time he was with us that Merle said to me one day as we were going down the road, "You know, Buck, you oughta call your band the Buckaroos."

Chapter Fifty

WE WENT BACK TO CAPITOL STUDIOS in February of 1963. By then, we'd had all the fun and excitement with Moose that we could stand, so I'd replaced him with a drummer named Ken Presley. We did three sessions in three days that February, but that first one turned out to be the one that pretty much changed everything for me.

I don't know how many stories I've heard over the years about "Act Naturally" and how I came to record it. The song is credited to Johnny Russell and Voni Morrison. Johnny told me he wrote the song and then ended up sharing the writer credits with Voni because she was the one who brought the song to me.

Johnny lived up in Fresno. One day he got a call asking him to go down to a recording session in LA, which meant he'd have to tell his girlfriend that he wasn't going to be able to get together with her like they'd planned. When he told her he couldn't see her that night because he had to go to Hollywood, she asked him what he was going down there for. Johnny said something like, "They're gonna put me in the movies and make a big star out of me." Well, when you're a songwriter, sometimes you realize instantly when you've got the makings of a good song. So, Johnny came up with "Act Naturally" right away—and then, for two years, he couldn't get anybody to cut it.

I've heard the story that a couple of years after he wrote it, Voni brought the song to me and I didn't like it, but that's sure not the way I remember it. I remember that Voni brought me four or five songs that

Johnny had written—or maybe Johnny and Voni had written 'em to-gether, depending on who's telling the story—and they were on these acetates.

In the days before cassette tapes or CDs, songwriters would have their demos cut onto acetates. An acetate looked like a regular vinyl re-cord, and it played on a record player just like a regular record. The dif-ference was it was usually blank on one side, and it wore out a lot faster than a record made in a pressing plant.

Johnny's gone now, but he used to tell everybody about how I'd originally picked a different song from that stack of acetates, and that I'd said I didn't want to record "Act Naturally" at all, but I don't remember any of that—mainly because that's not what happened.

Voni came into my office with these acetates, and each acetate had one song on 'em. Don was there with me. I listened to several of 'em and didn't hear anything that I thought would work for me. When Voni was down to her last acetate, she started to hand it to Don, but then she said, "Oh, I'm pretty sure you won't like this one."

Don said, "Well, since we're here, let's hear it."

When Don put the needle down on that last acetate, I heard Johnny singing the first line of "Act Naturally," and I said, "That's the one."

It wasn't until later that I found out Johnny had been trying to get that song cut for a couple of years and nobody'd wanted it. But the sec-ond I heard that first line, I was sold.

So, we went into the studio and recorded "Act Naturally" and a cou-ple of other songs, including one I wrote called "My Heart Skips a Beat." I knew that was a good one, too, but I wasn't happy with the way it'd come out, so I decided I'd try it again some other time.

One of the main things I remember about that recording session is that it was the first time I had my whole band playing with me in the studio. Don played lead guitar and fiddle; Jay McDonald played steel; Kenny Pierce, who'd just joined the band, played bass; and Ken Presley—who'd replaced Moose—was the drummer. I finally had the same band that went with me on the road—the Buckaroos—backing me up on a session. Who knows? Maybe the fact that we were so tight made that record a little bit better than anything I'd recorded before.

For once, Capitol didn't mess around. Less than a month after I'd recorded it, they had the singles pressed and out the door. Now, you talk about having a record on the charts with a bullet! That single started shooting down everything that was above it until it met up with Hawkshaw Hawkins and Bill Anderson.

One of the records above mine was Hawkshaw's single, "Lonesome 7-7203." He was Jean Shepard's husband—the woman who'd recorded "A Dear John Letter" with Ferlin Husky. Just a couple of days after Hawkshaw's record came out, he was killed in the same plane crash that killed Patsy Cline and another country singer named Cowboy Copas. Can you believe that? Here the man hadn't had a hit since the early '50s, and he ends up being killed in a plane crash right before he has the biggest hit of his career. It wasn't just a bunch of country fans being sympathetic either. "Lonesome 7-7203" was a great record.

On top of that, Bill Anderson had a record out then called "Still." Bill had a lot of big hits, but "Still" is the probably the one he's most famous for.

While my single of "Act Naturally" was working its way up the charts, "Still" was sitting at number one. It was up at there at the top for three weeks, and then here came "Lonesome 7-7203." Hawkshaw's record was number one for a week, and then Bill's record came right back and *it* went back to number one for three more weeks. Sure enough, after Bill's record had sat up there those three weeks, here came "Lonesome 7-7203" again.

So, for eight weeks, I watched these two records battling each other while "Act Naturally" was floating around number three or four. I was scared to death that my record was going to turn around and start heading back down the other direction before those two singles were done fighting over which of 'em was going to be number one that week.

Finally, on June 15th, 1963, I had the first number one record of my career—at least according to *Billboard*—which was the chart that mattered to me. I was on top of the charts and on top of the world—until the next week, when "Lonesome 7-7203" took my spot.

Then, on June 29th, "Act Naturally" went back up to number one again. So now I'd not only had a number one hit—I'd had a number one hit for two weeks. I thought, "Now we're gettin' somewhere"—until the next week when "Still" passed my record and Hawkshaw Hawkins' record and went back to number one again. I'd never seen anything like it.

But "Act Naturally" was just a great song, and I thought it was the best record I'd made up to that point—so I wasn't really surprised when it finally knocked "Still" and "Lonesome 7-7203" out of the way and went back to number one for a couple of more weeks.

There's no telling how long it would've stayed up there, but then Johnny Cash came along with "Ring of Fire" and just took over that top spot for weeks and weeks.

Now, I'd had three singles before "Act Naturally" that had gotten up to number two, so you wouldn't think one little spot would make that much difference. But once I had that first number one single, it was like the floodgates opened up. Between September of '63 and July of '67, I put out fourteen more singles with me and the Buckaroos—and every damn one of 'em went to number one.

Chapter Fifty-One

A MONTH AFTER I RECORDED "ACT NATURALLY," Capitol finally put me and Rose Maddox back in the studio together. It'd been over two years since we'd had that two-sided hit with "Mental Cruelty" and "Loose Talk." Now, in the music business, two years is a really long time. By the time me and Rose got together to record that second single, most folks had probably forgotten all about that earlier one we'd done. So, whatever momentum we might've had from that first record was long gone.

Anyway, in March of '63, me and Rose recorded four more duets together. For me, the special thing about that session was that Cal Maddox was there to play guitar. So, along with all the other guys in the studio, we had a "Maddox Brother and Rose."

Even though I was writing songs about as fast as I could churn 'em out, I decided to take "Sweethearts in Heaven"—another song from my

Pep Records days—and turn it into a duet. Then we did one I wrote with Rollie Weber called "We're the Talk of the Town." The other two songs we cut that day were one of mine called "No Fool Like an Old Fool" and "Back Street Affair," which had been a big hit for Webb Pierce back in the '50s.

Well, wouldn't you know it—the same damn thing happened that had happened with our first record. The A-side of the single was "We're the Talk of the Town," and the B-side was "Sweethearts in Heaven." "We're the Talk of the Town" hit the charts in early August, and the next week "Sweethearts in Heaven" was on the charts, too. I couldn't believe it. That single didn't do as well as our first record had, but both sides ended up in the Top Twenty.

When the disc jockeys are fighting over which side of the record is supposed to be the hit, one of three things is going to happen—one side will eventually win out, neither side will become a hit, or both sides will be a hit. For me and Rose, we were lucky that the two sides of the record didn't cancel each other out. Like I said, I recorded a lot of duet records over the years, but those two singles I did with Rose were the only two where both sides of the single became hits at the same time.

Chapter Fifty-Two

BACK WHEN DON AND I FIRST STARTED going out on the road together—in late '60, early '61—I knew I'd need somebody to help book us into clubs. In the beginning I had a couple of different booking agents. One was Eddie Crandall, and the other was Bob Neal. Bob's big claim to fame was that he'd been Elvis Presley's manager before Colonel Tom Parker came along and turned Elvis into a superstar. Eddie and Bob were both based in Nashville, so I guess that was one thing Nashville turned out to be good for.

When "Act Naturally" hit, things just exploded. I had to take advantage of having such a big record, so I wanted somebody who could really take over the booking for me—and not just booking clubs, either.

Suddenly, I was being asked to play in big venues and to appear on network TV shows and things like that. So, I needed somebody to handle all that stuff, but I didn't want it to be somebody in Nashville that I'd never see. I needed somebody to be out here in California with me.

As it turned out, there was a guy named Jack McFadden in Sacramento who was doing some part-time booking of country acts. Jack was a salesman's salesman. He'd sold shoes and cars and radio advertising and I don't know what all. I was playing a show up around Sacramento when he came to see me. He told me he had booked shows for some pretty big country artists, and that he wanted to do the same for me. In fact, he said he didn't want to just book shows for me—he wanted to be my personal manager, too. Until that night, I'd never heard of Jack McFadden, but he was a real amiable guy, so I gave him my phone number. He started calling me right away, telling me if I'd give him a fifteen percent commission, he'd book me for so much more money than I was making at the time that I'd be making more money if I used him—even after he took his commission.

He called me, it seemed like, every day. And every time he'd call, I'd say, "Jack, I'm still thinkin' about it." One day he called and I said, "OK, Jack. I've got a show booked in Washington and a show booked in Oregon. What I want you to do is to get me eight more dates and turn it into a ten-day tour." I told him what I was going to get paid for those two dates so he'd know what kind of money I was looking for.

He called me back just a day or two later and said, "Buck, I've got you sixteen more dates, and they're all going to pay you more than those two dates you've already got booked—even after I take my fifteen percent off the top."

Well, with that kind of action, I decided it might be time to give him a job. So, in the summer of '63 he moved to Bakersfield and we went to work. From that point on, in all the years that Jack and I were together—and that was up until his death in June of '98—I never had another manager or another booking agent. It was always just Jack. We were a business team just like Don and me were a musical team. Jack's favorite saying was always "whatever it takes." When he came to work with me, he said that was going to be our motto—and I guess he was right because it didn't matter what we set out to do, we were going to do it, whatever it took. And believe me, we did it.

Chapter Fifty-Three

SINCE I WAS ABOUT THE ONLY COUNTRY ACT AROUND who had the same band in the studio that I had with me on the road, I decided that my albums should start featuring the guys in the band. That way, in our live shows, I could put the spotlight on each of 'em to give the show more variety. I wanted my concerts to be a lot more than just me singing one song after another like most of the other acts were doing.

So when my next album, *On the Bandstand*, came out in April, it included Don singing the lead vocal on "Sally Was a Good Old Girl," Kenny Pierce singing the lead vocal on "Touch Me," Don playing fiddle on "Orange Blossom Special," and Jay playing steel on an instrumental version of "Release Me." Of course, there was plenty of me on there, too, including that hit Wanda Jackson had written, "Kickin' Our Hearts Around."

What it didn't have on it was "Act Naturally."

Here I'd had the biggest hit of my career up to then, and Capitol didn't put the song on the album, even though it had been cut during the same sessions all of the songs from *On the Bandstand* had. There was a live recording of it that got released in November of '63, but the original hit version didn't appear on an album until Capitol put out *The Best of Buck Owens* over a year later.

In July of '63, while "Act Naturally" was right there at the top of the charts, I went back into the studio because I wanted to make an album of Tommy Collins songs like I'd made that album of Harlan's songs. At the same time, Capitol wanted me to get in there quick and record a follow-up single to "Act Naturally."

Now, in '63, and part of '64, my ex-wife Bonnie went out on the road with me. By then, she'd had a hit of her own with a song called "Why

Don't Daddy Live Here Anymore." Yeah, I guess you can imagine how I felt hearing her singing that one. Anyway, I'd written a song called "Love's Gonna Live Here," so I sang it for her. I'll never forget—we were in Indianapolis when I let her hear the song. When I told her I hadn't decided if I was going to record it or not, she said, "Buck, if you don't record that song, I'll just record it myself." After she said that, I was starting to feel pretty confident about it being a good one.

On the way to the session, Jack McFadden asked me to play him the song I'd picked to be my big follow-up to "Act Naturally." He was driving and I was sitting up there next to him with my guitar, so I sang him "Love's Gonna Live Here," and he said something like, "Really. *That's* gonna be your next single?"

Here I'd decided it was a damn good song—especially since Bonnie had liked it so much—and now my manager was acting like it was the worst thing he'd ever heard.

But we were on our way to go record the thing, so it wasn't like I had much of a choice in the matter. We had a couple of days booked at Capitol Studios to record my next single and the whole Tommy Collins album, so on the first day, the first thing I did was to cut "Love's Gonna Live Here."

We'd had a tragedy in the band less than a month earlier. The Buckaroos' drummer, Ken Presley, had been killed in a car wreck on June 16th—just one day after "Act Naturally" had reached the top of the charts. Ken was married and had three kids, so it was a really tough time for all of us, even though we were in the middle of having this big hit record.

There was a pretty good drummer from Bakersfield named Mel King. He always kept a good beat and didn't play anything too fancy. He just played nice and clean. So, Mel became my new drummer, and he hadn't been with me but just a few days when we went into the studio.

It was a baptism by fire for ol' Mel because when that record light turned red, we went to town. We ended up recording "Love's Gonna Live Here," a song called "Getting Used to Losing You," and that whole Tommy Collins album—fourteen songs in all—in two days.

Chapter Fifty-Four

WHEN FOLKS TALK ABOUT THE CLASSIC LINEUP of the Bucka-roos, they're usually talking about the band I had from January of '64 through August of '67. Of course, going back to the beginning, there was always Don on fiddle and guitar. The next member of that classic lineup to join was Doyle Holly. Doyle came on board in August of '63, taking Kenny Pierce's place on bass guitar. But Doyle didn't just play bass—he also sang bass. He had this great big, deep, rich voice. He also had this wonderful "Peck's Bad Boy" image. Doyle could get away with saying just about anything—he was the comic of the group, onstage and off. Over the years he was with me—from '63–'70—he quit three or four times. I kept taking him back every time—well, every time but the last time, I guess. I always called him "Dashing" Doyle because he was a handsome guy, and because he had a way with the ladies like nobody I'd ever seen.

A month after Doyle joined the Buckaroos, "Love's Gonna Live Here" came out. I'd been nervous about the song ever since I'd recorded it because I knew I needed to keep the momentum going since "Act Naturally" had been such a big hit. It would've been bad news if my next single had done poorly. Lady Limelight only shines on you for so long, and then she's gone.

Turns out I didn't have anything to worry about because "Love's Gonna Live Here" ended up being the biggest hit single I ever had. Nowadays, I doubt if most people think of "Love's Gonna Live Here" as being as big as something like "Act Naturally" or some of my other number one records—but as far as the charts were concerned back in 1963, it hit the top on October 19th, and it was still number one when everybody was celebrating New Year's. And then it just stayed there through the whole month of January, and then on into February. That thing was number one for sixteen weeks in a row.

Now, maybe you don't pay a lot of attention to how long a song stays at number one on the charts. Most people who aren't in the business probably don't keep track of something like that. So just in case you're wondering if sixteen weeks is a long time for a record to stay at number one, I guess the best way to put it is to tell you this: it's never happened again, and it ain't never gonna happen again. In all the years since "Love's Gonna Live Here" came out, there've only been a few singles that stayed at the top of the charts for even close to that long—and they were all by the same artist. But I'm just too damn modest to tell you who that artist is.

After all those years of being told you can't make a country record if you don't record it in Nashville, and you can't be a country star if you don't live in Nashville, and you're not considered a real country singer until you get invited to join the *Grand Ole Opry* in Nashville, we proved 'em all wrong with one record.

Chapter Fifty-Five

BELIEVE IT OR NOT, Herb Henson's TV show, *Cousin Herb's Trading Post*, was still going strong in September of '63. Since Cousin Herb had featured so many Capitol artists on his show over the years, Ken Nelson decided he'd get a bunch of us together to do a concert in Herb's honor at the Bakersfield Civic Center to celebrate the *Trading Post*'s tenth anniversary. The plan was for Capitol to record the show, and then they'd put out a live album of the concert.

Ken rounded up Rose Maddox, Joe and Rose Lee Maphis, Jean Shepard, Merle Travis, Roy Nichols, and some other folks, and we had a good ol' time doing this big event for our friend Cousin Herb. There was even a young artist there that night who'd just had his first hit on Capitol a couple of months earlier called "Tips of My Fingers." His name was Roy Clark.

On November 11th, my album *Buck Owens Sings Tommy Collins* was finally released, and a week later Capitol put out the Herb Henson tribute album. I remember it was called *Country Music Hootenanny with Cousin Herb Henson Featuring Country Music's Greatest Stars!* I guess the guy at Capitol who came up with that one was getting paid by the word.

Less than a week after *Country Music Hootenanny* came out, there was that awful day in Dallas on the 22nd, when President Kennedy was assassinated.

The Buckaroos and me were actually in Texas, too, when it happened. Of course, none of us had ever experienced anything like that, so we didn't know whether we should do our show that night or not. But we had a job booked at the Maverick Club in Corpus Christi, so we went.

President Kennedy's assassination had come as a shock to the whole country, but a lot of us in Bakersfield and country music in general had another sad shock just four days later. On November 26th, 1963, Herb Henson—the man we'd just done the big tribute concert for a couple of months earlier—died of a heart attack at the age of thirty-eight.

Chapter Fifty-Six

OUR PERFORMANCE OF "ACT NATURALLY" at the show we'd done for Cousin Herb ended up being the last recording of mine that our steel guitarist, Jay McDonald, would play on. Don came to me not long after the Herb Henson concert and told me that Jay wanted to leave the band. I hated to see him go, but we had a lot of shows coming up, so we had to start looking for someone to replace him pretty quick.

Luckily, I remembered a session that Don and I had played on a couple of years earlier for a Capitol artist named Al Brumley Jr. There'd been a great steel player on that session—in fact, it was Al's brother, Tom—so I started looking for him. It turned out he'd moved to Texas and gotten into the house-building business. Well, I finally reached him and managed to convince him to get back into the music-making business—and I'm sure glad he did. He played on his first session with me on January 6th, 1964, and he ended up playing on all of my biggest hits over the next four years.

*   *   *

One night—in fact, Mel King's last night with the band—we were playing a show in Albuquerque at the Civic Auditorium. It was January 25th. Some of the other acts on the same show that night were Glen Campbell and Willie Nelson.

A lot of folks might not know that Willie actually had his first hit back in '62 with a song called "Touch Me" on Liberty Records. Then he made the mistake of signing with RCA Records for about a decade where he made one album after another, and just about every track he cut had lots of background singers and lots of strings on it. Chet Atkins and a couple of other RCA record producers kept trying to fit Willie into that syrupy Nashville Sound mold they were so fond of. Well, the day finally came when Willie put his foot down and said he wanted to do things his own way, use his own band, and record the songs he wanted to record. Sound familiar? Sure enough, once Willie escaped from RCA and started making the kind of music he wanted to make in the early '70s, he became one of the biggest country stars of all time.

The way the show was going to work at the Civic Auditorium that night back in '64 was that the Buckaroos were going to be the band for everybody on the bill. While the Buckaroos were out setting up, I was in the dressing room talking to the show's promoter, Ray Moran. All of a sudden, in walked Doyle Holly.

He said, "Chief, Don wants to see you out on the stage."

I said, "What's the matter, Doyle?"

He said, "I'll let Don tell you."

Now, I have to explain that we always set up the same way. The steel guitar player would be on my left; Don would be on my right; and the bass player would be to the right of Don. There would be a row of amplifiers behind us, and there'd be a space between the amplifiers where the drum kit would be—pretty much directly behind me.

When I walked out onto the stage, I saw that Mel's drums were set up right in front of the microphone where I was supposed to stand. I looked at Don Rich and said, "What's the drums doing there, Don?"

Don said, "That's where Mel set 'em up, Chief. He said he was tired of us beatin' him down, so he wasn't gonna sit back there next to the amps anymore. He just kept sayin' that he was tired of us beatin' him down—so I fired him."

Like I said, this was January 25th. From the 9th through the 22nd we'd played at the Golden Nugget in Las Vegas—six forty-minute shows a day with twenty-minute breaks between shows. On the 23rd we'd done a show in Farmington, New Mexico, followed by a show the next night in Phoenix. The show in Albuquerque was going to be our seventeenth night in a row without a break. It was the last show of the tour before we were going to head back to Bakersfield. Everybody was tired and frustrated. Tempers were starting to shorten up a bit—including mine.

So, I picked up the snare drum and threw it off one side of the stage. Then I grabbed the tom toms and tossed them off the other side of the stage. Then I picked up the bass drum and flung it off the back of the stage. The cymbals didn't survive, either. When I was all done, I went back to the dressing room where Ray the promoter was sitting there with Willie. I said, "Ray, you're gonna have to get us a drummer."

He said, "My God, man! It's fifteen minutes to show time."

I said, "Yes, it is. But some things can't be helped, and it's too late to change what's happened, so you've gotta get us a new drummer."

The show ended up starting a little late, but Ray managed to find this older gentleman that he swore was a professional drummer. I don't know what kind of drums the man played, but he couldn't play with any of the acts onstage that night. To be fair, if you've ever heard Willie sing, you know that being his drummer is a hell of a tough job. And, of course, Glen Campbell was playing all of that fast stuff on guitar, so that poor guy couldn't even come close to keeping up with him.

When I got out there to play the last half of the show, I told the drummer to just go over and stand by the side of the stage and I'd call him when I needed him. Well, I never did call him because I knew he'd never be able to keep up with us, either.

I ended up having a bit of an altercation with Mel before the evening was over. I don't remember who said what, and I don't remember who swung the first fist, but I do remember that was Mel King's very last night as a Buckaroo.

Chapter Fifty-Seven

O N JANUARY 28TH, I went back into the studio. Don was play-ing lead guitar on most of my sessions by then. Once he'd started playing lead guitar for me, he'd only play the fiddle on a session if I told him he had to. That day the lineup included Don on lead, Tom on steel, Doyle on bass, and a different Mel—Mel Taylor—on drums.

If his name sounds familiar, it's probably because he was the drum-mer for that great instrumental group, the Ventures. The Ventures had originally gotten together up in Tacoma while I was still living there. In fact, one of their guitar players—Nokie Edwards—had played in the band with Dusty and me on the *Bar-K Jamboree* for a while. The music world can be pretty small sometimes.

Two of the songs we cut at that session with Mel Taylor on the 28th were ones I'd written—"My Heart Skips a Beat" and "Together Again." If you're familiar with some of those hits by the Ventures, then you know what a showman Mel was on the drums. Since I had him playing for me that day, I got him do this flashy little drum thing on the cho-rus of "My Heart Skips a Beat" that ended up making the song sound pretty unique—especially for a country record. In fact, I had some fans complain about it. I guess they thought drums were there to be seen but not heard. Hell, those guys at the *Grand Ole Opry* had a rule back in the early days that said drums weren't even allowed on their sacred stage. I guess that's one more thing that me and Nashville didn't have in common.

Even though Tom Brumley had played steel on only one other ses-sion of mine by that point, he managed to find a way to fit in perfectly with my sound. Truth be told, he helped to create some of the Buck Owens sound himself when he played that steel guitar solo on "To-gether Again." That was his forte—to play those beautiful, slow lines. In fact, he really set the standard for all steel players forever with what he played on "Together Again." The tone, the feel—everything he did on that song was exactly right. You ask any steel player about the perfect use of a steel guitar on a record, they'll tell you to listen to Tom Brumley on "Together Again."

I can't tell you how many times I've been asked to sing at events when I didn't have my band with me. Well, when I'm asked, I sing. And if there's a steel guitar player in the band, he'll always ask me to sing "Together Again." I know those steel players don't really want to hear me sing. They just want the audience to hear 'em playing those beautiful steel guitar lines that Tom Brumley played on my record.

Of all the songs I've written, "Together Again" is the one that's probably been recorded the most, so a lot of people have asked me how I came to write it. Well, first I have to tell you that the most famous lineup of Bob Wills and His Texas Playboys was when he had a singer in his band named Tommy Duncan. When Bob and Tommy split up in 1948, it was a big deal. So when they made an album in 1960 for the first time in twelve years, that was an even bigger deal. The name of their album was "Together Again." That title stayed in my head for a long time, so one night I finally wrote a song about this couple that had been broken up, and now they'd gotten back together.

The funny thing about "Together Again" is that it's actually a happy song, but since the melody is kind of mournful sounding, most people think it's really sad. That's because they haven't listened to the lyrics. The singer is talking about how his tears have stopped falling and how his lonely nights are over because he's back together with the woman he loves. The guy couldn't be happier—but I put the lyrics to this slow, melancholy melody—and that's what causes folks to misunderstand what the song is really about.

Speaking of songs, plenty of young singers have come up to me over the years, asking me what it takes to have a hit record. I always tell 'em a hit record has three parts—the song, the singer, and the production. The most important thing is the song. The singer isn't as important as the song, and the way the song is arranged and produced isn't as important as either the song or the singer. I've heard lots of record that were screwed up by the production—by being over-produced. You can't ever let the arrangement or the production get in the way of the song.

When it came to recording "Together Again," I sure didn't let the vocal arrangement get in the way. If you're a fan of my music, you can probably hear that song in your head right now. And when you get to the chorus, you can hear Don singing along with me, doing that tight, high harmony part. Well, believe it or not, that's not the way it was on the original record. From beginning to end, the hit version didn't have any harmony vocals on it at all. It wasn't until we started performing "Together Again" live that Don added that incredible harmony part on the chorus. We ended up doing the song that way on so many concerts and TV shows and live albums that a lot of people have told me they were really surprised when they heard the original version without Don's harmony part on it. So that was a case where I might've made the vocal arrangement a little too sparse. But since nobody had heard it any other way when the record came out, they didn't think anything was missing. And I guess that kind of proves my point that the song itself is always the most important part of any hit country record.

Chapter Fifty-Eight

THE SAME DAY THE REST OF US WERE in the recording studio cutting "My Heart Skips a Beat," "Together Again," and a couple of other songs, Willie Cantu was flying from Corpus Christi to Bakersfield to become our next drummer. He was only seventeen years old at the time, but I'd decided he was the right man for the job. We had to get his parents' permission, of course, so I told 'em Willie could come live with me when we weren't on the road.

We had met Willie the night that we were playing in Corpus Christi—the same night President Kennedy had been shot. The club had a house band that played before we went onstage, and there was a teenaged drummer playing with 'em. Doyle and Don had gone to the club to check things out the night before, and they'd been real impressed with his drumming. So the night we played there, Doyle asked him for his phone number. Since Mel King was out of the picture, I needed a new drummer, so I'd called Willie and asked him to join the band.

Now that Willie was officially on board, the lineup was finally complete for what a lot of people consider to be the golden era of the Buckaroos: Don Rich on lead guitar and fiddle, Tom Brumley on steel guitar, Doyle Holly on bass, and Willie Cantu on drums.

In February, Capitol released my next single. It had "My Heart Skips a Beat" on one side and "Together Again" on the other.

Right around the time that record came out, my manager, Jack McFadden, got a call asking me to be on the *Jimmy Dean Show*. Jimmy'd had a huge hit in '61 called "Big Bad John." He was a real down-home kind of guy who had a good personality for TV. In fact, he'd already had a show on CBS for a couple of years back in the '50s. He got a new show on ABC in '63, and I guess he liked the way I came off on TV because he had me on his show in March of '64, and again in April, and then again in September.

Not long after my second appearance on the *Jimmy Dean Show*, "My Heart Skips a Beat" reached number one on the charts. That was on May 16th. Of course I was thrilled like I've always been when one of my records hits the top of the charts, but the funny thing was, I also kept hearing the B-side, "Together Again," on the radio a lot. Sure enough, I was looking at *Billboard* magazine one day and I saw that "Together Again" had hit the charts, too. Like I told you about those duets I had with Rose Maddox, if you're going to have hit records, you really want to have 'em one at a time. I don't mean to come off sounding like I'm greedy or ungrateful, but the point of making records is to sell records. That's why they call it the music *business*. You're not really looking to have a two-for-one sale, or a "buy one, get one free" kind of situation. But every time I'd look at *Billboard*, I'd see "Together Again" just keep going on up the charts.

So, "My Heart Skips a Beat" was number one for three weeks. And then, when I opened *Billboard* the next week to see how my record was doing, I couldn't believe my eyes. "My Heart Skips a Beat" had dropped to number two, and "Together Again" was the new number one hit. I'd had my number one record knocked off the top of the charts by the other side of my own record!

The week after that, I opened up the new issue of *Billboard*, and the chart looked just like it had the week before. "Together Again" was still sitting at the top, and "My Heart Skips a Beat" was still there at number two. I thought, "Well, okay, I had 'My Heart Skips a Beat' for three weeks and 'Together Again' for two weeks. I wonder who's gonna come along and knock 'Together Again' out of that number one spot."

Ray Price had a song called "Burning Memories" that had been moving up, and Loretta Lynn had one called "Wine Women and Song" that was doing the same thing. So, I figured one of those two would hit the top once "Together Again" had run its course.

Well, I was wrong. Believe it or not, after two weeks at being number one, "Together Again" had dropped down to number three—right between Ray's record and Loretta's record—and "My Heart Skips a Beat" had gone back up to the top of the charts one more time. In fact, that second time around it ended up staying at number one for four weeks in a row.

They tell me that's the first and only time that both sides of a country single has done that—where the A-side reached the top of the charts, then the B-side reached the top of the charts, and then the A-side reached the top of the charts again.

Now, the businessman in me can't help but think about the fact that we would've sold twice as many records if those two songs hadn't been on the same single, but I'm still proud of the fact that we did something that had never been done before in the history of country music—and once again, we did it a long way from Nashville.

Chapter Fifty-Nine

IN 1964, NOBODY THOUGHT there was anything the least bit strange about somebody putting out more than one album a year. These days you're lucky if an act puts one out every twelve months. Hell, Capitol put out five Beatles albums in '64, so I guess I looked downright lazy by only having three.

In June, Capitol released an album of my hits called *The Best of Buck Owens*. The next month, out came another one. That album was called *Together Again/My Heart Skips a Beat*. Really rolls off the tongue, don't it? But that's what Capitol came up with for the title.

Despite what they named it, it went to number one on the country albums chart, and it even managed to reach number eighty-eight on the Top 200 pop albums chart. In those days, country albums usually didn't sell nearly as well as pop albums. Country fans were mainly buying singles back then. But my albums were selling so many copies that they started showing up on the pop charts sort of by default.

*   *   *

Between the releases of *The Best of Buck Owens* and *Together Again/My Heart Skips a Beat*, we'd gone back into the studio, recording what would become the third of my three albums that came out in 1964.

I thought we'd been pretty fast back when we'd managed to record *Buck Owens Sings Tommy Collins* in two days. This time around, we recorded eight songs for our next album in just six hours. We did one three-hour session on the morning of July 8th. Once we finished the morning session, we took a half-hour break for lunch, and then we went back in for another three hours. By 4:30 that afternoon, we had those eight songs in the can.

The first one we cut that morning was a song I wrote that would be released as my next single. It was called "I Don't Care (Just as Long as You Love Me)." I sang the lead vocals on most of the songs we recorded that day, but I had Doyle sing lead on the Johnny Cash song, "Understand Your Man" so I could have my next album feature the Buckaroos individually on several tracks, like I'd done before.

By then, I'd also decided to include more instrumentals on my albums when I could, because I wanted to show off everybody's musicianship. For this album, just for fun, I decided to show that I could still play a little bit of lead guitar myself, so we recorded one I called "Buck's Polka."

Since eight songs wasn't enough to fill an album, we included four tracks that had been recorded at earlier sessions. One was of Don singing lead and playing the fiddle on "Louisiana Man." Another one was Doyle singing again, on a hit by George Hamilton IV called "Abilene."

When Tom Brumley had first come on board, I'd had him cut a steel guitar solo of a thing called "Bud's Bounce," so we included that. Then we reached all the way back to 1961 and put my duet of "Loose Talk" with Rose Maddox on it. Since that cut hadn't ever appeared on an album before, I guess Capitol figured nobody would complain, even if it was three years old by then.

This time around, instead of making the album title two song titles with a slash in the middle, Capitol decided to go the opposite direction and call it half of the title of my new single. The single, "I Don't Care (Just as Long as You Love Me)," came out in August, and the album, *I Don't Care*, came out in November. The title of the album was fine with me. At least you could say the whole thing in one breath.

When *I Don't Care* came out in November, the single was sitting at the top of the charts, where it stayed for six weeks. Then the album went to the top of the country album charts, so I was starting to think things couldn't get much better that year. Turns out I was wrong again—but this time, for once, I didn't mind being wrong.

Chapter Sixty

AFTER HARLAN HOWARD AND HIS WIFE, Jan, had moved to Nashville, I didn't get to see 'em very often anymore. Harlan and I had written some good songs together early in my career, but now he was busy down in Nashville writing hits for just about everybody in town. And, of course, I was either in the studio or on the road.

When Jan Howard was on the road, a lot of times Harlan would travel with her, so when me and Jan got booked to do some shows together down in Texas in 1964, I figured this was my chance to finally write some songs with Harlan again. By then, the Buckaroos had finally run my ol' camper into the ground, so I'd bought us this green Dodge motor home that the guys in the band called the Green Goose. I let the Buckaroos travel in the motor home without me while I rode with Harlan and Jan in their Cadillac.

Jan drove, I sat in the front seat with her, and Harlan sat in the back. I know that might sound a little funny, but that's the way we traveled. The reason I recall the seating arrangements so well is because I remember Jan threatening to stop the car and throw us both out on more than one occasion.

We were together like that for several days, trying to write songs, and just nothing was coming. I was starting to think we might have lost that magic we'd had in the late '50s and early '60s when the two of us were writing hits like "(Excuse Me) I Think I've Got a Heartache" and "Foolin' Around" and "Under the Influence of Love."

Then Jan went driving by one of those old Esso gas stations. There was a big sign out front that had a cartoon of a tiger on it, and the Esso slogan in big letters. It said, "Put a Tiger in Your Tank."

When I saw that sign, it made me think of that old line about having a tiger by the tail. So, I looked back at Harlan and said, "How about 'Tiger by the Tail' for a title?"

And that's all it took. Harlan sat back there, scribbled away for maybe five or ten minutes, and then he just threw the piece of paper into the front seat between me and Jan. I picked it up, read the lyrics, started singing the melody that came into my head, and the song was done—just like that. The words and melody I sang in Harlan's Cadillac that day were the same ones I sang on the record.

I just loved what Harlan came up with. When you've got a tiger by the tail, you can't let go of that tail or the tiger'll just turn around and eat you up—unless you can outrun it. And if you're holding it by the tail, when you let go, you don't have much room between you and the tiger to get yourself a head start. Well, Harlan had taken that and turned it into the story about a man whose woman is just running him ragged. And if he tries to leave her, he knows he's not going to get very far.

We went into the studio on the first day of December and only got three songs recorded, but one of 'em was "I've Got a Tiger by the Tail" and another one was "Cryin' Time," so it wasn't a bad day's work.

Chapter Sixty-One

SOMETIMES YOU HAVE A RECORD THAT YOU JUST KNOW is going to be a hit—or at least you think you know. Well, this was one of those times when I absolutely knew without a doubt. I knew "I've Got a Tiger by the Tail" was going to be big, which meant I had to get back into the studio before the year was out because we'd need to have an album's worth of songs ready when the single of "Tiger by the Tail" started flying up the charts. Nobody's ever accused me of lacking confidence.

But first we had some gigs up in Washington and Oregon where I did something I'd never done before—and once I'd done it, I never did it again. When we were on the road, I was the only one who had a copy of the itinerary. I was in charge of the whole operation, so I'd always tell the guys how many days we were going to be gone and where we were going, but I didn't pass out a copy of the itinerary to everybody in the band. We'd be in someplace like Olympia, so I'd tell 'em, "Tomorrow we go to Spokane," and the next day we'd be off to Spokane with enough time to spare to be able to unload, set up, and change into whichever uniform we were going to wear that night.

We were on the Oregon leg of this tour of Washington and Oregon, so I looked at the itinerary and said, "Okay, boys, tomorrow we're going to be in Baker City." We got to Baker City about an hour before show time. The itinerary had the name and address of this great big 'ol dance hall there, so we drove over to it. The place was locked up tight, and there was nobody there to let us in. An hour before show time there's always somebody there, so I thought, "Well, something's gotta be wrong here."

So, I dug out the itinerary and looked again, and that's when I realized we were supposed to be in Pendleton—and by this time there was no way to get to Pendleton from Baker City in time to do the show.

My old buddy "Pecos" Pete Brown, who was the manager of a radio station in Pendleton, Oregon, was promoting the show there, so I had to call the venue in Pendleton—where there was a packed house waiting for me—and tell him what had happened.

We ended up playing a make-up date for him early the next year for free because he had to rent the venue twice, get security twice, promote it twice, and everything else you have to do when you're putting on a show. You can bet I looked very closely at every single itinerary for every tour we did for all the rest of my years on the road—and we never missed another show like that again.

We came off the road for Christmas, and then rushed in the studio for two days at the end of the year. Like I said earlier, Bonnie had toured with me during '63 and part of '64, and while we were on the road together she and I had written one called "If You Fall Out of Love with Me." By this time, Don was starting to do some songwriting, too. I guess maybe Bonnie pulled him out of his shell a little bit because the three of us wrote two songs together. One was called "Fallin' for You," and the other one was called "Wham Bam."

On December 28th and 29th, we cut those three, with Don singing lead on "Wham Bam." I had Doyle Holly sing that old cowboy song, "Streets of Laredo," and I had him sing it in a real low key because it sounded so good when he was hitting those deep bass notes.

Red Simpson and I had managed to write a few together when I was off the road, so I recorded two we'd written together—"Gonna Have Love" and "Let the Sad Times Roll On"—and one he wrote by himself called "The Band Keeps Playin' On."

Harlan had sent me one called "Trouble and Me," so we did that one. And then we did one more that got me in some serious trouble with some of my fans.

I've always thought that Chuck Berry was a great songwriter. They call his stuff rock & roll, but I've never heard a song of his that wasn't one of those good ol' story songs. If you took anything he ever wrote, slowed it down, and added a steel guitar to it, everybody would call it country. Some of the songs he wrote were funny, some were happy, and some were sad. But they always told a story like a good country song does. "Memphis" was one of those sad ones. It's about a guy who's talking to a telephone operator, trying to get her to connect him with his six-year-old daughter who he hasn't seen since he and his wife split up. Now don't that sound like a country song to you? Yeah, me too. But some country fans didn't see it that way, and they sure let me know about it.

Well, we managed to record nine songs in all over those two days in December. The album included all of 'em but "Gonna Have Love," which we saved for later. And, of course, it included "I've Got a Tiger by the Tail" and "Cryin' Time," as well as the other song I'd recorded at the same session when I'd recorded those two. It was called "We're Gonna Let the Good Times Roll."

Finally, I wanted to slip in an instrumental, so I included a piece featuring Don on fiddle called "A Maiden's Prayer" that we'd recorded back in January.

By the time we went into the studio to record those songs that I'd written with Don and Bonnie, Bonnie had already stopped touring with me to go tour with Merle Haggard. They'd had a duet hit together in late '64 called "Just Between the Two of Us," so it made sense for her to start traveling with him instead of me. He wasn't Merle Haggard the country superstar yet, but he'd had a big hit called "Sing a Sad Song," and he was about to have a whole bunch more.

Chapter Sixty-Two

A S EXCITING AS THE PREVIOUS COUPLE OF YEARS HAD BEEN, 1965 was the busiest year of my entire career—in fact, maybe of my entire life. Capitol put out "I've Got a Tiger by the Tail" in January, and less than a month later it had already hit number one on the country charts.

I don't know how you can get more country than "I've Got a Tiger by the Tail," but there was something about the song that appealed to a whole other audience—an audience that had probably never bought a country record before. I was every bit as surprised as the folks at Capitol were when that record started going up the pop charts. In '64, I'd had a couple of records that'd just barely grazed the bottom of the Top 100 on

Billboard's pop singles chart, so it wasn't like it'd never happened before. It'd just never happened like this.

We'd recorded "Tiger by the Tail" at the same place we'd recorded everything else. The musicians were the same guys that had played on my last few records. Ken Nelson was the producer, like he'd been on all my other records. And, of course, it was me singing. So, that has to mean there was something about the song itself that caused it to have such broad appeal. Maybe it was because that Esso Gas tiger was so popular at the time. Hell, I don't know. Maybe it made people think of Tony the Tiger from the cereal commercials. Or maybe it was just a damn good song. Whatever it was, for some reason, that record crossed over into the pop singles chart and started heading in an upward direction fast. It finally topped out at number twenty-five.

Today that might not sound very high, but the pop charts were a different thing in the '60s. For instance, just about everybody on the planet knows Glen Campbell's "Gentle on My Mind." It never got higher than number thirty-nine on the pop charts. And his single of "By the Time I Get to Phoenix" stopped at number twenty-six. It's not like Glen was on a label that didn't get his records distributed properly, or out to radio stations fast enough. He was on Capitol just like me.

In those days, anything on pop radio that made it into the Top Forty was considered a hit. I'd spent years watching those Nashville record producers doing everything they could to come up with a record that would cross over. Whatever the current trend was in the pop market, they would try to sprinkle a little bit of that onto their country records to try to goose 'em up enough to get 'em some pop radio airplay.

The funny thing was, it really didn't hardly ever work at all. Except for Eddy Arnold's "Make the World Go Away" and some other big ballads like that, those Nashville records didn't become hits on Top Forty radio. They just ended up being over-produced, watered-down, bad country records.

And now here I'd come from way out in Bakersfield, playing with my little band of honky-tonk pickers, and gone and scored a hit that had reached the top of the country charts and the Top Twenty-Five on the pop charts. If the Nashville folks didn't like me for not playing their game before, they sure as hell didn't like me now.

Chapter Sixty-Three

Back when I was a kid in Texas, wearing hand-me-down clothes and living on the wrong side of the tracks, I'd made up my mind that someday I was going to be somebody. Well, after five number one records, I knew I *was* somebody. And I knew I'd gotten where I was and I'd become as successful as I was because an awful lot of folks really liked the kind of music I was making.

The Nashville establishment might not have liked what I was doing, but they weren't the ones buying my records and coming to my shows. Sure, it bugged me a lot that I had worked so hard to get where I was, only to be ignored by that little clique down there who did everything they could to control what everybody's definition of country music was supposed to be—but what mattered the most to me was keeping my fans happy. And what I wanted my fans to know was that I would always stay loyal to 'em and to my kind of music.

And I wanted those bigwigs in Nashville to know the same thing, so in March of '65—right in the middle of the five weeks that "I've Got a Tiger by the Tail" was sitting at the top of the charts—I took out a full-page ad in this Nashville trade paper called the *Music City News*. I called it "Pledge to Country Music." It said:

> I shall sing no song that is not a country song.
> I shall make no record that is not a country record.
> I refuse to be known as anything but a country singer.
> I am proud to be associated with country music.
> Country music and country music fans have made me what I am
>   today.
> And I shall not forget it.
>
> —*Buck Owens*

Many folks have asked me over the years why I'd do something like that. Mainly, I did it because I meant it. I was telling the Nashville music industry and everybody else that I was the real deal. A lot of my records were up-tempo—and they had a lot more of a beat to 'em than most other country records. But to my mind, that's real country—the same kind of music I'd made at the Blackboard in the '50s. It was fast and loud so people could get up and dance to it if they felt like it. Or, if it was a ballad, it had a steel guitar on it, playing those pretty steel guitar licks that left no doubt that I was singing a stone country song.

But in March of 1965, since "I've Got a Tiger by the Tail" had crossed over onto the pop charts, I also wanted to assure everybody that I was still a country singer singing country songs, even if I'd hit on one that got played on Top Forty pop radio stations—and was bought by a whole lot of younger folks who usually wouldn't be caught dead with a country record in their collection.

Chapter Sixty-Four

WHEN I SAID 1965 WAS A BUSY YEAR, I wasn't kidding. I spent 302 days on the road that year—and it wasn't even a leap year—so that means I only had sixty-three days when I wasn't either doing a show or on my way to one.

By the time we were able to get back into the studio, it was late March. Capitol had released the *Tiger By the Tail* album on March 1st, and it was already heading up the charts when we started recording the next one on the 25th.

Now, Doyle Holly was the bass player for the Buckaroos on our live shows and sometimes on our records, but like I mentioned before, a lot of times in the studio I'd have Bob Morris play the bass. Bob played on a whole bunch of my records, going all the way back to when I'd done that album of Tommy Collins songs. I used him pretty frequently because he was a really solid studio musician. "Dashing" Doyle didn't sit around in the studio and do nothing, though. He played rhythm guitar on the sessions that Bob played bass on. And of course, he had his share of lead vocals over the years, too. Plus, since Doyle was a great entertainer, he was a lot more at home on the stage than he was in the studio.

By '65, we'd gotten pretty good at getting in the studio and getting out of there in just a couple of days with most of our next album in the can. This time around, we did two four-hour sessions in two days, and came away with ten songs.

Back during those years when we were having such a long stretch of number one hits, people used to ask me, "How long do you and the band practice a song before you go in the studio and record it?" The truth is, we didn't rehearse at all. There wasn't any time for rehearsals. When we'd get in the studio, I'd have in mind what songs I wanted us to record, and how I wanted things to go—like where I wanted the instrumental break to come, or whether I wanted Tom to take a steel solo instead of Don taking a guitar solo or a fiddle solo on a particular song. But as far as being specific about exactly what I wanted 'em to play was concerned, I hardly ever gave anybody any kind of detailed directions. I'd just tell everybody what the chord progression was, and then I'd count off the song and we'd go. I know that might sound crazy to a lot of folks and a lot of my fellow musicians, but that's how we did it—and looking back now, I can safely say that it all worked out just fine.

So, on March 25th and 26th, I had my core guys—Don, Tom, Doyle, and Willie, along with Bob Morris on bass, and another guitar player named Jim Seals. In those days he was Jimmy Seals. Jimmy's big claim to fame back then was being one of the guitar players on that song "Tequila" by the Champs, but in the '70s he became Jim Seals and got real famous as half of a group called Seals and Crofts. With the seven of us in the studio, we cut five songs each day. The very first one we did that first day was one Don and I had written called "Before You Go."

Except for a few ballads we'd hit the charts with—like "Under the Influence of Love" and "Together Again"—just about everything else we'd done that had become big hits for us were up-tempo songs. "Act

Naturally" and "Love's Gonna Live Here" and "My Heart Skips a Beat"—they all had that beat to 'em that my fans had come to expect from me. Well, on "Before You Go," the opening verse was up-tempo, but when we got to the chorus, everything stopped—and then the song turned into a slow ballad on the chorus. Then it would kick back into that fast up-tempo beat again on the next verse—and then back to a ballad on the chorus again.

I knew it was a hell of a gamble. It was the kind of thing that people might love because it was so different—or they might hate it for the same reason. But I didn't want to reach the point where people would start accusing me of just recording what sounded like the same song all the time with different lyrics, so I decided to really shake things up a bit and see what would happen.

*   *   *

By '65, me and Jack McFadden had decided to start branching out into some other business ventures. Of course, I already had Blue Book Music, which had my songs in it, and the songs Don Rich and other people co-wrote with me. We also started signing other writers, including Merle Haggard. As I'm sure you can imagine, once Merle started writing all those hits of his, he helped to turn Blue Book into a pretty impressive music publishing company.

I also started a booking company with Jack. We called it OMAC. That stood for Owens McFadden Artist Corporation. We had acts on the roster like Dick Curless, Tommy Collins, Joe and Rose Lee Maphis, Wynn Stewart, and Bonnie and Merle.

Well, by 1965, I'd had so many hits on my own that it didn't make sense, businesswise, for me to be anybody else's opening act. So, one of the reasons for OMAC was to create our own package shows, with Buck Owens and the Buckaroos as the headliners. We called our package "Buck Owens' American Music Show."

Chapter Sixty-Five

IN APRIL, Capitol put out "Before You Go" as my next single. I just kept my fingers crossed and hoped for the best. I'd had six number one singles in a row, and I knew this one was a real roll of the dice. I mean, it's one thing to have a song that has real slow verses and then kicks in fast on the chorus, but I don't think anybody'd ever had a hit with a song that did it the other way around.

This was all back before the days of CMT, or some other country music network playing videos of your latest song on TV. The only way we could let people hear our latest single was by staying on the road, playing it night after night, and by me working those radio stations. While the Buckaroos would be back at the Holiday Inn, resting up for that night's show, I'd be going to every country radio station in whatever town we were in, talking to program directors and disc jockeys, telling them about my latest record. It was hard work, but I was used to hard work. I'd already done my time in those little honky-tonks. Like I said before, it was a lot cooler in those honky-tonks than it was out in those peach-pickin' orchards—and it was even cooler in those nice air-conditioned radio stations.

* * *

We were on the road just about the whole month of April—from Columbia, South Carolina, to Augusta, Georgia, to Greenville, South Carolina, to Fairfax, Virginia. One day we were in Fairfax, and the next day we were in Europe. For the rest of the month, we mostly did what a lot of country acts had been doing for years—playing those US Army and Air Force bases, mostly in Germany. That's where I learned about there being no speed limit on the autobahns.

There was a gentleman named Herman, who'd been a major in the Luftwaffe. He had a Rolls Royce that he drove us around in while we were in Germany. We called him Hermie the Germie. Well, I'd never been in a car that had a speedometer that measured the speed in kilometers. We were on the autobahn when I looked over at the speedometer and saw it said we were going about 150. I looked over at Hermie and said, "My God! Why are we going so fast?"

He said, "There's no speed limit, so we can go as fast as we want."

I said, "But we're going 150 miles an hour. If you have a flat tire, we'll all be killed!"

Hermie just started laughing and said, "You're reading it wrong. Those aren't miles per hour. They're kilometers. We're only going about 95 miles per hour—not fast at all."

I sat there and thought to myself, "If 95 miles an hour ain't fast, I wonder what they consider fast on this road."

Hermie drove us from Frankfurt to Hamburg to West Berlin to Munich to Guttenberg, and we managed to get to all those military bases in one piece.

While were we in Europe, we also played at places in England and Ireland and France and Spain. One of the things I learned about Europe was that they drank everything there at room temperature. It didn't matter if it was beer or milk, it was the same temperature—which wasn't nearly cold enough for me. Jack McFadden and I ended up going to stores and buying gallons of milk, and then having whatever hotel we were staying in put 'em in their refrigerator. Then later, when I'd go to the restaurant at the hotel and ask 'em to bring me a glass of my milk from the refrigerator, the waiter would look at me like I was crazy. And then when he'd see me drinking it, it'd about make him gag.

As soon as we got back from Europe, we headed to LA for another two days of recording sessions. Two of the songs we cut on May 4th were a couple more I'd written. One was called "Gonna Roll Out the Red Carpet," and the other one was "Only You (Can Break My Heart)." Writing those up-tempo songs like "Gonna Roll Out the Red Carpet" was getting pretty easy for me to do by that point. Lord knows I'd written a ton of 'em by then. But coming up with pretty ballads took a lot of effort. "Only You (Can Break My Heart)" was one of those ballad songs, and I was real happy with the way it came out.

The next day we recorded three more songs, and we still had some studio time left, but I just didn't have anything left to cut. I'd been writing song after song while we were on the road because I knew those sessions would keep getting booked, but I was just plain flat out of material. Ken Nelson was sitting at the control board, doodling on a pad of paper like he always did while we were out in the studio recording. He turned on the talkback mic and said, "We've got fifteen minutes left. Have you got one more?" I was shaking my head when Bob Morris said, "I've got one." We all looked at him kind of dumbfounded. I mean, we all knew he was a good songwriter. I'd even recorded some of his songs before. But he wasn't the kind of guy to suggest a song while a session was going on. Well, he put down his bass and picked up a guitar and started playing this really catchy little instrumental tune. We gathered around, learned it right there on the spot, and Ken told the engineer to hit the "record" button.

When we were done, I asked Bob what it was called. He said he didn't have a name for it, so I just said, "OK, we'll call it 'Paris.'" And that was it. We'd cut eight songs in two days. And then, just like always, we headed back out on the road.

Chapter Sixty-Six

I USED TO JOKE ABOUT WHAT THE REQUIREMENTS were to be a country singer. You had a have a bass player in the band who doubled as the comic of the group. I had that with Doyle Holly, for sure. You had to have a steel guitar player, of course—and I had the best one with Tom Brumley. You were supposed to drink a lot, so I didn't fit the mold there because I never touched the stuff. And as far as records were concerned, you had to make at least one gospel album and at least one Christmas album. The trick was to stick around long enough as a recording artist to do that gospel record and that Christmas record before Lady Limelight stopped shining on you.

By 1965, I'd been with Capitol for eight years, so I was a little behind schedule on the gospel and Christmas records. Now, one of the things that most people who aren't in the business probably don't think about is that you've got to record a Christmas record a long time before Christmas—and it's pretty hard to get in the mood to record a bunch of Christmas songs in the middle of summer. It's even harder to write 'em, but I didn't want to record the same ol' Christmas songs that everybody else was doing. I decided if I was going to have a Christmas album, I'd go with a bunch of new Christmas songs that nobody'd ever heard before. So, Don and I wrote some, and Red Simpson and I wrote some—Don and Red even wrote one together. We got one from Bob Morris that he'd co-written, and another couple from other songwriters. The only traditional Christmas song we did was "Jingle Bells." I was kind of breaking my own rule there, but it's pretty hard to make your first Christmas record without putting "Jingle Bells" on it.

So, even though it was hot outside, we recorded all of those Christmas songs in June and July. Well, I guess the plan worked out okay because one of the songs that me and Don came up with was called "Santa Looked a Lot Like Daddy." That one still gets played every year at Christmas time, and not just my version of it either. Last time I checked, that song had been recorded by a couple of dozen artists.

*   *   *

I was real relieved when "Before You Go" went to number one that June. And that's where it stayed for the next six weeks. My fans had stuck with me, even though I'd done something a little different than what I called those "freight train" songs. Don used to say those up-tempo records we made sounded like a runaway locomotive coming right through the radio, so that's why I've always called 'em freight train songs.

Speaking of the radio, the reason my Capitol records sounded the way they did—real heavy on the treble—was because I knew most people were going to be listening to 'em on their AM car radios. In fact, in those days, even the radio in most people's houses was an AM radio. And of course, those early transistor radios were all AM radios, too.

When I told Ken Nelson why I was going for that trebly sound, he didn't waste any time. He had the tech guy at Capitol Studios install some little mono speakers in the control booth. When we'd mix my singles, we'd always play 'em through those little speakers to make sure that sound really cut through loud and clear.

At the time, nobody else was doing anything like that, but it just seemed like common sense to me. And it was one more reason that you knew it was a Buck Owens record as soon as it came on the radio—because it just didn't sound like those other records that always came out sounding like the bass player was standing in front of the singer.

Chapter Sixty-Seven

I'VE GOT TO GET BACK to Bonnie and Merle for a little bit. There's a story about me and Merle Haggard that a lot of people have gotten wrong over the years.

Now, you already know that Bonnie and I got divorced, and then I got married to Phyllis, and then Phyllis and me split up, and then we got back together again. So, by the time Merle and Bonnie got together, Bonnie and me had been divorced for so long that we'd actually gotten past all of the anger and sadness that comes with a divorce. We'd gotten over it to the point that we'd become good friends. We wrote songs together. We toured together. We enjoyed each other's company. She's really a wonderful woman. But, except for having two great kids together, our marriage hadn't worked out so well—and I've already admitted that it was pretty much my fault since I couldn't seem to keep my eyes and hands off of other women. But, believe it or not, I can't tell you how many times I've read about how Merle stole Bonnie away from me. Well, nothing could be further from the truth. He stole her away all right—just not from me.

Like I told you earlier, Bonnie and Fuzzy Owen had recorded "A Dear John Letter" on a small record label before Ferlin Husky and Jean Shepard ended up having a big hit with the song on Capitol. Bonnie and Fuzzy were also on *Cousin Herb's Trading Post*. This was back in the '50s and real early '60s. They were on there all the time, and Cousin Herb would always say something like, "And now we're gonna hear a song from our lovebirds." So, Bonnie and Fuzzy were an item. They were together for quite a while. And of course, when Bonnie and Fuzzy first got together, Bonnie and I had been separated for a long time and were already in the process of getting divorced.

Fuzzy Owen and Lewis Talley not only had that little recording studio in Bakersfield, where I'd cut some of my Pep singles; they also had a label called Tally Records together, and Fuzzy eventually bought out Lewis's share. Once Fuzzy owned the label, he started putting out records by his girlfriend, Bonnie. Pretty soon, Fuzzy discovered Merle Haggard, became his manager, and signed him to Tally Records, too. Most people who know about Merle's career know about him having a lot of his biggest hits on Capitol. Well, before Ken Nelson signed him to Capitol, Merle's first couple of big hits were on Tally.

Anyway, once Merle met Bonnie, it didn't take long for him to fall in love with her. Nobody could blame him for that. A whole lot of men who met Bonnie fell in love with her. I sure did. So did Fuzzy. And then so did Merle. Merle's marriage was already falling apart at that time, and Bonnie was helping to take care of his kids and stuff, so Merle just fell more in love with her.

Now, Bonnie was still with Fuzzy, but she decided to take this steady job singing in a club way up in Fairbanks, Alaska. I guess she'd decided to get just about as far away as she could from everybody for a while. So, she went up to do this long-term gig in Fairbanks, and before long Merle managed to find his way up there, too. Well, it gets pretty cold up in Alaska, and when it's cold, folks have got to find a way to stay warm. The next thing you know, Merle was calling Fuzzy to break the news to him that Merle and Bonnie were going to get married.

And that's the real story. Merle didn't steal Bonnie away from me. He stole her away from Fuzzy Owen.

Now, while Merle was calling Fuzzy to tell him about the upcoming marriage, Bonnie was calling to tell me the same thing. But mainly she was calling me to tell me that she wanted Buddy and Mike to come live with me and Phyllis. Bonnie knew she and Merle were going to be on the road a lot of the time—and she knew I was going to be on the road a lot of the time, too—but she thought with Phyllis being there with

Phyllis's two kids and Johnny—the son Phyllis and I had together—it would be a good solid home for Buddy and Mike to be a part of.

By that time we'd moved to a twenty-acre ranch near Edison, just east of Bakersfield. I had some cattle and some horses out there. We had a swimming pool, too, so I thought it was a great idea to bring Mike and Buddy out there, and so did Phyllis. When the boys came on board, our household went from three kids to five kids overnight. I remember after Buddy and Mike moved in, Phyllis used to laugh when she'd tell people that *her* two kids and *my* two kids were out in the yard fightin' with *our* kid.

Even though I wasn't there very much, I was really happy to finally be able to spend what time I did have at home with Buddy and Mike before they were completely grown. In the middle of all that constant touring and recording, it was always nice to come home to the ranch and have this big bunch of kids hanging out in the yard. They were wonderful days while they lasted.

Chapter Sixty-Eight

IN JULY OF '65, MY NEXT SINGLE CAME OUT. It was that pretty ballad I liked called "Only You (Can Break My Heart)." I guess the folks at Capitol Records had decided the public just couldn't have too much Buck Owens because—get this—on July 26th they released two Buck Owens albums on the same day. The year was just barely half over and I'd already had three albums released in 1965.

Once again—and I made sure it was the last time—they'd named one of my albums after two song titles with a slash between 'em. This one was called *Before You Go/No One but You*. So, obviously, it included what had been my latest number one hit single, "Before You Go," and the B-side of that single, "(I Want) No One but You."

It also fit the pattern I'd created of featuring some instrumentals, and some of the other guys in the band. Tom Brumley did "Steel

Guitar Rag." Don sang the lead vocal on a song I'd written with Bonnie called "Number One Heel." We did another instrumental that I played lead guitar on called "Raz-Ma-Taz Polka." And we even managed to piss off some fans again by doing an old Coasters hit by Leiber and Stoller called "Charlie Brown." Some people called that song rock & roll. Other people called it rhythm & blues. We did it our own way and called it country.

Oh, and this album didn't include my current single, "Only You (Can Break My Heart)," but it did include the B-side of that single, "Gonna Have Love." I was beginning to realize that the only way I was going to be completely happy with my releases was to figure out a way to get more control over my albums than I already had. Capitol had let me have some of the guys in the band sing the lead vocals on some of the songs on my albums—which I knew was a unique situation—but they didn't seem to put much thought into the album titles or some of the song selections.

The other album that came out on the same day as *Before You Go/No One but You* was *The Instrumental Hits of Buck Owens and His Buckaroos.* I liked the idea because it showed off what great musicians I had in my band. It also showed that I could still play pretty good myself. The only problem was that most of the album was instrumental stuff we'd already released on my earlier albums. In fact, it included the two instrumentals that were on my other album that came out the same day.

But despite everything, there were two really good things that came out of the release of that instrumental album. One was that it led to the Buckaroos getting their own recording contract with Capitol.

The other was that it included the Bob Morris tune we'd cut at the end of that recording session back in May—the one I'd named "Paris." Well, at the last second, before they did the artwork for the *Instrumental Hits* album, I told 'em to change the name of that one from "Paris" to "Buckaroo."

The next month, we went back into the studio for three days in a row and knocked out about a dozen more songs, including "Sam's Place," "Waitin' in Your Welfare Line," and "In the Palm of Your Hand."

And then things started to get interesting.

Chapter Sixty-Nine

AFTER WE WRAPPED UP THE LAST of those three days of sessions in August of '65, I headed home to Bakersfield. The next day, I was sitting in my office when Jack McFadden walked in and said, "They want you to play Carnegie Hall in March."

I said, "Jack, we've been on the road since January, and we're booked through the end of this year. I've already decided I really need to take a break, so I've been planning on taking off the first three months of next year to have some time with my family. Tell 'em maybe we'll do it some other time." I'd heard of Carnegie Hall, and I knew it was some famous place—I just didn't know how famous.

Jack said, "My man, you don't understand. You don't call Carnegie Hall. They call you!"

He told me that it would be real important for my career to be able to say I'd played Carnegie Hall, and of course, he was absolutely right about that. But I still had some serious misgivings about it—not so much because of the venue, but because of where it was located.

If you don't already know, let me tell you—of all the towns and cities in America where country music is popular, New York ranks about dead last. Things have improved some since the mid-'60s, I guess, but in those days—if you played New York City at all—you played in a club. There were some rare exceptions, of course, but I sure as hell didn't like the idea of going into New York and playing to a half-full house—especially not at a place as prestigious as Carnegie Hall.

Well, Jack called Ken Nelson and talked to him about it, and by the time their conversation was over, Ken had said if I'd play the Carnegie Hall gig, Capitol would record the whole thing and put it out as a live album. I had about a dozen albums out by then, and the closest I'd come to a live album was having one song on that Herb Henson tribute record—so the thought of doing a whole live album of just me and the Buckaroos made the idea of playing Carnegie Hall sound a lot more interesting to me. But I was still having a hard time believing we could fill up a place like that in the middle of Manhattan, so I agreed to play there

146

the following March, but only with the understanding that I could back out of the deal if I felt that ticket sales were too weak to justify making the trip.

*   *   *

Back in February of '64, while "Love's Gonna Live Here" was still sitting at the top of the country charts, the Beatles were having their first number one pop hit in America with "I Want to Hold Your Hand." Oh man, I can't tell you how angry some country artists got when the Beatles started having so much success. There were plenty of older country stars going all the way back to the '50s that thought rock & roll was the worst thing that ever happened. They said it was the Devil's music. They didn't just think that it was turning kids into juvenile delinquents—they thought it was turning kids away from country music. Which it was. And when the Beatles came along, you can bet that teenagers wanted to hear the Beatles a lot more than they wanted to hear Eddy Arnold or Ernest Tubb.

If you were a country singer, you weren't supposed to like rock & roll. But I never was one to follow other people's rules, and I never believed that you had to like one kind of music to the exclusion of all other kinds. I like Bill Monroe and Bob Wills and Lefty Frizzell and George Jones, but I like Little Richard and Elvis and Chuck Berry and the Beatles, too. And I guess that's one of the things I loved about the Beatles. They weren't just great performers—they also had the same attitude that I had toward "the Man." You could see it in their press conferences and their TV appearances and their movies. They didn't bow down to people who considered themselves authority figures. Instead, they made fun of 'em. I remember seeing 'em on TV when they first arrived in America. They were at the airport doing a press conference, and one of the reporters was giving 'em a hard time because they wouldn't sing for the press.

The reporter said, "Are you not singing for us because you can't sing?"

John Lennon looked him in the eye and said, "No, we're not singing because we need money first."

I just thought that was so refreshing, to have these guys barely out of their teens, refusing to let anybody push 'em around. I liked their music and their attitude, but I was still old-fashioned enough not to like their hair. Back then I thought only women should wear their hair that long. In the early '60s, I wore my hair short—and I thought other men should wear their hair short, too.

After the Beatles arrived and started having one hit after another, me and the Buckaroos did a little comedy section in our shows where we wore Beatle wigs and sang "Twist and Shout." At the end of the song, one of the guys would pull Tom Brumley's wig off and throw it on the floor. Then Don Rich would act like he thought it was some kind of critter, so he'd pull out this big ol' blunderbuss pistol and shoot it at the wig. Sometimes he'd fill that pistol with way too much gunpowder, and then plug it with a wad of paper. Ol' Don's aim was pretty good. A lot of nights that paper wad would hit that wig just right and it'd go flying up in the air. And when he'd shoot that thing, the noise was deafening. There'd be smoke everywhere, too. I don't think anybody ever fell asleep at one of our shows, but if they did, they sure as hell woke up when Don fired his blunderbuss.

Even though we made a little fun of the way the Beatles wore their hair back then, it wouldn't be too many years before I'd be wearing my hair over my ears. Hell, I even had a beard for a while. So, the Beatles didn't just change music—they changed culture. And they were great songwriters, too.

They'd covered some other people's songs on their early records, but by late '65, they were mainly recording their own original songs. That's why I was so surprised when I found out they'd recorded "Act Naturally."

Of course, I didn't write the song, but I knew the reason they cut it was because they'd heard my record—and the reason I knew they'd heard my record was because Ken Nelson had told me that the Beatles had asked Capitol to send 'em copies of my albums every time a new one came out—which was pretty often in the '60s.

I thought having the Beatles do "Act Naturally" was just the ultimate. You can't imagine that feeling. It's a feeling all unto itself, and probably only to me, because a whole lot of people heard about Buck Owens for the very first time after the Beatles cut a song that I'd made famous. Like they say, you can't pay for that kind of publicity. Suddenly

I started developing a whole new audience of young people that had never bought my records or been to my concerts before. I guess they figured if the Beatles recorded one of my hits, then I must be all right.

The Beatles' recording of "Act Naturally" came out first on their album, *Help*, in August of '65. Most of the songs on that album were from the soundtrack to their new movie, so I was lucky—"Act Naturally" was one of the other songs they decided to fill out the record with.

The next month, they put "Act Naturally" on their new single. By this time, they were so hot that a lot of times both sides of their singles would become hits on the radio. It happened to me a few times, but with the Beatles it happened practically every time they put out a record. On this one, the A-side was "Yesterday," and "Act Naturally" was on the B-side, with Ringo singing the lead vocal.

Not long after the Beatles' version was a hit, I was on a plane sitting next to a lady who didn't know who I was. When she asked me what I did for a living, I told her I was a country singer. Well, she started going into great lengths about how she hated country music. She said she thought it was common and crude—and in the very next breath she was saying how much she loved the Beatles. I asked her if she liked "Act Naturally," and she said, "Oh yes. That's one of my favorites."

And as hard as I tried, I couldn't convince her that "Act Naturally" was a country song.

Chapter Seventy

AS 1965 WOUND DOWN, Jimmy Dean had me come back and perform on his show two more times. I was really starting to get the hang of being on national television.

In early October, "Only You (Can Break My Heart)" finally made it to number one on the country charts. The single had come out way back in July, so that one really took its time reaching the top, but it did—making it my eighth number one single in a row.

When Capitol put out "Buckaroo" as my next single, I figured my streak of chart-topping singles was finally going to come to an end. I mean, whoever heard of a country instrumental making it to number one?

That same month, my fourth and final album of the year was released. It was called *Christmas with Buck Owens*. Capitol even put out "Santa Looked a Lot Like Daddy" as a single. So, now that I had a Christmas album under my belt, I figured it was time for that gospel album.

I did the same thing with it that I'd done with my Christmas record, cutting a bunch of original gospel songs instead of just picking things out of the Baptist Hymnal. We went down to Capitol Studios in November for a couple of days to record most of the songs that ended up on the album. I wrote some of the songs with Red Simpson, and I even gave my mother a co-writer credit on some that she had been the inspiration for. One of the songs I wrote was called "Dust On Mother's Bible." That one was inspired by my grandmother. We'd been through a lot together, going all the way back to that trip from Texas to Arizona back in 1937, but she had passed away before I'd gotten famous, so that one was for her.

I have to laugh when I think about making that gospel album— at the end of the second day we had some time left over, and since we didn't ever want to waste any of that precious studio time, we did a couple of instrumentals, including one called "Tom Cattin'." I'm sure there are a few church folks who would've thought it was downright sacrilegious for us to be recording an up-tempo steel guitar instrumental called "Tom Cattin'" right after we'd finished doing a bunch of songs with titles like "Where Would I Be Without Jesus," but when you've got time left over in the studio, you've got to take advantage of it. After all, in the book of Ephesians it says to make the most of every opportunity. So that's what we did.

*   *   *

After 302 days on the road, four album releases, and three number one singles, I was ready to call it a year. But then, right before Christmas, I took a look at that final issue of *Billboard* for 1965.

In that last issue every year, they always used to list the top Christmas records—not just country Christmas records now, but all the

Christmas records that were on the Christmas chart for that year. And it wasn't even just Christmas albums that had been released in 1965. It was all the most popular Christmas albums that had been bought that year, and it included ones going all the way back to Bing Crosby's Christmas album from 1945. Well, I'm proud to tell you that *Christmas with Buck Owens* was number twelve on that chart. My album was right up there with Elvis and Andy Williams and Nat "King" Cole. And as far as "Santa Looked a Lot Like Daddy" was concerned, it was listed at number two—right below the Harry Simeone Chorale's recording of "Little Drummer Boy," and right *above* Bing Crosby's "White Christmas."

But that wasn't all. When I looked at the country singles chart, I couldn't believe what I was seeing. "Buckaroo" was sitting at the very top. So, the impossible had happened. My fans had made my one instrumental single a number one hit.

I didn't know it at the time, but a few years later, Ralph Emery—the famous disc jockey and TV host—told me that "Buckaroo" was the first instrumental to ever go to number one on the country charts. Last time I checked, it was also the last instrumental to go to number one on the country charts.

Chapter Seventy-One

I STARTED OUT THE NEW YEAR IN PRISON.

On January 1st, 1966, me and the Buckaroos did a concert at San Quentin—the same San Quentin where Johnny Cash recorded his famous live album three years later. It was also the same San Quentin Merle Haggard had gotten out of six years earlier.

The warden at San Quentin had heard we were going to be playing a New Year's Eve gig up in San Francisco. So, since he knew we were going to be right there in the area, he called Jack McFadden and asked if we could play San Quentin the next day. Jack told me what the warden wanted, and I told Jack it was fine with me. Of course, when I said it was fine with me, I had no idea how scary that place was.

About an hour before the show was supposed to start, I stepped out onto the stage to see what I was getting myself into. The prisoners hadn't been led to their seats yet, so the place was still empty. What I noticed immediately was this heavy-gage chain link fence that completely surrounded the stage. Now, I'd played a few places early in my career that had chicken wire between the stage and the audience, but I'd never seen anything like this.

Since we had about an hour before show time, the warden gave us a tour of the prison. I asked him if we could see the gas chamber, but he told me he couldn't do that anymore. He said the last time he'd done it, somebody from the press heard about it and wrote a story accusing him of using the gas chamber as a tourist attraction.

Now, I've been on some pretty interesting double-bills in my career, and this was definitely one of 'em. Believe it or not, the opening act was Eartha Kitt.

Me and the Buckaroos were back in the warden's office while she was onstage, so I didn't get to see her perform—but I do recall the loud cheering. Eartha's a very talented singer, and she's very attractive, too—so those men were probably having as good a time looking at her as they were listening to her sing.

When we finally got out onstage, I saw there were security guards everywhere. It seemed like there were almost as many guards as there were inmates. I think I might've sung a little faster than I usually do, but we did all the hits we'd had up to that point—and everybody seemed to like us, which was a big relief. Then, as we were coming off the stage, the warden came up to me and said, "There's no press here today, so if you promise not to tell anybody, I'll take you and one other person and show you the gas chamber."

Well, naturally, Don Rich volunteered. When the warden took us in there, I noticed they had two chairs inside the chamber, and there were two stethoscopes hanging on the outside of the chamber. I guess they needed spares in case anything went wrong.

The warden told us we could step inside the chamber, so we did—and as soon as I stepped in there, I began to smell this substance I'd never smelled before. I started getting woozy and dizzy. I felt like I needed to lie down because I was getting downright nauseous. I asked the warden if there was any chance there could be a gas leak. He just chuckled and assured me there wasn't a leak, and that he'd seen this same thing happen to other people who'd visited the chamber before. Well, this time it was happening to me, and I wasn't enjoying it one bit—especially when he said, "Mr. Owens, if you'd really like to have the whole experience, why don't you take a seat in one of the chairs? We can even have one of the security guards fasten you in with the straps if you'd like."

That warden was having way too much fun, so I stepped out of the chamber and said, "Maybe next time." I've had some interesting New Year's Days over the years, but that's one I'll never forget—even though I'd really like to.

Less than a week after my gas chamber experience, Capitol released my next single, "Waitin' in Your Welfare Line." The B-side was a song I wrote called "In the Palm of Your Hand."

"Waitin' in Your Welfare Line" was written by me, Don Rich, and Nat Stuckey—and the way that one came to be written is a hell of a long story that starts way back in 1957.

In November of '57, there were four of us from Bakersfield who were getting ready to go to the annual Country Music Disc Jockey Convention in Nashville. It was me, Lewis Talley, Fuzzy Owen, and a guy named Bill Carter, who was a recording artist on Tally Records. The convention was held at the Andrew Jackson Hotel, and it was the place to be if you had a record to promote. The deejays from a whole lot of country radio stations from around the nation would set up there, doing remote broadcasts. And if you were anybody, they'd interview you on the radio.

Well, as me and the other guys were getting ready to leave Bakersfield and head to Nashville, I got to thinking that it would be a good idea to see if I could get myself on the *Louisiana Hayride* radio show in Shreveport while we were on our way to the convention. My first single on Capitol had just come out, so I thought that would be a real good way to promote myself and promote my new record. That way, when we went to the disc jockey convention, I could tell all those radio guys that I'd just played the *Louisiana Hayride*, which was a big deal in country music back then—probably the most important country radio broadcast around outside of the *Grand Ole Opry*.

I'd heard about a guy named Tillman Franks who lived in Shreveport. He managed Johnny Horton and Webb Pierce and some other big country acts. Of course, he had no idea in the world who I was, but I called information and got his phone number and just called him up and told him that I had a new single out on Capitol Records, and that I was coming through town and would like to play the *Hayride* while I was there. I guess he didn't think I was completely crazy because he said he'd call Frank Page, the emcee of the *Hayride*, and check it out for me.

He called me back a little while later and said that Frank said it was okay with him. So, on our way to the disc jockey convention, we went to the Shreveport Municipal Memorial Auditorium. Fuzzy played the bass, and Lewis and me played guitars. I sang both sides of that first single—"Come Back" and "I Know What It Means to Be Lonely"— and that was it. The next morning we headed on to Nashville for the convention.

Like I said, that was in 1957. In 1960, they decided to end the radio show. So that one night in November was the one and only time I ever played the *Louisiana Hayride*. But for some reason, Frank Page, the emcee of the show, never forgot about me. I guess he must've kept an eye on my career, even though it wasn't until a couple of years after I did the *Hayride* that I finally had a hit.

So, now we go forward to 1965. One day, out of the blue, Frank Page sent me a tape of songs by a guy named Nat Stuckey. None of us knew who Nat Stuckey was then because he hadn't had his first hit as a recording artist yet. But I'd always appreciated Frank letting me be on the *Hayride*, so I listened to the tape. One of the songs on there was just a couple of lines. It was like Nat had come up with a good idea for a song, but he hadn't finished it. Either that, or he'd written the shortest song you ever heard. This little thing he'd written was about a guy who had the "hongries" for this woman's love, so he was waitin' in her welfare line.

Don and I got a big kick out of that line, so we sat down and wrote some verses to go with it, and we made the part that was on Nat's tape the chorus of the song. I called Frank and we got the co-writer credits worked out with Nat, and then we went in the studio and cut it in

August of '65. And that's how "Waitin' in Your Welfare Line" came to be written and recorded.

*   *   *

I don't mean to sound like I'm biting the hand that fed me all those years, because I'd be the first to tell you that I'd never have been as successful as I was without Capitol Records. That's just a fact.

But, at the time, I thought it was a crazy move on Capitol's part because my first album of 1966—the one that somebody at Capitol named *Roll Out the Red Carpet for Buck Owens and His Buckaroos*—didn't include any hits.

Hell, even my album of instrumentals had a number one hit on it. This one didn't even have a song on it that Capitol wanted to release as a single. It was a collection of songs we'd recorded in May, July, and August of '65, and except for the fact that it didn't include any of my recent hits on it, it was like my last few albums had been: I sang most of the songs, but there was also one called "I'm Layin' It on the Line" that Don sang lead on, and one that Doyle Holly sang called "After You Leave Me." It also had a couple of instrumentals on it, which were the ones we'd recorded at the tail end of the gospel album sessions.

Luckily, my fans were loyal to me, because they bought enough copies to push it to the top of the country albums chart—even though there wasn't a song on it that any of 'em had ever heard before.

Chapter Seventy-Two

A WEEK AFTER THE *Roll Out the Red Carpet* album came out, we went back in the studio for a couple of days and cut nine more songs, including a pretty good one called "Think of Me."

Now, I'm not meaning to sound like I'm bragging, but I wasn't too surprised when "Waitin' in Your Welfare Line" went to number one on the country charts in mid-February. But I'd be lying if I didn't tell you I was really surprised when another act had a hit with one of my earlier songs that same month.

My version of "Cryin' Time" had been the B-side of "I've Got a Tiger by the Tail," and I guess the A-side was so strong that none of those country deejays even bothered to turn the record over. But Ray Charles must have turned the record over because he'd recorded it in late '65, and put it out as a single that December. To be honest with you, I don't know how Ray heard "Cryin' Time," but I knew even before he recorded it that he was a big country fan because a few years earlier he'd recorded this great album called *Modern Sounds in Country and Western Music.*

By the middle of February, Ray's single of "Crying Time" had become a huge hit. When I'd done it, I'd dropped the "g" at the end of the word "crying." My record came out as "Cryi*n*' Time." Ray's record came out as "Cryi*ng* Time." The other difference was that his version had gone to number six on the pop charts, number five on the R&B charts, and it had spent three weeks at number one on what they used to call the "easy listening" charts. When my record of "Cryin' Time" had come out in '64, it didn't hit any chart anywhere. After Ray's record of "Crying Time" did so well, I decided dropping that "g" on my record had probably been a bad idea!

I had originally recorded "Cryin' Time" the same year I wrote it. What had happened was I'd been doing a show that had several artists on it, including Bobby Bare. It was 1964, and me and Bobby were the two main acts. He'd had two or three hits by then, including "Detroit City."

That last night of the tour, we were up in Madison, Wisconsin, and I had a red-eye flight booked because I needed to be in Los Angeles the next day. Usually, I was the last to go onstage, but since I had that plane to catch, Bobby agreed that he'd let me go on before him. I never met a singer yet who didn't want to close the show, so I guess he wasn't too upset about it.

As soon as our set ended, I jumped in this rental car and hightailed it for the airport. I was flying down the highway going way above the speed limit when I got to wondering if I was going to get there before that plane took off. I knew I had to be in LA the next morning, so I said to myself, "Man, if I miss that plane, it's gonna be cryin' time."

When you're a songwriter and a phrase like "cryin' time" pops into your head, the song's practically written already. It turned out not to be cryin' time after all because I made my flight—and before the week was out, I'd written the song.

After Ray had a hit with it, everybody from Elvis to Dean Martin to Barbra Streisand recorded the song. So, I'm real grateful to Ray for being a country music fan. But he didn't stop there. His next single was "Together Again," and that one was a hit on the pop charts and the R&B charts, too—and just like "Crying Time," it went to number one on the easy listening charts.

I'd already been a fan of Ray's going all the way back to "What'd I Say" and "Hit the Road, Jack"—but after he had those two hits with my songs back-to-back, I became about the biggest Ray Charles fan you ever saw.

To be serious about it, I admired Ray a great deal because he showed that you could take country songs and turn 'em into pop hits and R&B hits and even easy listening hits. A great song is a great song—it doesn't matter what style it's performed in. That's why I'd made that pledge in the *Music City News*. I might record a song written by Chuck Berry, but nobody was ever going to mistake me for Chuck Berry. If I recorded one of his songs, it was going to come out country—because the song was good enough to work in any style of music.

Chapter Seventy-Three

I ALREADY TOLD YOU THAT 1965 was probably the busiest year of my career, but looking back on things now, the busiest month of my whole career was March of 1966. Half a year earlier I'd been planning on taking the first three months of '66 off to have a chance to rest up and to spend some time with my family. But it turned out that I wasn't any good at being idle.

The first thing I did that month was to finally break down and buy a tour bus. Some of the guys in the band had started to give me a hard time about the Dodge motor home, so I decided it was time to start traveling in the same kind of luxury that a lot of the other country stars were. Our bus wasn't anywhere near as fancy as some of those tour buses you see today—the ones that have bathrooms and kitchens and a big master bedroom in the back—but with our new tour bus, everybody finally had a bunk to sleep in, and there was plenty of room for all of our equipment, so it was a big improvement over the ol' Green Goose.

Like I said earlier, back when we'd borrowed Cousin Herb's camper, the guys drove off without me that time in Artesia, New Mexico. You'd think that sort of thing couldn't happen in a big ol' tour bus, but it did. We'd stopped at a gas station and Willie Cantu had gone to the bathroom. Those nice bunks in the bus had curtains, so when we took off everybody thought Willie was in his bunk with the curtain closed. We were thirty miles down the road when I went back to his bunk to ask him a question. I pulled open the curtain—no Willie.

Doyle turned that big ol' tour bus around and we headed back to that gas station. There was Willie Cantu, sitting out front where he'd been waiting for over an hour—waiting to see if we were ever going to come back and get him or not.

When there's five of you traveling around the country, no matter how organized you are, those things are just going to happen. Of course, the next few days after we accidentally left Willie behind, we were extra careful to make sure everybody was on board before we took off down the road. But time went by and I guess just about everybody got left behind at one time or another—but usually we didn't go more than a block or two before we realized what had happened. During the couple of years we had that tour bus, Willie ended up holding the record as the Buckaroo left behind the most amount of miles.

Now just because I'd spent all that money on a tour bus, that doesn't mean I was looking to throw money away. A lot of other country acts had professional bus drivers, but we didn't go that route—and it wasn't just about trying to save money, either. We were on the road so much that no one person could've driven that bus without needing to sleep every once in a while. When you're playing one night up in Colorado

Springs and the next night down in Houston, you don't want to be depending on one guy to stay awake and drive for fifteen hours straight—especially not if you're going to have a twenty-five hour drive from Houston to Bakersfield the next day. So, the bus drivers were Doyle and Tom and Don and me. Doyle was so good at it that many years after he left the Buckaroos, he became a professional tour bus driver for a bunch of big country acts.

Well, we were down around Oklahoma City one time when ol' Buck was behind the wheel. Doyle was navigating, and he got us just a little off course. He told me to exit the freeway before we were supposed to, and we ended up on this two-lane road. Doyle apologized for having me get off at the wrong place, but I said, "Don't worry. I'll just turn this thing around and get us back to the freeway."

There weren't any cars coming from either direction on this little road, so I pulled off to the right as far as I could. Then I made a sharp left turn and pulled across the road. Well, the embankment was too steep on that side to keep going, so I put it in reverse—and that's when we had a little problem. When I'd backed up, I'd backed off the road and onto some grass that was so slick, the bus wouldn't go forward when I put it back in first gear. That bus just sat there, blocking both lanes of the road, while the back tires spun on that wet grass until smoke was coming off of 'em. And that's when the traffic started showing up. A couple of minutes before, we'd been the only ones on that road for as far as you could see in either direction—and now it looked like rush hour on the 405 freeway.

The cars just kept coming, and they were coming from both directions. One thing we learned that day was that the Buckaroos might be the best musicians in the world, but all four of 'em together couldn't push a bus off of wet grass.

Finally, one guy who was stuck there waiting for us to move got out of his car and told us he'd make a U-turn and go get us a tow truck. I don't know where he went to get it, but it was an hour before that tow truck finally showed up. That was about the longest hour of my life, too, because I've never been more embarrassed. Here was this big ol' sign on both sides of the bus that said, "Buck Owens and the Buckaroos," so everybody could see exactly who was causing the problem.

As the minutes went by, some people got out of their cars and came to say hello to me. Some of 'em told me they were big fans and asked for my autograph, which I was happy to give 'em. Then they'd go back and tell the folks behind 'em that Buck Owens was up there. So, more people got out of their cars and came to chat with me and ask for my autograph. Finally, this big ol' guy came walking up to me and said, "Where the hell is Buck Owens? I'm going to give that son of a bitch hell for causing this fiasco!"

I looked him right in the eye and said, "I don't have no idea where Buck Owens is." When he turned around and walked away, I climbed in that bus and stayed out of sight until the tow truck showed up.

I know I waited a long time before I finally bought that bus—way too long if you asked the guys in the band—but I've always been careful with my money. I guess one of the advantages I had was that my first real big success didn't come in my teens or even my twenties. When I had my first number one hit with "Act Naturally," I was almost thirty-four years old. Hell, a lot of big country stars have already had their *last* number one hit by the time they're thirty-four. For all I knew back in '63, "Act Naturally" could've been the only number one hit I was ever going to have. So, I didn't spend all the money I'd made on a tour bus back then because there was no way of knowing if I was ever going have another big payday like that. But once I'd had *ten* number one hits, I knew that buying a tour bus wasn't really going to put that big of a dent in my bank account.

And while I was spending money, I decided to invest some of it in a business I already knew something about. In Bakersfield there was—and still is—a radio station called KUZZ. It was owned by a couple of guys who were losing money on it hand over fist. When the station first went on the air in the '50s, it was called KIKK. In '62, Cousin Herb Henson had gotten hired to be the station manager. So, with the blessing of the owners, he had the call letters changed to KUZZ. I thought that was some pretty smart self-promotion on his part. If everybody in town knows you as Cuz, why not name the radio station something that makes everybody think of you?

Well, the station became available, so I bought it in March of '66 for $133,000. Bakersfield was a growing town, so I thought it was a good investment. The bigger a town gets, the more revenue a radio station can bring in from selling ad time. I'd learned about that at KAYE up in Puyallup.

When I bought the station, it was operating out of this little house that was probably no more than a thousand square feet. It wasn't a very classy looking place. All my life I've wanted to represent country music with more dignity, more integrity—more class. I wasn't satisfied having the station in that little ol' house, so I got to thinking the perfect place for it would be in this great big motel in town called the Wonder Lodge. It had around three hundred rooms in there, so I went over and negotiated with the owners to let us move KUZZ into their motel. Those motel rooms were huge, so we took a bunch of 'em that were located just off the lobby, knocked down some doors and some walls, and ended up operating the station out of the Wonder Lodge for several years.

Now, just because I owned a radio station, that doesn't mean I wasn't still naïve about some things in life. Every Thursday on the radio station we'd have a big promotion for that night's wrestling match, and a couple of wrestlers would come to the station to talk about what they were going to do to each other that evening. They'd come into the studio during my son Buddy's shift, and they'd sit there and make all kinds of threats towards one another. They'd call each other pencil-neck geeks and all sorts of things—and I thought they were dead serious.

One of 'em was Buddy "Killer" Austin. One time he said on the air that he got the nickname "Killer" because he'd once killed a guy with a wrestling move called a pile driver—and I believed him! "Killer" Austin had a big rival named "Classy" Freddie Blassie. The two of 'em would come into the studio and just threaten the hell out of each other. I was worried they were going to start in on each other right there in the studio and tear the place up.

I swear to you, I had no idea it was all just a show. I thought they were really wanting to kill each other in that ring. Then one day I came to find out they'd driven up from LA to Bakersfield in the same car. Then somebody saw the two of 'em eating dinner together after the wrestling match was over. And that's when I finally figured out that it was all just an act. Here I was, thirty-seven years old, and I'd gone all my life thinking that wrestling was—well, I thought it was wrestling.

So, I might've been a little naïve, but by March of '66, I had a music publishing company, a booking agency, and a radio station. My records were selling real well and my shows were selling out. And, as if that wasn't enough, I ended up hosting a television show—but this one was a little bit bigger than the *Bar-K Jamboree*.

Chapter Seventy-Four

I HAD A COUPLE OF FRIENDS named Bud and Don Mathis. They owned a business called Mathis Brothers Furniture in Oklahoma City. Now, they were real successful at selling furniture, but they decided they'd like to get involved in the entertainment industry in some fashion, so they came up with the idea of creating a country music TV show. Since the two brothers were friends of mine, they came to me and asked me to be the host of this new show they were going to put on.

I told 'em there was no way I could do a TV taping every week because most of my time was going to be spent either in the recording studio or on the road. That turned out not to be a problem because they said that me and the Buckaroos and all of the guest stars could come to Oklahoma City four times a year, and then we'd tape a bunch of half-hour shows at once. Now, to end up with enough shows to run every week for fifty-two weeks, that meant every few months we'd have to go tape thirteen shows in a row over the course of a few days.

There was a TV station called WKY in Oklahoma City that the Mathis Brother had gotten the airtime from, so I had them build a set there at the station that looked like a ranch house. We called it *The Buck Owens Show*, but there was a sign that hung there on the set that said "Buck Owens Ranch" on it. So, folks started calling it *The Buck Owens Ranch Show*, and that name kind of stuck.

We had a pretty young singer named Kay Adams who was on with us every week. The whole show pretty much consisted of me and the Buckaroos singing and playing some songs, Kay singing a song or two, and then there'd be a special guest on each show who would perform a couple of times. Bud Mathis wanted to be on TV, too, so we gave him the title "ranch foreman," which meant he'd announce Kay and the guest acts, and every now and then he'd come out and plug my albums and songbooks and whatever else we had for sale.

Well, after I'd bought the bus and closed the deal on the radio station, we headed to Oklahoma City—and on March 15th we started taping those first thirteen episodes. For several years, when we taped those shows, we did 'em absolutely live. Later on we'd use taped backing tracks and do things in a more professional manner. But when the show first started, it was all done live. The tape would start rolling, we'd start playing "Buckaroo," and the announcer would say, *"The Buck Owens Show* with Buck Owens, the Buckaroos, and Kay Adams, playing and singing their great American music." Then he'd say who that week's guest star was going to be, and we'd be off and running.

Here's how primitive it was in the beginning: When I say we did those shows live, I mean we literally shot live to tape. When it was time for a commercial break, we'd stop for exactly that minute or two where the commercials would go in, and then we'd go live again until it was time for the next commercial break. Then we'd come back on and do the rest of the show. In other words, the tape would start rolling when the show started, and the tape would stop rolling a half-hour later. If we made mistakes, we just plowed right on ahead because you couldn't stop and do a re-take. There weren't any editing facilities at all in the beginning. Luckily, I already knew what it was like to do a live TV show because of my days back at KTNT, so I knew how to keep the show moving, and how to just laugh when things went wrong because there wasn't really a choice in the matter.

I still remember that very first show we did. Me and the Buckaroos played a couple of songs, and then I introduced our ranch foreman, Bud Mathis. Bud came out wearing a tuxedo and said, "How do you like my suit, Buck?"

I said, "I like it real well."

He said, "In case this show dies, at least I'll be dressed for it."

He was kidding, of course, but none of us really knew whether we'd make it past those first thirteen episodes or not. But we sure did. My deal with the Mathis Brothers was that they'd air the show locally first, and then we'd try to get it aired on other stations. Porter Wagoner had been having a lot of success with his syndicated TV show, so I figured that with a little effort we could do the same thing. Well, the show just took off. More and more stations around the country started picking it up to the point that we eventually had it on around a hundred stations.

But, back in March of '66, we didn't know what we had. We just knew that when we finished those first thirteen shows, it was time to get on the bus and head to New York.

Chapter Seventy-Five

A FEW MONTHS EARLIER, Jack McFadden had confirmed the date of March 25th for our appearance at Carnegie Hall. My concern from the beginning had been whether or not we'd draw a big enough crowd to a place like that—which is why I kept reminding Jack and Ken Nelson that I still had the option to bail out if the ticket sales turned out to be embarrassing. Well, that ended up not to be an issue because the place went and sold out a couple of weeks in advance.

So I was able to relax about that, but my new big concern was whether or not we'd be able to get through the whole show without screwing anything up. Remember now, we were recording a live album that night—and this was before the days when you could take the tapes back into the studio and edit out all of your flubs and then overdub new vocals and stuff. We had to get it right the first time or we'd have to cut out the songs that had any mistakes on 'em.

In March of '66, my current lineup of Buckaroos had been together since Willie Cantu came on board in January of '64, so the band was as tight as it could be. But this wasn't some fairground in Iowa we were playing—it was the most famous concert venue in America. On top of that, we were going to be playing in front of a bunch of New Yorkers—and those folks were known to be pretty selective about what they thought was a good performance.

Even though we were all professionals, our drummer was still just a kid. Imagine being nineteen years old, in the band for just over two years, and having to sit behind your drum kit at Carnegie Hall. And even though Don had been with me for what seemed like forever by that point, he was just twenty-four. That's hard to believe now, but it's true. So I'd be lying if I said I wasn't just a little bit worried that the guys might get the jitters.

The night of the show, the Buckaroos and me wore these suits that had been designed by Nathan Turk. By then, a lot of country artists were wearing Western-style outfits with lots and lots of rhinestones and all sorts of fancy embroidery on 'em. Like I mentioned earlier, the first time I ever saw a country act wearing flashy clothes like that was when I saw the Maddox Brothers and Rose back when I was a teenager in Mesa. As time went on, the outfits all of us country acts were wearing just got flashier and flashier. Nathan Turk was one of the designers a lot of us went to. Another guy we used who was probably the most famous of those gaudy-Western-suit designers was named Nudie Cohn. He called the outfits he designed for us "Nudie suits." I always thought that sounded like we weren't wearing anything at all. I didn't know how well we were going to perform in front of that audience, but at least I knew we were sure going to look good.

The Carnegie Hall show was like a lot of those package shows we'd been doing. A group called the Homesteaders were the openers. After them came Marion Worth, who'd had several country hits by then. Then Archie Campbell came out, told some jokes, and sang a song. He was followed by Johnny Paycheck, who'd just had his first hit with a song I'd recorded a couple of years earlier called "A-11."

Jack McFadden had managed to get several of our OMAC artists on the bill, so after the intermission, Kay Adams sang my song, "Gonna Roll Out the Red Carpet." Then my old songwriting partner Red Simpson came on. By '66, he'd gotten signed to Capitol Records, and he'd immediately had a hit with a song Tommy Collins wrote called "Roll Truck Roll." Dick Curless followed Red, and just about stole the show when he did "A Tombstone Every Mile." The audience kept calling for Dick to do an encore, which got me a little nervous, knowing I was going to have to follow that.

The emcee for the night was Lee Arnold. Years later he'd become one of the most famous country deejays around with his syndicated radio show, *On a Country Road*. But back in '66 he was a disc jockey at a radio station in New Jersey, which was probably the closest country music station they could find.

Well, Lee introduced us. He said some nice things about me, including something about me being America's number one country artist. Then he said, "Ladies and gentlemen, a warm Carnegie Hall welcome for Buck Owens!" We started the introduction of "Act Naturally," and the applause was so loud and so long, we had to just keep playing the intro over and over until the crowd calmed down enough for me to start singing. I couldn't believe my ears or my eyes. From the opening song, we had that crowd in the palms of our hands. And I swear to you, when we finished the last song a little over forty-five minutes later, not one of us had hit a wrong note, missed a beat, or flubbed a single word. After all of those years in the recording studio doing everything we could to make sure we got at least four songs recorded in three hours, we'd literally recorded a perfect album in less than fifty minutes.

I've never had a show—before or since—that went as seamlessly as that one did at Carnegie Hall. And even though New York City isn't exactly known for having much of a country music fan base, the crowd that night was as receptive as any I'd ever experienced. After we did our last song, I felt like I needed to make a little speech—and in that little speech, I told those folks that I'd been making music for over twenty years, and that they were, without a doubt, the warmest audience I'd ever had the opportunity to perform for. And I meant it. I still wouldn't live there if they gave me the whole damn town, but that night sure changed my mind about not wanting to play there.

After the concert was over, we all went back to the Americana, which is the hotel they'd put us up in while we were staying in New York. They'd given me a big suite there, so that's where the crowd had gathered after the show. There were some record promoters and some of the other acts who'd played that night, and several other music business people in there. But mainly there were a lot of pretty young women in my suite. All of a sudden, "Dashing" Doyle Holly came strolling in and said, "Well, looky here! All right girls, which one of you pretty young

"Now that there were three of us, I bought a Chevy truck and put a camper on it so we'd have enough space for everybody in the band, and for all of our equipment."

(*Left to right*) Wayne "Moose" Stone, Don Rich, Buck, Jay McDonald, and Merle Haggard, 1962. "It was during that short time he was with us that Merle said to me one day as we were going down the road, 'You know, Buck, you oughta call your band the Buckaroos.'"

(*Left to right*) Buddy, Buck, and Michael outside a Las Vegas motel during one of Buck's two-week engagements at the Golden Nugget, 1962.

(*Left to right*) Oliver "Mooney" Lynn, Phyllis Owens, Buck, and Loretta Lynn, 1964.

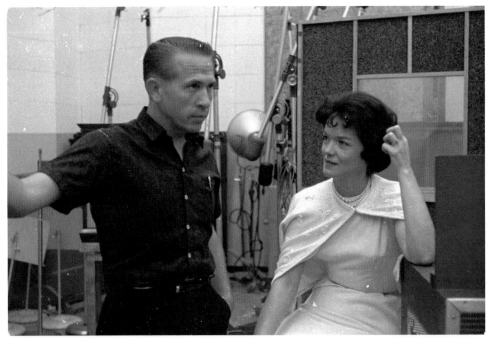

Buck with ex-wife Bonnie Owens at Capitol Studios. "By then, she'd had a hit of her own with a song called 'Why Don't Daddy Live Here Anymore.' Yeah, I guess you can imagine how I felt hearing her singing that one."

Buck at Capitol Studios. "There wasn't any time for rehearsals. When we'd get in the studio, . . . I'd just tell everybody what the chord progression was, and then I'd count off the song and we'd go. . . . Looking back now, I can safely say that it all worked out just fine."

EXPIRES

IS AN ACTIVE MEMBER

OF THE

Buck Owens fan club

"BUCK'S CONTINUED
FAME . . . IS OUR AIM"

P. O. BOX 128 — EDISON, CALIFORNIA 93220

Buck in his newly acquired radio station's Volkswagen Bus. "I decided to invest some of it in a business I already knew something about. . . . The station became available, so I bought it. . . ."

(*Left to right*) Willie Cantu, Tom Brumley, Buck, Don Rich, and Doyle Holly. "I can guarantee that was the first time anybody ever got their picture taken in front of Carnegie Hall wearing outfits like the ones we had on."

The Buck Owens Ranch Show. (*Left to right*) Doyle Holly, Don Rich, Buck, Willie Cantu, and Tom Brumley. "We called it *The Buck Owens Show*, but there was a sign that hung there on the set that said 'Buck Owens Ranch' on it. So, folks started calling it *The Buck Owens Ranch Show*, and the name kind of stuck."

Publicity photo for the album *Buck Owens and His Buckaroos in Japan!* "We recorded that one at Kosei Nenkin Hall in Tokyo. . . . It was packed out—standing room only—and the crowd was about as enthusiastic as any crowd we'd played for in America."

(*Left to right*) Tom Brumley, Wayne Wilson, Don Rich, Buck, Buck's record producer Ken Nelson, and Willie Cantu.

Buck with his manager, Jack McFadden. "Jack's favorite saying was always 'whatever it takes.' When he came to work with me, he said that was going to be our motto—and I guess he was right because it didn't matter what we set out to do, we were going to do it, whatever it took. And believe me, we did."

things would like to make love with Ol' 'Dashing?'" Of course, everybody in the room cracked up, but that was Doyle's approach to life. He'd just played Carnegie Hall, but the show was over and it was time for him to move on to more important things. When it came to women, he had this "I'm here, so let's get it on" attitude, and it served him mighty well over the years.

I found out later that Carnegie Hall has a seating capacity of over 2,700, and I sure was glad we'd managed to get that many people to come out to see us in Manhattan. But wouldn't you know it—the next day we did the same show again with all those same acts at a place called Symphony Hall in Newark, New Jersey, and we had almost twice as many people show up. Then we hauled everything and everybody back over the state line again and played a sold-out show at the Brooklyn Academy of Music. And after that, we finally headed back to Bakersfield for a few days.

Chapter Seventy-Six

WHEN I SAY WE HEADED BACK to Bakersfield for a few days, I'm not kidding. A week later, we were back in LA at Capitol Studios again. I'd written a song called "Where Does the Good Times Go" that I'd already recorded a couple of times before, but I could never seem to get it to come out just right. It took us a long time to get a couple of more takes of it down at that session, and then we only had time to record one other song. It was called "Open Up Your Heart," and for that one I'd brought in the great James "Chicken-Pickin'" Burton to play lead guitar.

James had been Ricky Nelson's guitar player since the late '50s, and just a few years later he'd be Elvis's guitar player. But on April 6th, 1966, he was my guitar player, and I loved what he did on "Open Up Your Heart." Me and Don just sort of strummed along and let James handle the guitar intro and the instrumental break both. It was kind of funny to me because I knew if that one became a hit, Don would have to learn all those licks James played so it'd sound right when we did the song live.

Now speaking of Don, there were people who'd wanted to hire him away from me going all the way back to when the two of us first started touring together—back when it was just me and him driving from town to town, using pickup bands at those old clubs and honky-tonks we used to play in.

Even back then there were big country stars that wanted him to be in their bands. There were managers who wanted him to go solo so they could manage his career. There were record companies that wanted to sign him. In fact, the first time he got offered a record deal, he came to me and told me about it. I said, "Well, Don, we want to do what's best for you."

He said, "I'm gonna do what's best for me, and what's best for me is to stay with you."

Of course, I was real happy he felt that way, but I'd still kid him about it. After we'd had several big hits and were starting to get pretty famous, I'd look at Don and say, "You're still here?"

He'd always say, "Oh yeah, Chief. I ain't goin' nowhere."

As time went on, I'd say, "Don, let's go into the studio and record something on you." We managed to get a few songs recorded, but it was like pulling teeth to try to get him to let me record a whole album of him as a solo artist.

I've always been so motivated and had so much drive and ambition that I couldn't understand why somebody with his talent wouldn't want to try to become a recording artist like I'd done—to have the crowds applauding for them night after night, and to have all the nice things that fame and money bring. I'd done it, and I felt like the opportunity was there for Don to do it, too.

One time I finally came right out and asked him to explain it to me. He just smiled and said, "Aw, Chief, I don't need to be any more famous than I am now. I like it right where I am. I don't have any pressure. You get to have all the pressure. You thrive on that stuff. I wouldn't want to have to deal with all that, so you just keep doing what you're doing and I'll be your straight man. Every time you say something that you need me to agree with, I'll just sit here and say, 'You bet your sweet ass!'"

He was making light of the situation, but he was dead serious. He was perfectly happy being second fiddle. He didn't mind at all that I was the one getting all the attention.

I pretty much forced him into the spotlight on those albums where I'd make him sing a solo now and then. And at our shows, he seemed okay with letting that spotlight hit him for a song or two—as long as he wasn't the main act on that stage that everybody'd come to see. He didn't want the pressure of having to fill all those seats.

Since he'd been with me the longest, he just naturally became the leader of the Buckaroos. The personnel changed a lot over the years, but as long as he was with me, he was in charge of making sure the band had their act together and was ready to play.

Once we reached the point where the Buckaroos were Don, Tom, Doyle, and Willie, the band developed its own personality. And, since I liked to give everybody nicknames, I figured each member needed his own nickname to match his individual personality. I already told you about "Dashing" Doyle. Don Rich became "Dangerous" Don because he was so dangerous on the Telecaster. Tom Brumley was "Tender" Tom, because of those tender steel lines he played. And Willie Cantu became "Wonderful" Willie because he was a wonder on the drums.

I'd played on our album, *The Instrumental Hits of Buck Owens and His Buckaroos*, but it was obvious the band was so tight that they should be making their own albums without me.

Like I told you earlier, in November of '65, I recorded most of the songs for my first gospel album. Well, a couple of days before we did those sessions, the Buckaroos went down to Capitol Studios and recorded what would become their first album. I'd come up with this idea of having them record instrumental versions of a dozen of my songs. Then I got Capitol to agree to include this sheet inside the sleeve that had all the lyrics to those twelve songs on it. So, the Buckaroos' first album turned out to be a karaoke record before there was such a thing as karaoke.

When the album came out in '66, it was called *The Buck Owens Songbook: Instrumental Backgrounds of Owens Favorites Played by the Buckaroos Under the Direction of Don Rich*. I guess that guy at Capitol who got paid by the word to come up with album titles was still working there.

In mid-April of '66, I remember opening the new issue of *Billboard* and looking at the country charts. "Waitin' in Your Welfare Line" was still hanging around, sitting at number two on the singles chart after being number one for the previous seven weeks; *Roll Out the Red Carpet for Buck Owens and His Buckaroos*—the album that didn't have any hits on it—was sitting at number one on the country albums chart; and, lo and behold, the Buckaroos' album was there, too, sitting in the number ten spot. That was a pretty good week for all of us.

As the years went by, the Buckaroos ended up making a dozen albums. All of those records had plenty of instrumentals on 'em, of course, but Don and Doyle and some of the other guys would sing on 'em, too. I'm proud to say that some of the ones that Don sang on got released as singles and some of 'em made the charts.

But he was never interested in stepping out entirely on his own and becoming a star. All he really wanted to do was make music with me and the Buckaroos. And, when I needed his approval, he'd always be there to nod his head and say, "You bet your sweet ass!"

Chapter Seventy-Seven

IN MAY OF '66, Capitol released my gospel album, *Dust on Mother's Bible*. That same day, they put out my next single, "Think of Me."

"Think of Me" was the first song Don co-wrote with somebody besides me that turned out to be the A-side of one of my singles. By 1966, I'd been having hit records for seven straight years. What that means is that for seven straight years I'd been getting songs and poems in the mail from all over the place.

Sending a successful recording artist an unsolicited song and expecting him to actually record it is like sending a famous actor an unsolicited movie script and expecting him to actually make the movie. It's a pretty unrealistic proposition. But people do it all the time, and at least 99.9 percent of the time absolutely nothing comes of it.

I guess it must've been a slow mail day or something, but when I got this poem in the mail from a woman named Estrella Olson, I actually sat there and read the thing. I thought to myself, "Hey, this is pretty good." Don was sitting there with me, so I handed it to him and said, "What do you think?" At first he thought I was kidding, but then he read it and said, "I think I can do something with this." So, he came up with a melody and we went in the studio and cut it in February of '66.

It wasn't one of those fast "freight train" songs like we'd done so many of by then, but it wasn't a slow ballad like "Together Again" either. As far as the tempo was concerned, it sort of fell between the two—but the result was the same because it went to number one in July and stayed up there for six weeks.

That same month, Capitol released our first live album. It was called *Carnegie Hall Concert with Buck Owens and His Buckaroos*. They'd taken photos of us there in Manhattan that afternoon, the day of the show, so the album's cover photo was a picture of me and the Buckaroos in our Nathan Turk suits, standing in front of Carnegie Hall. We got a lot of funny looks on the street that day, even from those New Yorkers who don't usually pay attention to stuff like that. Hell, they wouldn't act like they noticed you if you were walking down the street in your underwear. But they noticed us—I can guarantee that was the first time anybody ever got their picture taken in front of Carnegie Hall wearing outfits like the ones we had on.

When we did that concert, I'd managed to figure out a way to squeeze in damn near every hit I'd had up to that point. When it came to "Act Naturally" and "Together Again" and some of other really big ones, we did the whole song. But for the most part we did a lot of medleys. Don and Doyle performed their comedy routine that they did at all of our shows, and we even did our skit with the Beatle wigs. But the folks at Capitol wanted to cut out most of the talking and comedy. So, the album itself was one hit after another in front of this very excited audience. And like I said, as far as the musicianship was concerned, it was just a night of perfection. Back then, a live country album wasn't real common. There'd been some, of course. Flatt & Scruggs have even recorded a live album at Carnegie Hall a few years earlier. But when *Carnegie Hall Concert with Buck Owens and His Buckaroos* came out, it was a big deal. That thing shot to number one on the country album charts, and it even crossed over onto the pop album charts.

I was real proud of that record when it came out, and I'm still real proud of it. Of course, since it did so well, Capitol wanted me to make more live albums. At the time I was a little concerned because I knew I'd have to shake up my set list on each one since I knew nobody'd want to buy another live album by me with the same songs on 'em. But it ended up working out okay. Over the next few years we had plenty more hits to add to the set list.

Chapter Seventy-Eight

IN AUGUST OF '66, my next single came out. The A-side was "Open Up Your Heart"—the one that James Burton had played his "chicken-pickin'" guitar licks on. By this time, the whole operation of my career had become what you'd call a well-oiled machine. If you've ever wanted to know what it was like to be a major country star in those days, you're probably beginning to get a pretty good idea. You'd either be in the recording studio or on the road or on somebody's TV show or back home finding out what all you'd missed while you were gone.

In my case, I was doing all those things, plus I was taping my own TV show four times a year. I also had my music publishing company and my radio station, and Jack and I had our booking agency. I know that sounds like I was working a lot harder than I might've needed to. But when I started getting into all those business ventures, one of the main reasons was because I'd seen what had happened to a lot of other folks who had been big country stars and weren't anymore.

I'd watched some of those stars grow old, lose all of their money, and end up having to play a bunch of places like they'd played when they were first starting out. They didn't really have a choice. If they wanted to eat and have a roof over their heads, they had to work—and they had to take the jobs they could get.

Well, I sure as hell didn't want to find myself back at the Blackboard after the hits stopped coming and the fans had lost interest in me. A lot of people over the years have said they thought I was more of a businessman than a musician. That's okay. I've never much cared what anybody thought about me anyway, except for my fans. So I stayed on that treadmill. I just kept touring and making records and doing TV shows. And every now and then, I'd actually get to go home and spend time with my family.

Like I told you, Bonnie wanted Buddy and Mike to come and live with me and Phyllis since Bonnie was on the road so much with Merle. I had missed out on my sons' early years, so I was glad to be able to spend what time I could with 'em now that they were teenagers.

Buddy was always a wonderful, cheerful young man. He was about sixteen and a half when he and Mike moved in with Phyllis and me. Both of my two sons I had with Bonnie were great kids and they're great adults. They worked for me starting when they were youngsters, and they've been hard workers all their lives. They have the accomplishments to show for it, too.

But they were both typical teenagers, and they also both liked to drive—fast. One time Buddy was driving his friend Ray McDonald through town when he got real excited talking about something, and he proceeded to run through a red light at the corner of 18th and Chester Avenue.

In those days, that was about the busiest intersection in Bakersfield. He didn't cruise through the light right as it was changing—he just flat out ran the red light. And, wouldn't you know it—a motorcycle policeman coming from the opposite direction saw it happen. It took that motorcycle cop a little while to get turned around, but when Buddy saw him, he decided to try to lose him, so he made a quick cut to the right. The only problem for Buddy was that quick right turn took him straight into an alley that came to a dead end. There he was with no way to turn around, so he cut off his lights and just sat there.

Of course, the motorcycle officer pulled up right behind them. Since Buddy was a juvenile, the motorcycle policeman called the juvenile officer on duty, who happened to be a man named Jim Cash—a guy I'd known since my days at the Blackboard.

When Jim finally arrived, he walked up to the car, looked inside, saw Buddy, and said, "My God, you look just like Buck Owens. Are you kin to Buck?"

Well, Buddy's face lit up and he said, "Yes sir, I'm his son!"

So Jim gave him a good stern lecture, but he knew Buddy hadn't technically run away from the police because the first officer had never turned on his siren. Jim told Buddy if he was ever caught running a red light again, he'd be in serious trouble.

Buddy is so much like Bonnie, he's impossible not to like. So Jim didn't take him down to the police station or impound his car or anything like that. In all the years I've known Buddy—which is all his life, of course—I've never met anyone who had a bad word to say about him. That doesn't just go for Buddy. That goes for his mother, too.

My son Mike is quite a remarkable, ambitious, hard working, hard playing, straight up guy. He was a really good athlete when he was a youngster, as was Buddy. They were always battling each other in basketball and football. We used to have some great football games out at the ranch on Sunday afternoons. Buddy and Mike would each have three or four of their friends out there a lot of times, and when I was home, I always liked to join in.

Ever since I'd had what they called "brain fever" as a child, I couldn't run very fast. To tell the truth, I couldn't punt very good either. Since there were only four or five guys on each team, my job was to play quarterback for both sides. And the number one rule was to *never* hit the quarterback. Some of those boys actually played on the high school football team, so I'd wear this bright red shirt just to make sure they'd see me. When you play guitar for a living, you can't be getting your fingers broken playing football with a bunch of teenagers.

Speaking of football, the only time I can ever remember Mike getting into trouble had to do with a football game at his high school.

Phyllis and I had gone to Miami because I was doing Jackie Gleason's TV show that he taped down there. Anyway, while me and Phyllis were down in Miami, Phyllis's aunt was in charge of watching the kids. At the time, I had a red '66 Corvette with a big ol' 427 engine in it. It was a beautiful car and it would run like you couldn't imagine. Well, Mike told Phyllis's aunt that I had given him permission on this particular Friday night to take the Corvette out so he could pull the victory bell around the track at the North High football game. That's where he went to school, and it was homecoming night, so apparently he had volunteered my Corvette to be the bell-pulling vehicle. The only problem was he had sort of "forgotten" to get my permission. Of course, Phyllis's aunt didn't know that, so she said to Mike, "If your dad said you can, then it's fine with me."

Well, Michael took off, and it wasn't long before a motorcycle policeman chased him down and told him he'd clocked him going a hundred and five miles an hour. Since Michael was just a teenager, the motorcycle cop told him the car would have to be impounded and Michael would have to be taken to the police station, and then someone would have to get him out and take him home. So a second policeman arrived at the scene to take Mike away, while a tow truck came to take the Corvette to Cheeseman's Garage—the place where they always took impounded cars.

On their way over to the police station, Mike was saying "yes sir" and "no sir" and explaining to the officer that the motorcycle policeman had been absolutely right to stop him for speeding and that he had been totally in the wrong for driving so fast, but that the reason he had been in such a hurry was because he was late getting to the football game where he was supposed to pull the victory bell around the field there at homecoming.

By the time they got to the police station, Michael had used his charm and persuasion so well that the officer decided that rather than keep him there until somebody could come pick him up, he would just give him the speeding ticket and then take him over to Cheeseman's Garage so he could get the car back and go to the football game. So, over to Cheeseman's they went, and the officer told the guy at the garage to release the car to Mike.

Mike hopped into the car, got to the school, and drove out onto the track that ran all the way around football field. My Corvette had a trailer hitch on the back, so they took the little trailer that the victory bell sat on and hooked it onto the trailer hitch. Finally, Mike took off driving

175

around the track with the victory bell ringing—and wouldn't you know it—after everything he'd gone through that night, the car ran out of gas halfway around the track.

I got back from Miami two nights later, went to the office on Monday, and everything seemed just fine. Nobody said anything to me about what had happened. I went to work on Tuesday, and in the mail there came a bill from Cheeseman's Garage for towing my Corvette the previous Friday.

I figured that had to be a mistake because I'd been in Miami doing the Gleason show the day the bill from the garage said my 'Vette was being towed. While I was sitting there trying to figure out why the garage thought they'd towed my car, Buddy passed by my office. I said, "Buddy, come here a minute." He came in and I showed him the bill, and he started to back out the door saying, "You've got to talk to Mike."

I said, "Talk to Mike? You don't know what this is about?" But Buddy just ran on out the door.

So, I asked Mike about it, and he told me the whole story. When he was done, I asked him the name of the officer that had given him the ticket. He gave me the man's name, so I called him on the phone and he confirmed exactly what Mike had told me.

I don't know if this is still how they do it today, but in those days if you were classified as a juvenile, you couldn't just pay the ticket. You had to go to traffic court, and you had to take at least one of your parents. As it turned out, I was off the road for a few days, so I went to court with Mike and listened as the judge told him that going a hundred and five miles an hour through the middle of town was a really serious offense. And then he gave him a pretty stiff fine—something like seventy or eighty dollars, which was a pretty big fine in 1966.

The judge said, "So, you have to pay the fine, and I'm going to leave the file open on you. If you get another speeding ticket during the next year, the penalty will be a lot more than just a fine." Then the judge looked at me and said, "Does that sound okay to you, Mr. Owens?"

I thought about it for a minute, and then I stood up and said, "Your honor, I don't think that's severe enough. I think we need to do something that will make my son understand the seriousness of his actions."

The judge said, "You know, you might be right. How about if we take his driving privileges away for two months? He can drive to school and he can drive to work, but other than that, no driving for the next eight weeks."

I said, "That sounds like a good idea me."

Boy, let me tell you, when I was driving us home from traffic court, Mike was very unhappy with me. He thought, at the tender age of sixteen, that I should have just agreed with what the judge's original sentence was. But I felt that Mike needed to know what a bad thing he'd done. In fact, he'd done several bad things. He'd lied to Phyllis's aunt. He'd taken my car without my permission. He'd been caught going over a hundred miles an hour. After all that, I thought that just having to pay a fine wasn't sufficient.

But I have to say this about Buddy and Mike: in all the years they were growing up, those are the only two problems that I can remember ever having with either one of those boys. They were great kids, and they've both accomplished a lot as adults—so I couldn't be more proud of 'em.

Chapter Seventy-Nine

IN LATE OCTOBER OF '66, "Open Up Your Heart" hit the top of the charts. That made an even dozen number one singles in a row for me. I was glad to have another big hit, but I was sorry that I'd lost Doyle Holly.

Doyle was a really important member of the Buckaroos, but he and I had a real love/hate kind of relationship. Sometimes I loved him and he hated me, and sometimes it was the other way around. By the time we went back into the studio in early November, he'd been out of the band for several weeks—but only temporarily. He'd eventually come back and then leave again. To tell you the truth, over the years I kind of lost count how many times he came and went.

When we went to Capitol Studios for three days in November, the Buckaroos' new bass player was Wayne Wilson. Just like we'd done on most of our sessions, Bob Morris played bass when we were recording, and Wayne played bass on our live shows. And just like I'd done with Doyle, I had Wayne play rhythm guitar when we were in the studio.

On November 7th, our first day of recording without Doyle in almost two years, things didn't go very well. We only managed to get two songs in the can over the course of four hours. We got back on pace the next day and recorded four songs, including a ballad I'd written called "Your Tender Loving Care."

On December 26th, Capitol released my next single, "Where Does the Good Times Go." The next day, they put out my sixteenth Capitol album, *Open Up Your Heart*. This time around, unlike *Roll Out the Red Carpet*, it was an album that included some hits on it—"Open Up Your Heart," "Think of Me," "Waitin' in Your Welfare Line," and one that would become a hit a few months later called "Sam's Place." But the great minds at Capitol had struck again—God forbid they put 'em out in time for people to buy 'em for Christmas presents.

Chapter Eighty

B Y THE BEGINNING OF 1967, we'd played every place there was in America for an act like us to play—and we'd played most of 'em at least twice. We'd also played in Europe at those military bases. So, Jack McFadden and I decided it was about time to go to the Far East and see what kind of reaction me and the Buckaroos would get there. We knew the folks in Japan were huge fans of country music, which meant they were big fans of mine—so Jack booked shows for us in a bunch of places, including Kyoto and Osaka and Tokyo.

In the meantime, it was back to the studio again—but this time I was in the control room with Ken Nelson. In January, the Buckaroos recorded their second album, *America's Most Wanted Band*—and it took 'em three whole sessions to do it. Doyle wasn't back yet, so Wayne Wilson didn't just take Doyle's place playing bass—he also sang one by himself and did a duet with Don. There were a dozen songs on that album, and Don sang four solos on it, so I was starting to think there might be some hope for a Don Rich solo album yet.

It wasn't long after those sessions that we headed off for Japan. I have to tell you, it's a terrific country with the kindest, nicest, most polite people you'd ever want to meet. I really loved Japan and I really loved the people, and they really seemed to love me and the Buckaroos.

When we arrived at the airport in Tokyo, it was like the Beatles arriving in America—only bigger. It seemed like there were thousands of people to greet us when we came off the plane. And, of course, all the press was there with their cameras. When they all started taking pictures of us at the same time with those motor-driven Nikon F cameras, it sounded like machine guns going off.

Well, as you can imagine, the first thing we had to do was get to the nearest electronics store and buy ourselves some Nikon F cameras. You could get 'em in America, but back then a Nikon F cost about twice as much in the US as it did in Japan. I bought one, all of the Buckaroos bought one, Jack McFadden bought one—and so we spent three weeks in Japan, playing shows and taking pictures. But Jack, he just got real carried away. I'll never forget—he went through thirty-five rolls of film on that trip. I told him, "Jack, just because it's a thirty-five-millimeter camera, that don't mean you have to take thirty-five rolls of film."

Since the folks at Capitol Records knew having me and the Buckaroos playing shows in Japan was a pretty unique situation, they'd decided they wanted us to record another live album while we were there. So, when we played Tokyo, Ken Nelson had tape rolling. Now, we hadn't been the first country act to record an album at Carnegie Hall, but no other country artist had ever recorded a live album in Japan before. Hell, up until our show was recorded on February 6th, 1967, at Kosei Nenkin Hall in Tokyo, no country artist had ever even made a live album outside of America before.

I had to come up with a whole new set list and even wrote a couple of new songs so we wouldn't duplicate anything we'd done on the Carnegie Hall album. But I didn't mind at all because that night we were making history.

Now, the whole three weeks we'd been in Japan, all of us but Jack had been getting our film developed in whatever town we were staying in along the way. But not Jack. He said he was going to wait until he got back home to get his developed. Back in those days, there weren't any x-ray machines at airports yet, so nobody gave any thought about him packing his film in his luggage and waiting until he got home. Well, we got back to Bakersfield, and Jack took his thirty-five rolls of film in to be developed—but not a single one of his 1,260 pictures had come out because every time he'd loaded a roll of film in his camera, he'd put it in backwards.

For the longest time after that he didn't want to come anywhere near any of the guys in the band because they really tortured him every time they'd see him, asking him to show 'em those pictures he took while we were all in Japan.

A week or so after we got back from the Far East, "Where Does the Good Times Go" went to number one on *Billboard*'s country singles chart. What do you do when you've had thirteen number one hits in a row? Well, I looked around, but there wasn't a soul to ask because nobody'd ever done that before. Other country stars would've probably just bought another Cadillac or something. I bought another radio station. In fact, I bought two. One was an FM station in Bakersfield that was called KBBY when I bought it. The other one was an AM station in Tempe, Arizona.

My older sister, Mary Ethel, who still lived in Arizona, called me one day to tell me about this 50,000-watt AM station for sale there in Tempe. The call letters were KYND, so the station was called "Candy." I thought, "Well, let me see what they want for it." I went out to Arizona to see it, and it wasn't much to look at, but the guy who owned it sold it to me for $30,000 down and $1,500 a month for the next ten years or so. I mean, this station was held together with bubble gum and baling wire, and it was located in a former Sizzler Steak House—but it was a 50,000-watt station, so I couldn't turn it down. When I bought it, they were playing this sort of middle-of-the-road pop music. So, the first thing I did was change the call letters to KTUF, and I changed the format to country.

Chapter Eighty-One

AS YOU CAN TELL, I'm pretty proud of what I've accomplished, but I can't begin to explain to you how proud I was when Ray Charles won not one, but *two* Grammy awards in March of '67 for his version of "Crying Time." Ray won for "Best Male R&B Solo Vocal Performance" and for "Best R&B Recording." Some of the songs I'd written in the past had become hits for other artists, but none had done as well as Ray's recording of "Crying Time." I was real happy for Ray that night—and I was real happy for me, too.

In addition to *The Buck Owens Ranch Show* that was still going strong, I kept getting asked to be on other shows. I did Mike Douglas's and Joey Bishop's and Dean Martin's. Then, about a week after Ray Charles picked up his Grammy awards, they finally aired the *Jackie Gleason Show* we'd taped while Mike was having all that fun in my Corvette. Jackie called it "an all-star salute to country and western music." In addition to having me and the Buckaroos perform three songs that night, he'd also rounded up Roy Acuff, Homer and Jethro, Boots Randolph, and several others, including that guy who'd been one of the performers at that tribute concert for Herb Henson four years earlier—Roy Clark.

On March 13th, my single of "Sam's Place" was released. Me and Red Simpson had written that one. We got the title from the name of a club I used to play up in Northern California. Like I told you earlier, Bob Neal—the guy who'd been Elvis's first manager—was one of the guys who used to get me bookings back when Don and I first started going on the road together. Bob really wanted to manage me, but back in 1961 I told him, "I don't want to be getting no manager yet. It's way too early for that."

He said, "Well, let me book you some dates there in your neck of the woods, then."

I said, "You can book me anywhere you can get me paid, but I already know most of the joints from Southern California to Northern Washington. I can book those myself."

Bob said, "Do you know a club up around Richmond, California called Sam's Place?"

Well, I'd never heard of that one, so the next time I had some gigs up in Northern California, I called Bob and told him I still had some dates open up there, so sure enough, he booked me and Don to do a show at Sam's Place.

When the date arrived, me and Don showed up early, as always. At first I thought it was just like every other joint we'd played on the tour—until the owner got so loaded that he tried to drive his car through the front door of his own honky-tonk. Well, he might've just been trying to park near the entrance, but he ended up almost getting his Cadillac all the way through the front door. I never knew for sure what his intentions were, but we played the gig anyway—even though it was pretty drafty that night since the entrance to the club was a little wider than it had been when we got there.

About three months later, we were up there again. The front door was fixed and everything seemed like it was pretty much back to normal until the owner decided to show the crowd how much he was enjoying having me and Don there. When we finished singing "Under Your Spell Again," he came running right up toward the stage with a .38 revolver in his hand. I'm telling you, one thing you don't ever want to see is a big ol' drunk guy running toward you while he's holding a gun. If he had tripped over the lip of that stage, that gun could've gone off and he could've accidentally put an end to a very promising career—namely mine! Luckily, he managed to get up on the stage without incident, and then he just started shooting that pistol off, straight up in the air. You would've thought we were in a saloon like in an old Western movie.

I called up Bob Neal the next day and said, "You can keep booking me, but you can take Sam's Place off your list." After watching that owner drive his car into the front door, and then having him unloading his pistol right next to me, I decided it wasn't worth the seventy-five bucks to find out what might happen the next time.

* * *

When May rolled around, our second live album, *Buck Owens and His Buckaroos in Japan*, came out. Like I said, we recorded that one at Kosei

Nenkin Hall in Tokyo. The venue wasn't anywhere near as big as Carnegie Hall, but it was packed out—standing room only—and the crowd was about as enthusiastic as any crowd we'd played for in America.

Don had been my lead guitarist for a long time by then. One of the things about Don was that he loved to play guitar so much that he didn't really like to play the fiddle anymore. I used to tease him all the time. If he started horsing around onstage, I'd tell him, "Okay, Don, time to get out your fiddle."

Well, I'd heard that the Japanese really like to hear a good country fiddle player, so I put Don to work that night. He'd written an instrumental piece called "Fiddle Polka," so I had him do that one. Bob Morris had written a song called "Fishin' On the Mississippi"—which was a Cajun-type song—so Don played fiddle on that one, too.

The whole show was similar to a lot of the albums we'd been recording during the last few years. I sang most of the songs, but Don sang lead on a song, too. Tom Brumley played a steel guitar instrumental. I played a guitar instrumental called "Tokyo Polka" that I'd written for that night's show. On that one I tried to blend a little Far East-sounding music with country music. I even had Willie Cantu do one he'd come up with called "Drum So-Low." And since Doyle was out of the band, I had his replacement, Wayne Wilson, sing another one of Bob Morris's songs called "Don't Wipe the Tears That You Cry for Him on My Good White Shirt."

A couple of weeks after the new live album came out, "Sam's Place" went to number one on the charts. And then a few weeks later, so did *Buck Owens and His Buckaroos in Japan*, even though it seemed like that album ended up with as much talking on it as it had music. We had a Japanese interpreter there to tell the folks what I was saying between songs. We couldn't pronounce his name, so we just called him Ted. Every time I had something to say, he'd repeat it to the audience in Japanese. Hell, it took three or four minutes just for me and Ted to introduce the band.

Chapter Eighty-Two

IN EARLY JUNE WE WERE BACK IN THE STUDIO. Don and I had spent a lot of our time on the road writing songs, so we cut several of 'em over those three days. On the third day we did one of mine called "It Takes People Like You (to Make People Like Me)." That was what I always said to our audiences at the end of all our shows. I wrote that one as a tribute to my fans.

Later that month, my thirtieth Capitol single came out. Both sides were songs I'd written, and we'd recorded both of 'em at those sessions in November of '66, right after Doyle had left the band. The A-side of the record was "Your Tender Loving Care."

After our big success at Carnegie Hall, other important venues began to realize that our kind of country music had started reaching an audience that was a lot broader than what most other country acts were reaching. On July 7th, we played the Hollywood Bowl. All of the biggest stars in the world had played there, from Frank Sinatra to the Beatles.

The Hollywood Bowl is this huge, outdoor amphitheater that holds about 18,000 people. But I wasn't as worried about it as I was Carnegie Hall and its 2,700 seats because I knew Southern California had plenty of country music fans. While Cousin Herb Henson had been doing his country TV show up in Bakersfield in the '50s and early '60s, there had been TV shows in Los Angeles like *Hometown Jamboree* and *Town Hall Party*. There was plenty of country radio and lots of live country music in LA, too.

They called the show "The Country Sound at the Hollywood Bowl." They could've called it "The Capitol Sound at the Hollywood Bowl" because all of the performers were signed to Capitol Records. There were ten acts and two emcees—and I was the headlining act. I was proud to be a part of it, and I was also proud to have Bakersfield so well represented. Merle and Bonnie were there. So were Ferlin Husky and Wynn Stewart and my longtime songwriting partner, Red Simpson. The other acts were Glen Campbell, Dick Curless, the Geezinslaw Brothers, and the great cowboy actor and singer, Tex Ritter. The ads leading up to the show said it was going to be "The Most Spectacular Country Show Ever"—and for it's time, it just might've been.

A month later, Capitol released my next album, *Your Tender Loving Care*. Because of all the TV appearances and my own TV show and all of our live shows, we hadn't been in the studio much so far during '67—at least not much compared to the previous couple of years. So along with both sides of my latest single, Capitol dug up enough tracks from '65 and '66 to put out an album with a dozen songs on it. They even included "Sam's Place," despite the fact they'd put it on my *Open Up Your Heart* album the year before.

By the time me and the Buckaroos went in the studio in late August, "Dashing" Doyle Holly was back in the band. I was happy to have all of my old lineup back together, and I was also happy because we had ourselves a real special guest in the studio for those two days.

Early on I told you about how Bill Woods made me be the singer at the Blackboard when I just wanted to play guitar—and how Bill had told me if he'd just wanted a guitar player, he would've hired Jimmy Bryant. Of course, he couldn't have afforded to have Jimmy Bryant in his band because Jimmy was *the* guitar player back in the '50s. He was on the *Hometown Jamboree* TV show for years, and he'd made a lot of records on Capitol with his partner, Speedy West. Well, they might not have been able to afford him at the Blackboard, but by 1967 I could afford to have him play with me, so I brought him in to record with us.

Like I told you, Merle Haggard was one of the songwriters I had signed to my publishing company, Blue Book Music. Merle had already had a big hit with "Swingin' Doors" in early '66, but I liked the song so much, I recorded it myself at one of those August sessions. We also did one I wrote called "How Long Will My Baby Be Gone." It was a fun couple of days in the studio even though we only managed to get seven songs cut. Hell, I was so happy to have Doyle back, I even let him play bass instead of using Bob Morris like I usually did. Now that I think about it, that might explain why we weren't able to get more songs recorded during those two days.

Chapter Eighty-Three

SHORTLY AFTER "YOUR TENDER LOVING CARE" went to number one in September, Capitol released "It Takes People Like You (to Make People Like Me)." The B-side was another one I wrote called "You Left Her Lonely Too Long."

I don't know if I was talking to myself or what when I wrote that song on the B-side, but one thing's for sure—by late '67, my marriage to Phyllis was on pretty shaky ground. We hadn't filed for divorce or anything like that, but things weren't going well at all. Despite how things were between us, I just kept hanging around, and she just kept hanging on.

When "Your Tender Loving Care" went to the top of the charts, that made fifteen number one hit singles in a row. I'd become successful beyond anything I'd ever imagined. Not only was my career going great, so were my radio stations and my publishing company and the booking agency. I was thirty-eight years old, and had finally begun to stop worrying about being poor again. Well, that's not quite true. When you've been as poor as I was growing up, you never really stop worrying about being poor again—but I was able to relax enough to accept the fact that we could afford to start flying to our shows instead of going everywhere in the tour bus.

In October of '67, we flew into Wichita, Kansas, to play a big ol' hall there called the Cotillion Ballroom—they called it "The Round Mound of Sound."

If you know anything about that part of the country, you know there's lots of cowboys and cowgirls around there. Well, when we played those kinds of places in Texas or Oklahoma or Kansas, we didn't stop. Those folks wanted to dance and have a good ol' time like those folks did at the Blackboard back in the '50s. So, if it was a weeknight, we'd play from eight o'clock to midnight. On Saturdays we'd play from nine to one in the morning. We just played the whole four hours. There were plenty of times when people would come up to me after one of those four-hour shows and ask me, "How can you play four hours in a row without stopping?" I'd just tell 'em, "Hell, it wasn't all that long ago that I was playing eleven hours straight without stopping, so four hours is easy."

By then, I was older than a lot of the other country stars who were around in '67, but I still had a lot of energy and the willingness to put it out there every night because I always wanted to give folks their money's-worth.

That night at the Cotillion Ballroom we'd been picking for about two hours when I felt Don's guitar neck touch my back. I'll never forget it. We were in the middle of "Truck Drivin' Man" when he did that. I glanced at him, and he cut his eyes over to the left. So, while I kept singing, I casually looked over that way and there sat two girls on the edge of the stage. I don't remember what the other girl looked like, but the one that got all of my attention had long, dark hair down to her waist, and the most gorgeous legs I'd ever seen.

I found out later that one of the security guards had told 'em they could sit there after they told him they were afraid they were going to get stomped on because all of those big ol' cowboys were out there dancing around in their cowboy boots. I didn't have a problem with 'em sitting on the edge of the stage like that. My problem was the same old problem I've always had—trying to have too many women at the same time. It's always gotten me into trouble.

I thought, "I'm gonna take a break and see if I can meet her." It seemed plain to me that she wasn't attached since she was there with another girl.

Now, like I said, when we were at places like the Cotillion Ballroom, most nights we'd just play right through—so when I told the crowd we were going to take a little intermission, Doyle and Tom and Willie were pretty surprised. But not Don—Don knew exactly what the situation was.

Since I told everybody it was intermission time, those two girls got up to stretch their legs, and then they disappeared off into the crowd. So, my plan got off to sort of a bad start.

I hurried down to my dressing room, and in a minute or two, Jack McFadden and Mike Oatman, the promoter of the show, came in to make sure everything was all right. I said, "Jack, did you see that beautiful young lady sitting out there on the edge of the stage?"

He said, "Man, did I!"

I said, "Well, I need you to go find her."

Jack said, "Buck, there's five thousand great big drunk cowboys out there, and you want me to go find one little ol' girl? I'll never find her in that crowd."

Mike Oatman said, "Come on, Jack. I saw her, too. With two of us looking, I'm sure we'll find her."

About five or ten minutes later they came back into the dressing room with her. Now, I've never been known to be very shy, so I said, "Well, hello! I wanted to meet you because I couldn't keep my eyes off of you out there."

I think that embarrassed her a little bit, but I managed to stumble through a conversation with her. I found out her name was Jennifer Joyce Smith, that she was twenty-two years old, that she was in her last year of college, and that she lived in Oklahoma City. When she told me where she lived, I said, "Oklahoma City? I do a television show there."

She told me she'd seen my TV show, and that she'd actually come to see me a year earlier when we played the Trianon Ballroom there. I asked her, "How come you didn't come up and say hello to me that night?"

She said, "Because I was with someone else."

I said, "Well, hell, you could've ditched him. Now we've gone and wasted a whole year!"

I was pouring it on pretty thick, but I was just infatuated with her. I tried to get her to go out to dinner with me after the show, but she said she couldn't because she and her friend had to head back to Oklahoma. I asked her if I could have her phone number so I could call her the next time we were in Oklahoma City. She gave it to me, and then Jack came over to us and told me it was time for me to get back onstage.

We played for a couple of more hours there at the Cotillion, but I had a mighty hard time trying to concentrate on what I was doing.

*   *   *

There was another thing that happened in October of '67—an awards show in Nashville that I want to tell you about. By the time that awards show came around, I'd been receiving all sorts of honors and accolades for years. I was always thrilled every time any organization or publication selected me or one of my songs as being the best of the bunch. You know, a lot of those blues singers talk about paying their dues. If things hadn't worked out the way they did, I might still be playing at some place like the Blackboard every night. But those days were behind me. I'd paid my dues.

I already told you about *Billboard* naming me the "Most Promising Male Artist" of 1960, so I'll just mention a few others. In '64, I received an award from *Cash Box* for having the "Most Programmed Record of the Year" for "Love's Gonna Live Here," and for being the "Most Programmed Country & Western Male Vocalist of the Year." I won that male vocalist award from *Cash Box* in '65, too.

In February of '66, they held the First Annual Country & Western Music Academy Awards Show at the Palladium in Hollywood. That's the organization that later became the Academy of Country Music. They were giving out awards that night for the year 1965. My manager, Jack McFadden, won the award for "Best Talent Management." Bob Morris, who'd played on almost all of my albums up to that point, won the award for "Best Bass." Central Songs, the company that some of my songs were signed to, won "Best Music Publisher." Ken Nelson—the guy who signed me to Capitol—won for "Best Producer/A&R Man." And I won the awards for "Best Bandleader" and "Top Male Vocalist."

That same year, I was chosen as "Favorite Male Country Artist" in *Country Song Roundup*'s Readers' Poll Awards. And there were a lot more awards from *Billboard* and BMI and others.

Now, receiving those awards was really great. I cherish every one of 'em. But I've got to tell you, the biggest honor in country music is supposed to be receiving an award from the Country Music Association. That's the organization in Nashville that has their awards show on network television every year. When they held their first awards show in '67, it wasn't being televised yet. In those days, it was one of those events where they had a cocktail hour, followed by dinner, and then the awards got handed out. They held that first one at Nashville's Municipal Auditorium.

That night I was nominated in two categories: "Male Vocalist of the Year" and "Entertainer of the Year." And I was real proud of the

Buckaroos because they'd been nominated as the "Instrumental Group of the Year."

Well, when they handed out those trophies that night, the "Male Vocalist of the Year" award went to Jack Greene. And who got the "Entertainer of the Year" award? Eddy Arnold. Now, I've got nothing against Eddy Arnold, but I'd be lying if I said I wasn't pretty surprised that the voters would choose him for "Entertainer of the Year" over me. I know that probably sounds like a combination of bragging and sour grapes, but I'm just speaking my mind—which I've been known to do.

In 1967, I was the biggest-selling act onstage and on records—but I didn't live in Nashville. I wasn't part of their clique. I didn't do things their way. I had no interest in following their rules—and that night I found out what happened when you didn't play the game their way.

Of course, I was pretty disappointed that I walked away with nothing that night, but Bakersfield was where I wanted to be and it was where I was going to stay—even though the Nashville establishment had made it clear they were going to refuse recognition if you didn't live there. If you lived anywhere else, you weren't any good in their book.

I had number one hit after number one hit, but in that decade of the '60s—when I was the biggest country star in the world—I never won a single award from the Country Music Association. In fact, I didn't even get nominated for another one. It was as if I didn't exist.

Chapter Eighty-Four

THE YEAR ENDED THE SAME WAY IT BEGAN—back at Capitol Studios. But by then there'd been a big change in the Buckaroos. Since he'd joined the band in January of 1964, Willie Cantu had kept the beat for us on a whole lot of hit records and on hundreds and hundreds of live shows, including Carnegie Hall, Kosei Nenkin Hall in Tokyo, and the Hollywood Bowl. He'd also played on the first couple of albums that the Buckaroos had recorded under their deal with Capitol.

I'd watched Willie grow from a teenager to a fine young man with a wife and a baby daughter. Willie's wife was Canadian, and after all those years of Willie being on the road more than he was at home, I guess she'd decided it made more sense for her to live in Canada and be near her relatives than to stay in California and not see her husband very often. Well, Willie decided he'd better get his ass up to Canada if he wanted to stay married, so he left the band in late '67. The Vietnam war was going on then, and Willie was still young enough to get drafted, so I thought it was a smart move on his part to head to the North before he got sent to the Far East.

I was really sorry to see him go. From the first day he'd joined the band, he understood about playing on top of the beat when it came to those "freight train" songs of mine, but he also knew how to lay back on the slow ballads. When he left, it was the end of that classic Buckaroos lineup.

So, we brought in a young drummer named Jerry Wiggins to play on our last three sessions in December of '67. While we were in the studio, we got ten songs cut, including one I wrote called "Sweet Rosie Jones," and a couple that would be going on my next gospel album. We also recorded one that Don and I wrote called "If I Had Three Wishes." Well, if I had one wish, it would've been that my streak of number one hits hadn't come to an end right at the beginning of 1968.

Chapter Eighty-Five

THE VERY FIRST WEEK OF '68, my nineteenth Capitol album came out. It was called *It Takes People Like You to Make People Like Me*, which was also the title of what I figured would be my next number one single. Every single I'd had since "Act Naturally" in 1963 had gone to the top of the charts. Nobody had ever achieved anything even close to that in country music.

But my streak ended that first week of January when a song called "For Loving You" just wouldn't drop out of that top spot. It had gone to number one in December, and it stayed there the first couple of weeks of January while my record sat just below it. And wouldn't you know it—"For Loving You" was a duet by Bill Anderson and Jan Howard—Harlan's wife. And when their record finally dropped out of that number one spot, what took its place? "Sing Me Back Home" by Merle Haggard. I guess having my streak of number one hits broken was kind of bittersweet because Jan Howard had been a friend of mine since the '50s, so I was happy for her to finally have the first number one record of her career. And I probably shouldn't complain about Merle's hit either since "Sing Me Back Home" was in my publishing company, Blue Book Music.

I didn't really have a lot of time to think about my streak ending because I was back in the studio with the Buckaroos in early January, co-producing their next album with Ken Nelson. We got the whole album done in three days, took the weekend off, and then went right back into the studio for three more days so I could get some tracks of my own cut, including a few more for my next gospel album.

Things were really moving fast because Capitol had already put out another single, "How Long Will My Baby Be Gone," before the second week of January was over.

A couple of weeks later, it was almost time to head to Oklahoma City to tape some more *Buck Owens Ranch* shows, so I made a phone call to Miss Jennifer and asked her if she'd have dinner with me. When she said she would, I told her to make a reservation at the nicest restaurant in town for the next night. The next morning I flew to Oklahoma, rented a Mustang convertible, and then drove out to this little suburb of Oklahoma City called Edmond, which is where she lived. When I got there, she told me she'd made a reservation at this fancy French restaurant. Well, it turned out I couldn't read anything on the menu, but it didn't matter because I was happy just to be with her.

Once we finished taping our shows in Oklahoma City, I said goodbye to Jennifer and headed back to LA to do the Dean Martin Show. Dean had a way of making you feel so relaxed and welcome. When I walked onto the stage for rehearsal, he said, "There's my boy!" He loved country music, so he was a fan of mine just like I was a fan of his. Now, Dino and me had one thing in common—neither one of us took much stock in rehearsing. I remember the director telling him, "Now, you'll sing this verse and then Buck will sing that verse, and then here's where you'll both sing together."

Dean was a real good-natured kind of guy, so he just smiled at the director and said, "Now, how about if you do the directing and leave the singing to me and Buck?" Then he turned to me and said, "You sing when you want to and I'll sing when I want to, and we'll just have a good time." So, that's what we did.

That night, me and the Buckaroos performed "How Long Will My Baby Be Gone," and then Dean and me sang "I've Got a Tiger by the Tail" and "Love's Gonna Live Here"—and the two of us couldn't have done a better job on those two songs if we'd rehearsed 'em for a month.

I'd been doing network television going back to my first appearance on Jimmy Dean's show in March of '64. It just seemed natural to me to have that camera pointed in my direction. So, when Ken Nelson told me that Capitol was interested in making a promotional video of my next single, I told him I'd do it. It would be many years before there'd be a network that specialized in showing country music videos, so I didn't know where my little video would end up being shown. But, I've always liked to do anything unique to promote a record, so I was ready to give it a shot.

Ken told me that Bobbie Gentry had performed "Ode to Billie Joe" on a local TV show in Atlanta, and that Capitol had bought the rights to the tape and sent it to Ralph Emery. Ralph had a show on WSM-TV back in those days. Well, it got a big reaction when Ralph showed it, so Capitol had made a bunch of copies and sent them to something like forty TV stations.

When it came time to shoot my video, Capitol went all out. They brought in this Emmy-winning director who'd heard my song, "Sweet Rosie Jones," and wanted to create a little movie where the whole song would be acted out. "Sweet Rosie Jones" is about a guy who meets Rosie down by the river and falls in love with her. Then one day a tall, dark stranger comes to take her away, so she writes a letter to the guy who's in love with her, telling him she's leaving him for the tall, dark stranger. At the end of the song, the guy says he's going to jump in the river and drown because he can't live without Sweet Rosie Jones.

This director literally used the song for his script. He filmed me and the girl who played Rosie standing down by the river. Then he filmed the tall, dark stranger riding in on his horse. Then he filmed Rosie writing the letter saying she was leaving. Well, about that time, I was starting to get a little nervous because I was thinking he was going to say, "OK, Buck. Now in this next scene you jump in the river and look like you're drowning." But it turned out he just filmed this white cowboy hat floating down the river, so I was happy I didn't have to get my clothes wet for the sake of high art.

Chapter Eighty-Six

IN FEBRUARY I WENT BACK IN THE STUDIO to start working on my next Christmas album. Maybe my competitive streak was showing again since most country artists in those days usually made just one Christmas album and one gospel album during their careers. By the end of the month I was on my way to having my second Christmas album and my second gospel album in the can.

Capitol put out my second album of the year on April 1st. In fact, it was my second greatest hits record, *The Best of Buck Owens, Vol. 2*. That same day they released "Sweet Rosie Jones" as a single.

Less than a week later I was able to breathe a big sigh of relief when "How Long Will My Baby Be Gone" hit the top of the country singles chart. It only stayed number one for a week, but it was a week longer than my previous single had.

* * *

There was a variety show on television that ran for years and years called *Kraft Music Hall*. One of the things about that show that was different from most of the other variety shows is that the host changed a lot. It might be Dinah Shore one week and Rock Hudson the next week, and then Lorne Greene the week after that. Well, in '68, they decided to start having the same host for a while—and the first guy they chose to be their host for more than a week was good ol' Eddy Arnold.

Now to be honest, he was the perfect host for a show like that because the kind of saccharine country music he made appealed to a lot of folks that didn't even think of themselves as being country fans. I'm not knocking him. I loved Eddy's early records in the days before he started doing all of those middle-of-the-road songs with a ton of strings and background vocals on 'em.

Most of the guests Eddy had on the show were folks like Anita Bryant and Phyllis McGuire and Margaret Whiting and the Brothers Four, so I'm not sure what the show's usual audience must've thought when me and the Buckaroos came on that May. We did "I've Got a Tiger by the Tail" just to sort of remind folks who we were. Then we did both sides of my current single—"Sweet Rosie Jones" and another song I'd written called "Happy Times Are Here Again."

I couldn't help but notice that Eddy's career started going downhill almost immediately after he had that long stretch hosting *Kraft Music Hall*. This was a man who'd had dozens of records hit the top of the country charts starting back in the 1940s. He had one last number one single in '68—and then he never had another one. He never won another CMA award either. No Entertainer of the Year; no Male Vocalist of the Year; nothing.

The same thing happened with Jimmy Dean. After he'd had his TV show for a while, the number one hits just stopped coming. Television made Eddy and Jimmy a lot more famous than they'd been back when they were just known for their singing—but it took something away from them, too. It took away their mystique.

* * *

My son Buddy had shown an interest in music from the time he was pretty young. But even though his dad was Buck Owens and his stepdad was Merle Haggard, he started out performing rock & roll in a band he put together called the Chosen Few. Well, eventually he got interested in country music, and I thought he was a really good singer—still do—so he and I went in the studio in late May and recorded a couple of duets. One was called "Let the World Keep On A-Turnin'" and the other one was "I'll Love You Forever and Ever."

The next month, just as I was getting ready to go in the studio to record some more Christmas songs and co-produce another Buckaroos album, "Sweet Rosie Jones" peaked at number two on the charts. All of that effort and money spent on making that music video—not to mention performing the song in front of a huge viewing audience on *Kraft Music Hall*—hadn't been enough to push the song to the top.

My album, *Sweet Rosie Jones*, came out in July. That made three albums already in '68. A few days later, the two duets I did with Buddy came out, with "Let the World Keep On A-Turnin'" on the A-side.

In August, I acquired another radio station in Phoenix for $125,000. This one was an FM station that had that "beautiful music" format when I bought it. They played the same stuff on that station that you'd hear in an elevator. Well, I thought Phoenix was probably a little hipper than that, so I changed the format to progressive rock.

Now, that might surprise you, but I didn't buy radio stations just so I could hear my own records being played on 'em. I bought 'em because they generated income through ad sales. The music is mighty important, of course, because you have to have plenty of listeners to be able to generate ad sales—but I've always treated radio as a business. So, if there was a big enough market for a certain style of music, then that's the music we'd program the station to play. I eventually changed the format to country because country audiences had finally started paying attention to FM radio—and it wasn't long before KNIX-FM became the biggest country radio station in town.

That same month, I went back in the studio with a different kind of record I'd been wanting to do. I knew I'd be making an album that wasn't going to turn into a tremendous seller, but I had to make this one for *me*. Since Don had taken over as the main lead guitar player in the group, I hadn't had to do nearly as much lead guitar work myself. Now, like I said before, a lot of folks have accused me of being a businessman first and a musician second. I didn't go into the studio to make a record to prove 'em wrong—although it wound up doing that, too—I went in the studio because I had music in my head that I wanted to make with my guitar. Some of it had a Latin flavor, and I also had some polkas on there. When the album came out that October, it was called *The Guitar Player.* I played some of the instrumentals on my Telecaster, and I played acoustic guitar on the others. Ken Nelson wrote the liner notes on the back of the album. In the notes he said that one of the instrumental pieces—"Things I Saw Happening at the Fountain on the Plaza When I Was Visiting Rome or Amore"—was my "longest song title on record." I thought it was kind of funny that he'd say that since it wasn't as long as the titles Capitol had come up with for some of my albums.

During those same sessions, since the Buckaroos were there to back me up on my solo instrumental album, we took a little time out from making that record so we could cut one I sang on called "I've Got You on My Mind Again."

Nineteen sixty-eight was also the year several politicians started to take serious notice of me and my music. That was the year the governor of Texas, Preston Smith, appointed me to be Country Music Ambassador to the State of Texas. It was also the year Governor Ronald Reagan appointed me Country Music Ambassador of Goodwill for the State of California. I felt very honored, of course, to receive both of those accolades, but then I got a call from another gentleman in office, asking me to come perform for him—at the White House.

Chapter Eighty-Seven

ONE OF THE THINGS I'VE BEEN asked a lot over the years is whether I'm a Republican or a Democrat. The answer is I've been both. I don't vote for somebody just because they belong to one party or another. I vote for the person who has ideas I agree with, and who I think is best qualified for the job.

I've said it in many interviews, and I'll say it again: nobody loves America more than me. I know what I'm talking about because—like that old Hank Snow song says—"I've been everywhere." I've traveled all over the world, and I learned from going to all those other countries that there's a lot more I love about America than any other place I've ever been.

Of course, that's not to say that I don't get fed up with politicians sometimes. I don't like it one bit when some of those fellows vote for what they want instead of voting for what their own constituents want. And, I don't like the idea of vote swapping, either—where a guy says, "I'll vote for your bill if you'll vote for mine." So, sometimes I'm not happy with the way a lot of 'em conduct their business, but politicians come and go. The great thing about America is the people, and the freedoms we have that so many people in a lot of other countries don't.

When all of those protests started in the '60s, I didn't have a problem with young men who didn't want to fight in Vietnam. I was against that war, even though a lot of folks disagreed with the way I felt about it. I wasn't angry that people were protesting the war. What got me mad was when some of 'em started burning the American flag.

My reaction to that was to create a red, white, and blue guitar. I went to Semie Moseley—the man who had the Mosrite guitar company—and told him what I wanted. Semie and I designed a guitar for me. Then I got Don to paint one of his fiddles red, white, and blue. Doyle Holly's bass guitar was red, white, and blue, too. That red, white, and blue guitar of mine is my way of saying that I love America.

So, you can just imagine what it meant to me when I got that phone call asking me to play at the White House on September 9th, 1968. Lyndon Johnson was the President. He was a fellow Texan, and he was a country music fan. My sister Dorothy went with me, along with Buddy, Jack McFadden, and the Buckaroos, of course. It was the first time a country music show had ever been performed at the White House.

Now, President Johnson was a very busy man, so we were told to keep the show under an hour. The audience was the President and his family, and the White House staff and their families, so there were hundreds of people at the show. Billy Deaton—the Deacon of Music Row—was the emcee that night. He introduced us, and we opened with "Act Naturally." We wanted to do several of our biggest hits, so I didn't do much talking that night. We didn't even wait for the applause to die down before we went on to the next song. But, after we did "Together Again" and "Love's Gonna Live Here" and a couple more, we made time for Doyle to sing "Streets of Laredo," and for Don to play his fiddle on "Orange Blossom Special." My son Buddy had already started touring with us some by then, so he came out and did "Gentle on My Mind" and a song his step-dad Merle had written for him called "When I Turn Twenty-One." We wrapped things up with "I've Got a Tiger by the Tail" and "Truck Drivin' Man." When we got ready to do that last song, I told the audience, "For all the truck drivers here tonight, we're gonna do a truck driving song." That one even got the President to laugh.

Chapter Eighty-Eight

WE FLEW STRAIGHT FROM WASHINGTON, D.C., to Oklahoma City to tape thirteen more episodes of *The Buck Owens Ranch Show.* By '68, Bud Mathis had turned over his ranch foreman/emcee job to the famous Texas disc jockey, Bill Mack. Later, my son Michael would take over as the emcee. But in September of '68, I was real happy to get back to Oklahoma City so I could spend more time with Miss Jennifer. It seemed like the worse things got with Phyllis, the better things got with Jennifer.

We'd been doing the TV show for a couple of years by that time, so it would take us only about three days to get the whole thirteen episodes done. Then we'd be back on the road, and I'd have to say goodbye to Jennifer until it was time to shoot the next thirteen shows.

At the end of September, my thirty-fifth Capitol single was released. Like I said earlier, I'd recorded "I've Got You on My Mind Again" in early August—the same time I was recording my album of guitar solos. By that time I'd watched two of my recent singles—"It Takes People Like You (to Make People Like Me)" and "Sweet Rosie Jones"—only reach number two on the charts. Now, I know that might sound silly—especially since some country stars go their whole careers without ever having a number one record—but I was just the opposite. I'd come to expect my records to top the charts.

I've always looked at duets a lot differently than I do my solo records. What I mean is, I didn't expect the duets I recorded to be huge hits because—at least back in the '60s—a number one duet record was a very rare thing. I'm not talking about a duet act that always sang together. I'm talking about two successful recording artists who got together to make a record, like Johnny Cash and June Carter. Johnny and June never even had one of theirs hit the top of the charts. And if those two didn't have any, nobody should have! One of the few duets to go all the way to number one during those years was that one by Bill Anderson and Jan Howard—the one that kept "It Takes People Like You (to Make People Like Me)" from going any higher.

Well, my son Buddy and me came pretty damn close. Our duet of "Let the World Keep On A-Turnin'" reached number seven in September of '68, which was a hell of a month for country music. The week our record went as high as it was going to go, the top three singles were "Harper Valley P.T.A." by Jeannie C. Riley, "Only Daddy That'll Walk the Line" by Waylon Jennings, and "Mama Tried" by Merle Haggard. Today you'd be lucky to go a whole year and have three records as good as those three were.

Anyway, after I'd had those two solo singles that only made it to number two, I decided to go in a different direction for "I've Got You on My Mind Again." This one was a ballad, but instead of putting the focus on Tom Brumley's steel guitar the way we'd done on other ballads like "Together Again," we went with a piano introduction, and we kept the piano pretty far up in the mix throughout the whole song. Earl Poole Ball had been there to add keyboards to my guitar solo album, so I'd decided to use him on this song, too. And believe it or not, I gave my blessing to Ken Nelson to take the tapes down to Nashville and overdub the Jordanaires and the Anita Kerr Singers doing background vocals on the record. So, out it came as a single on September 30th. A week later, Capitol did that thing again where they put out two of my albums on the same day. One was my second Christmas album, called *Christmas Shopping*, and the other was my instrumental album, *The Guitar Player*.

*　*　*

Even though I let Ken add some background vocals to "I've Got You on My Mind Again," I wasn't trying to cross over onto the pop market. When songs of mine like "I've Got a Tiger by the Tail" hit the pop charts, I sure didn't complain about it, but I've always known that my audience was mostly a country audience. People who love country music are my kind of people, but I've always been happy to share my music with everybody who wants to listen to it. So, when Jack McFadden told me they wanted me to do a couple of nights at the Fillmore West, I was willing to give it a shot.

This was a venue where bands like the Grateful Dead and Iron Butterfly and Creedence Clearwater Revival had played. Until we appeared there on October 11th and 12th of '68, no country act had ever set foot in there.

I was real impressed with the place. It had a great P.A. system and a great big ol' stage, and a big open area where everybody either stood or sat on the floor to watch the show. It'd been a ballroom at one time, but there weren't any ballroom dancers the night we were there, that's for sure. The audience looked like what I figured the regular crowd looked like—which was a bunch of hippie-looking kids about half my age.

Me and the Buckaroos did just like the other acts did. We went onstage to tune up a few minutes before we were supposed to start. Well, the audience was right there in front of us, and there was a bunch of kids that were pressing right up against the stage. This one boy held out his hand like he had something he wanted to give me. So, I walked to the edge of the stage. He said, "Open your hand." I opened my hand and he put what looked like two rolled-up pieces of paper in my palm. I'd spent years having people hand me song requests on little pieces of paper, so I didn't think anything about it at first. But then the kid said, "Those are for you and Don."

Well, when I got to looking more closely, I saw they looked like two hand-rolled cigarettes. I put 'em on top of my amp, and then I turned to Don and said, "That guy right down front there said these are for you and me."

Don took one look at 'em and said, "Those are joints!"

I said, "What?"

He whispered, "They're joints—marijuana."

Until that moment, I'd never even seen a joint before, and now there were two of 'em on top of my amp. I got pretty nervous at first because, remember now, this was 1968—back in the days when you could get in serious trouble for having something like that. But when I looked out at the audience, I saw that there were several kids smoking 'em right out there in the open, so I calmed down a little bit.

When we finished our set, I noticed those two joints weren't on top of my amp anymore. I don't know what happened to 'em, but after the show that night, I couldn't help but notice that Doyle Holly seemed mighty relaxed.

Chapter Eighty-Nine

O N NOVEMBER 4TH, Capitol put out "Christmas Shopping" from my new Christmas album, and "Things I Saw Happening at the Fountain When I Was Visiting Rome or Amore" from my album, *The Guitar Player*. I think the guys at Capitol chose that one for the single just to see if they could get the whole title on the record.

By '68, Kay Adams had left *The Buck Owens Ranch Show*, so I'd replaced her with a singer named Susan Raye. I'd met Susan at a club up in Portland, Oregon, the night before her son was born. As you can imagine, she was very pregnant, but she got up and sang that night, and I liked her singing a lot. I liked her voice so much that I hired her to tour around with us every time we'd go up in that area. She was a beautiful girl, and she was always a real trooper to put up with me and the Buckaroos on the road. She was a great addition to the TV show, too. In December of '68, Jack McFadden told me that she was coming down to Bakersfield, so I had her come with me on down to LA to record a duet called "We're Gonna Get Together."

That same day, me and the Buckaroos made a recording that Ken Nelson wasn't too crazy about. I wasn't trying to change my sound. I was just trying to do something that still sounded like me, but that had a little something special to make it stand out.

Don Rich had gotten himself a fuzz box. That's a little metal box with some electronics in it that you run your guitar through. When you flip the switch, it makes the guitar sound real distorted. Semie Moseley had created a fuzz box he called the Mosrite Fuzzrite. A lot of the rock & roll guys had been using fuzz boxes for a while by then—like Keith Richards on "(I Can't Get No) Satisfaction." Blues guys and rock guys used 'em, but I don't know if any country guys had used one yet. If they had, they sure hadn't had a hit single with it. So, ol' Ken was pretty unhappy when Don flipped that switch, turned his amp up, and played the intro to a song I'd written called "Who's Gonna Mow Your Grass." On top of that, what Jerry Wiggins played on the drums that day sounded like something some of those other acts that played the Fillmore West might do. And when Don played the guitar solo on that record, I thought Ken was going to have a cow. You know, some of those early country-rock acts have said my music was an influence on their style, which was mighty nice of 'em to say. I'm pretty sure you'd call "Who's Gonna Mow Your Grass" a country-rock song—but with me singing it, I think it's safe to say it was a lot more country than rock.

A couple of weeks later, we were on a TV show called *Operation Entertainment*, which I was happy to do because it took place at a different military base every week. The week we were on, the show was at an Army base called Fort Leonard Wood in Missouri. Get a load of this lineup, now—it was Buck Owens and the Buckaroos, the Fifth Dimension, Richard Dawson, Jimmy Dean, an Italian singer named Dana Valery, and Richard Pryor. That week the show had a little something for everybody.

I really enjoyed being a part of that show, so I came back to Bakersfield feeling pretty upbeat. Then I saw the *Billboard* charts. My experiment of putting the emphasis on the piano and using Nashville-style background singers hadn't put me back on top of the charts. "I've Got You on My Mind Again" had gone up to number five, and then it just stayed there. I remember thinking, "If that's how my fans reacted to a little change in my sound, how are they going to react when they hear 'Who's Gonna Mow Your Grass'?"

Believe it or not, even though I'd already had five albums released that year, there was still one more to go. On December 30th, Capitol put out my last album of 1968, and they named it after the lowest-charting single I'd had in almost six year—*I've Got You on My Mind Again*. Six albums in one year. Can you believe that? At the time, I didn't even know what the word "overexposure" meant. I thought having so many albums constantly coming out indicated hard work and success. And to tell you the truth, we sold a lot of albums, so I was probably right to think that way. But in a few months I'd become the cohost of one of the longest-running television shows of all time—and before long I'd know *exactly* what overexposure meant.

* * *

There was one other thing that happened in '68 that I guess I did in a last-ditch attempt to keep Phyllis happy. I certainly didn't do it for me. I loved the ranch we had near Edison. It was out in the country, and it was the one place I could go to and relax when me and the Buckaroos would come off the road. Out there I didn't have to worry about any noisy parties next door or having a neighbor rant and rave because my cat got in their yard. I didn't have to hear car horns honk or tires squeal. To me, it was the ideal, perfect place to live.

But every time I'd come home, Phyllis would tell me she wanted to move into town. I didn't want to do it, but she'd say, "You're gone so much. Now that the kids are practically grown, I'd just rather live in town."

Finally, I told her she could go look for a place, and I'd buy it for her if it'd make her happy. Well, she went and found a place all right—all eight thousand square feet of it—on Panorama Drive in Bakersfield. So, I bought it and we moved in, but I was never happy there. It was just too fancy for me. I used to tell her, "This isn't a house—it's a hotel." It was a beautiful place, but it was never home to me. It was just the place I went to when I wasn't on the road.

Chapter Ninety

WHEN THE NEW YEAR ARRIVED, I went in the studio on the 8th and 9th of January. One of the songs we did was "Tall Dark Stranger." I also cut a few more tracks for that second gospel album I'd been working on.

And speaking of the New Year, Capitol sure didn't waste any time when 1969 rolled around. First they put out an album called *Best of Buck Owens, Vol. 3*. That one included my recent hits like "Sweet Rosie Jones," but it also had "Cryin' Time" on there, despite the fact I'd never had a hit with it myself. It even had songs on it that had been on my first "Best of" album. Although I was constantly in the studio making new records, Capitol didn't seem to mind recycling my old stuff—just as long as they could have something that said "Buck Owens" on it to sell.

That same day, January 13th, "Who's Gonna Mow Your Grass" came out—the one with Don and his fuzz box. The B-side was another one of mine called "There's Gotta Be Some Changes Made." I had no idea how many changes I was about to go through when I wrote that one.

One change had already happened that same month when Tom Brumley told me he was going to leave the band so he could focus on creating his own brand of steel guitars. Before he left, he suggested that I hire JayDee Maness to take his place. I took him up on that idea, so JayDee came on board in early '69.

* * *

While Capitol was busy putting out Buck Owens records, I'd gone and agreed to be in a movie. After all, I'd been singing "Act Naturally" for half a dozen years at that point, so I figured it was about time somebody really did put me in the movies. And it's a good thing I was already famous because that movie definitely wouldn't be making a big star out of me.

The plot, such as it was, was about two city slickers from up North who are on vacation in the South when their car breaks down. The two city slickers were played by Leo G. Carroll and Marilyn Maxwell. Well, along comes Marty Robbins in his tour bus. He gives 'em a ride into town, and while they're talking, he invites 'em to the *Opry*. They've never heard of the *Grand Ole Opry*, so they think he's inviting them to come hear an opera. I guess I don't have to tell you this one didn't win any Academy Awards.

I'd agreed to be in it when they told me that my old truck-driving buddy, Marty Robbins, was going to be in it, and also Charley Pride, Don Gibson, George Jones, Tammy Wynette, and a bunch of other country stars. They shot my scenes in Bakersfield at KERO-TV. Pretty soon, we got just about everybody in town involved. Merle, Bonnie, Susan Raye, my son Buddy, and Wynn Stewart all ended up being in the movie, too. And what do you think they called this epic film? They called it *From Nashville with Music*. Here I'd spent my career fighting that whole Nashville stigma, and now I'd ended up in a movie with Nashville right there in the title. I decided if I was ever asked to do another movie, the first thing I'd do would be to ask 'em what the name of the damn thing was going to be.

Chapter Ninety-One

NOW, I'VE ALREADY TOLD YOU about me being on a bunch of network TV shows—Jimmy Dean's, Dean Martin's, Jackie Gleason's, and so forth. Well, back in the '60s, there were only three networks to choose from—ABC, NBC, and CBS. There wasn't any Fox or CNN or HBO or anything like that yet. So, if you were watching the most popular network show that aired on a Sunday night at eight p.m., there were tens of millions of other people watching it, too. That means when I'd make a guest appearance on one of those popular variety shows, there were millions and millions of people watching.

Of course, that wasn't the case with *The Buck Owens Ranch Show*. My show was a "local" show. Different TV stations around the country bought the rights to air it, but it was only seen in those towns that carried the show. The network TV shows were broadcast everywhere in the country. The stations that carried my show could broadcast it on whatever day and at whatever time they wanted to. It was one of those shows that folks could watch before the primetime network TV shows would come on later that night. *The Buck Owens Ranch Show* was carried by a lot of stations, but it didn't hold a candle to the number of stations that the three networks reached.

The Jonathan Winters Show was one of those network TV shows. It was on CBS in the late '60s. Now, Jonathan Winters is kind of different.

He's a comedian, but the kind of comedy he does isn't easy to describe. I guess the best way to say it is that he's not one of those guys like Ed Sullivan or Dean Martin or a lot of the variety show hosts were. He appealed to a certain kind of person who got his sense of humor, so some folks really liked his show, and some folks weren't too interested in the kind of stuff he did. Since he didn't have the kind of broad appeal that somebody like Dean Martin had, Jonathan's audience wasn't nearly as big as a lot of the other variety shows were.

Now remember, there were only three networks for folks to watch, so those three networks were real competitive with one another. Just like in the radio business, television networks had to sell ad time. The more viewers they had for a show, the more they could charge for the commercials that aired during that show.

Since Jonathan's show was kind of lagging behind its competition, the guys at CBS decided they'd better bring in some new blood to be the producers. So, they hired these two Canadians named John Aylesworth and Frank Peppiatt. Well, the first thing John and Frank did was to check the show's demographics, and what they found out was that the show wasn't being watched by very many Southerners. Jonathan's sense of humor just didn't seem to appeal to 'em at all.

Being smart guys, John and Frank started booking guests for the show that they knew folks from the South would want to tune in to watch. One week they'd have Roy Rogers and Dale Evans, and then another week they'd have George "Goober" Lindsay. One week they had Minnie Pearl and Roy Clark on the same show.

Now, back in '68, there was another TV show that started over on NBC. It was called *Rowan & Martin's Laugh-In*. Nobody had ever done a show like that before. It had these two cohosts named Dan Rowan and Dick Martin, and a great big cast of people that were on every week. The regulars were Goldie Hawn and Lily Tomlin and Henry Gibson and Ruth Buzzi and Arte Johnson and a whole bunch of others.

Laugh-In had sketches and sight gags and all kinds of stuff. It would just cut from one thing to the next. The guests were movie stars and TV stars and professional athletes and even politicians. It was so different that it's hard to describe. But it was entertaining enough that it became the most popular network show on TV.

Meanwhile, Jonathan Winters's show wasn't doing nearly as well, so they kept booking the kinds of acts that they felt would get more Southerners to watch. Since I was a pretty big country star with a lot of fans in the South, I'd been booked to appear on the show in January of '69. I was in the dressing room getting ready to go on when there came a knock on my door. When I opened it, there stood John Aylesworth and Frank Peppiatt. I'd met 'em both before because they'd written for other variety shows I'd been on. They came in and told me they had an idea to do a country comedy show that they wanted to fashion after *Laugh-In*.

Now, I had lots of people approaching me during those years. They always had the same idea—to do a network television show with some kind of country music element to it. They'd always say they'd call me back in a couple of weeks. Well, a couple of weeks would go by, then a couple of months, then a couple of years. So, when these two guys told me their idea about a country version of *Laugh-In*, I just kind of shined 'em on. I told 'em, "If you've got the money, I've got the time."

Chapter Ninety-Two

ON MARCH 2ND, we left for a two-week overseas tour. Two days later we opened in Oslo, Norway, doing two concerts and appearing on a TV show there. Then we went over to Amsterdam where we did a show that started at midnight. The sun goes down a lot later there than it does here that time of year, but I still thought that was a strange time to start a concert.

While we were in Amsterdam, we also performed on this show called the Grand Gala du Disque. It was this big, international concert that went on for hours and hours. There were acts from Italy, Portugal, the UK, France, Holland, and the US. Along with me and the Buckaroos, the US contingent was Ike and Tina Turner, Little Peggy March, the Sandpipers, Gladys Knight and the Pips, Miriam Makeba, and Chet Atkins.

The whole thing was televised. For the Grand Gala every year, all these various record companies from around the world would send their top artists to perform on this one big TV broadcast. Out of all those acts, they told me I'd be going on next to last, and then Ike and Tina Turner would close the show. So, me and the Buckaroos just stayed at the hotel and watched the first few hours of the thing on the TV in my room.

Well, after a while we got tired of listening to all these people singing in foreign languages we didn't understand, so I changed to another channel to see what else there was to watch. But the other channel had the same show on. I called the bellman to find out what was going on, and he told me that the Queen had decided that everyone should watch the Grand Gala. Here was this country with only two TV channels, and the Queen had decided what everybody was going to watch that night.

Now, when we'd been in Norway a few days earlier, all of the channels had gone off at eleven p.m. The bellman at the hotel there had explained to me that the King had decided that people should be in bed by then, so he'd ordered that all the TV stations end their broadcasts by eleven every night.

This was 1969, remember—back when all these people in America were complaining about no freedom to do this and no freedom to do that. Meanwhile, in Norway the government had decreed what time you had to stop watching television, and in the Netherlands the government told you what you were going to watch. At least in America you could watch any damn TV show you wanted, and you could watch TV at two in the morning if you wanted to.

Anyway, we finally headed over to the venue to do our part of the show. By then, I was looking for any friendly American face I could find—and there stood Chet Atkins. He was the only person in the room I knew. Like I said, all these record companies from around the world had sent their top artists to be a part of this show. Capitol had sent me and the Buckaroos. Chet Atkins ran RCA Victor in Nashville, so I guess he'd sent himself.

When I got back to the States, somebody showed me a newspaper article that said my appearance was the "first time that a country and western act had ever appeared on the Grand Gala." I couldn't help but wonder what Chet Atkins must've thought when he read that—especially since he'd gone onstage before I had.

We flew from Holland to Liverpool and played a show there that night. The next night, on March 9th, we performed at the London Palladium. The guys at Capitol had watched my other two live albums go to the top of the country album charts, so they decided to roll out the recording gear for this one, too. I remember the recording engineer that night was Geoff Emerick—the same man who'd engineered a lot of the Beatles' records.

It was a full house and a great audience. Just like we'd done in Tokyo, we did an instrumental I'd come up with especially for the show. It was called "A Happening in London Town." I called it a country-rock number, although I'd have to admit that one was a lot more rock than country. But JayDee Maness played pedal steel on it, so a little bit of country snuck in there.

We did some of the old ones like "Love's Gonna Live Here" and "Cryin' Time," and we did some of the ones that were still new at the time, like "Sweet Rosie Jones" and "Who's Gonna Mow Your Grass." We also did some Cajun tunes that night. Like I already told you, since Don was such a great fiddle player, I always made him show off his fiddle-playing talents at our shows, even though he really preferred to just play his Telecaster. Back in '63 and '64, he'd taught me "Diggy Liggy Lo" and "Louisiana Man," so we did those two, and then he played one we'd written together called "Cajun Fiddle."

We closed the show at the Palladium with "Johnny B. Goode," another one of those Chuck Berry songs. Now, I've got to tell you, Don really outdid himself on that one. I'm not lying now. I've heard a lot of instrumental guitar breaks on a lot of records in my lifetime—I'm talking about thousands of 'em—and I've never heard a better one before or since than what Don Rich played on "Johnny B. Goode" that night. He just tore that one up like you can't believe. I'm mighty happy that Capitol recorded that show because it's given me the opportunity to listen to Don's solo many times over the years—and every time I hear it, I just can't believe what I'm hearing. As far as playing lead guitar is concerned, that was Don's finest moment.

Now, of course, that's one more instance where people have said to me, "Buck, that 'Johnny B. Goode' ain't no country song."

I tell 'em "Just listen to the words and you'll see that it most certainly is." Right there in the lyrics it says that he's a country boy. It says he lives in a log cabin. It even says he lives by the railroad tracks. Well, living by those railroad tracks is something this country boy can sure relate to.

*　*　*

Ten days later we were back on the road in America. On the 19th we were in Billings, Montana, then Victoria, British Columbia, then Spokane, Washington, and then Portland, Oregon. We went home for less than a week, and then it was on to Wilmington, North Carolina, Columbia, South Carolina, Jacksonville, Florida, and finally Macon, Georgia.

It was during the second leg of that tour when I found out "Who's Gonna Mow Your Grass" had gone to number one on the *Billboard* country singles chart. Here I'd been wondering if I was ever going to have a record at the top of the charts again, and it actually ended up staying there for two weeks in a row.

So, I was in a pretty good mood when Jack McFadden came walking into my office a few days later and said, "Remember John Aylesworth and Frank Peppiatt?

I said, "Yeah, I remember those guys. I saw 'em just a few months ago."

Jack said, "Well, they got the money from CBS to do the show they said they told you about, so they want you to go to Nashville in May to shoot the pilot."

It took me a minute to realize what he was talking about. Then I remembered that when they were in my dressing room the day I was shooting *The Jonathan Winters Show*, they'd told me their idea about doing a country version of *Laugh-In*.

I've always been a man of my word, so I didn't have much of a choice. Since they'd gotten the money, I was going to have to make the time. I didn't really give it a whole lot of thought. I knew enough about television to know that most of those pilots never ended up turning into a real series anyway. So, I told Jack to make room in my schedule for me to go to Nashville in May. I mean, hell—what's the worst that could happen?

PART IV

Hee Haw

Chapter Ninety-Three

B Y THE TIME I GOT TO NASHVILLE IN EARLY MAY, what was originally going to be a pilot had turned into an actual special that was scheduled to air on CBS the following month. And then, before we even finished taping the special, *The Smothers Brothers Comedy Hour* got cancelled. All of a sudden CBS was calling for a dozen more shows to be taped right away so they'd have something to replace the Smothers Brothers.

Tom and Dick Smothers were great comedians and a couple of pretty good folk singers, too, but they'd gotten way too controversial for the executives at CBS. In 1969, the whole Vietnam thing was still going on, and the Brothers had been using their comedy act as a way of protesting the war. A few years later, just about everybody realized that the Vietnam War was unwinnable and that the best thing to do was to just get the hell out of there. But in '69, people who protested the war were considered downright un-American. CBS kept getting more and more complaints about the kinds of things the Smothers Brothers were saying and doing on their show, so the network finally took 'em off the air.

So, thanks to the Smother Brothers being cancelled, I ended up staying in Nashville for several weeks, taping show after show so we'd have enough to fill up the rest of the summer.

Unfortunately, when I'd agreed to get involved with John and Frank's TV project, I'd made the same mistake I'd made back when I agreed to be in that movie, *From Nashville with Music*—I'd forgotten to ask 'em what the name of the damn thing was going to be.

John and Frank had a guy who worked with 'em named Bernie Brillstein. Bernie was a New Yorker who hated country music. It was bad enough that he had no appreciation for the music the show was going to be featuring. He was also the one who came up with show's title— *Hee Haw*. Here I'd spent more than a decade doing everything I could to present the kind of music I was singing and playing in a professional, dignified manner, and now I was going to be starring in a show with a title that sounded like it was making fun of country music and the whole rural way of life.

As much as I hated the name, I still thought the idea of having a weekly network TV show that featured country music was a great idea. So, I decided to live with the show's title, and I was more than happy to live with the show's money. John and Frank had agreed to pay me tens of thousands of dollars per episode, and they said that if the show lasted past the summer, they'd pay me $400,000 a year. Remember, this was 1969. Four hundred thousand dollars in 1969 money would be the equivalent of millions now—and that kind of money meant I wouldn't have to tour nearly as much as I had in the past.

Don't get me wrong. I've always loved playing in front of an audience. The problem in those days wasn't the shows themselves—it was the drain of getting from show to show. Things had gotten a lot easier since my days of traveling around in the camper, but it was still a pain in the ass to fly from one town to the next, check into a hotel, unpack, pack back up, check out of the hotel, fly to the next town—just doing that over and over—and not being home long enough to get settled down good before it was time to get on a plane again.

The producers of *Hee Haw* had figured out that if the TV show lasted past the summer, we could tape thirteen shows in one stretch, twice a year. That way we'd have twenty-six new shows, and then they'd rerun those twenty-six shows so there'd be enough to last all twelve months. Plus, at that time I was still doing my own syndicated TV show out of Oklahoma City four times a year. So, if everything went according to plan, I'd be on two different TV shows, and I'd still be able to do plenty of live concerts. I just wouldn't be on the road 250 to 300 days a year like I'd been doing.

So, I liked the large paycheck, and I liked the way they'd figured out how to tape the shows so quickly. I also liked the fact that they decided to put me in charge of the music. John and Frank didn't really know a whole lot about country music, so they got me to pick the acts, starting with that very first show. Then, after we found out *Hee Haw* was going to be on all summer, I got 'em to hire Jack McFadden to be the talent coordinator. I'd say who I wanted the performers to be for the show each week, and then Jack would be the one to coordinate with everybody's managers and booking agents. Plus, I got John and Frank to let me use the Buckaroos as the house band for all of the acts that appeared on the show.

Like they'd told me in my dressing room at *The Jonathan Winters Show* a few months earlier, John and Frank's plan was for *Hee Haw* to be kind of a rural version of *Laugh-In*. So, since comedy was going to be a part of the show, they rounded up a lot of great comedy writers and country comedians like Archie Campbell and Minnie Pearl. They also brought in Roy Clark to be the cohost of the show with me. Roy was as much a comedian as he was a musician, so he was in a lot of the comedy sketches.

Roy and me got along great, but I have to admit I got kind of tired of being his straight man all the time. Even on those rare occasions when Roy would do the set-up and I'd get to do the punch line, he'd still try to upstage me. But that was Roy. We didn't look as sophisticated as Dan Rowan and Dick Martin—especially since Rowan and Martin wore tuxedos and me and Roy wore overalls—but the two of us had a chemistry that worked really well on camera.

* * *

On May 5th, the same day we started taping *Hee Haw* in Nashville, Capitol put out my next single. The A-side was that live version of "Johnny B. Goode"—the one we'd recorded in London. Oh boy, you should've seen the reaction I got to that. I'd recorded Chuck Berry's "Memphis" a few years earlier, but that song had only appeared on one of my albums. When that single of "Johnny B. Goode" came out and started getting played a lot on the radio, things got real unpleasant. I got the usual letters from some angry fans who didn't think I should be recording a rock & roll song—which didn't come as a big surprise to me. But then one day a fellow sent me some pictures of a big bonfire with about a dozen people standing around it. In the photos, these people were throwing copies of my records into that big fire. It was a bunch of people from a radio station in Atlanta, and in the letter that came with the photos, the guy said that they'd burned every record of mine that they had at the radio station because I'd wandered off too far from what they considered to be country music. Well, he didn't say it nearly that politely, but that was the general idea.

I've already told you that I think "Johnny B. Goode" has all the elements of a great country song, but there was no way I could respond to so many letters from so many upset folks. So, just like with "Who's Gonna Mow Your Grass," I had to wait and see if the people who bought records were going to love it or hate it.

* * *

When that first episode of *Hee Haw* aired on June 15th, I didn't have to wait long at all to find out what the critics thought of the show. Some of those reviews compared it to *Laugh-In* all right, but not in a good way. And a lot of those critics wrote some pretty awful things about me, asking why was I up there acting like a buffoon when I was supposed to be a serious country artist. I wasn't used to that kind of criticism, but I figured if the public didn't watch it, the show would be gone soon enough.

Loretta Lynn and Charlie Pride were the musical guests on that first show. The critics sure couldn't complain about the music, because they were both great. Charlie told me later that it was the first really big exposure he'd gotten on television, and that he was glad of it because *he* knew he was the first major black country artist, but a lot of his *fans* didn't know it until they saw him on *Hee Haw* that night.

Anyway, those reviews for *Hee Haw*'s debut were so bad, I guess people must've watched the next week just to see if the show was as awful as those critics said it was. What they found out was that the comedy was corny as hell, but the music was definitely worth tuning in for. I'd gotten Merle Haggard to be on the second show, and he'd done a couple of his number one hits—"Mama Tried" and "Branded Man." At that point, Merle was one of the biggest country stars in the world, so I'm sure he helped to boost the show's popularity because the ratings started picking up right away.

Before the summer was over, John and Frank came to me and told me that CBS wanted to keep the show going. The only problem was, there wasn't a place for us in the fall lineup. So, we'd just have to wait for

one of the fall shows to get cancelled—and as soon as one of 'em did—
Hee Haw would be going back on the air.

Chapter Ninety-Four

J UST AS THINGS STARTED TO LOOK REALLY GOOD for my network television career, things started to turn really bad with Phyllis.
For the last few years, we'd stayed married just to stay married, I guess,
because I was seldom home—and a lot of the time when I could've been
home, I was with Jennifer Joyce instead.

In the late '60s, Phyllis had started taking some sort of mild medication for nervousness. A few months later, after that first medication
hadn't seemed to do much good, I noticed she'd graduated to Valium.
Now, Valium is very strong stuff. She and I talked about it, and she decided to try to get off of it, but that Valium, it snatches you. It grabs you
and it won't let go. She got to the point where she started sleeping a lot
more than she had before. And when I say a lot more, I mean she'd be in
bed all day. She might get up for just a little while, and then she'd take
that Valium and go right back to bed.

Her being asleep more than she was awake, and me being away so
much of the time—it was a bad combination. I wasn't happy about her
being hooked on Valium, and she wasn't happy about me not being
there for her.

I didn't realize how seriously unhappy she was until I was up in
Edmonton, Canada. I was getting ready to play a show when the phone
rang. It was my old friend, Wanda Markham, calling me from Bakersfield. I'd known Wanda since the '50s when she used to come to the
Blackboard. In fact, I'd introduced her to Don Markham—one of the
guys who'd been in my band in the '50s—and they ended up getting
married. So, there was Wanda on the phone, and she was telling me
that they had Phyllis in the 3-B ward at the hospital. Back in those days,
if somebody said something that you thought sounded a little crazy,

you'd say they ought to be locked up in 3-B. Everybody in Bakersfield knew 3-B was the mental ward at the county hospital. Wanda was calling me from the hospital, and she even put Phyllis on the phone with me for a minute. Phyllis didn't sound crazy to me. She just sounded really tired. When Wanda got back on the phone, I asked her what on earth had happened. She told me that Phyllis's daughter had gone over to the house and couldn't wake Phyllis up. When she discovered an empty medicine bottle on the night table, she'd called an ambulance. When the ambulance came, she showed 'em the empty medicine bottle and they rushed her to the hospital. And when the folks at the hospital found out about that empty bottle—after they made sure she wasn't going to die—they put her in the 3-B ward.

Now Phyllis never admitted to anything, but when I found out she'd taken all of those pills and couldn't be woke up, I wondered from then on if it hadn't maybe been a case of her just not wanting to ever wake up.

One thing was for sure—she wanted out of the hospital right away. But they had a rule that once you were in 3-B, you had to stay there for observation for at least seventy-two hours. So, there was Phyllis in the mental ward while I was 1,800 miles away in Canada. I tried to convince one of the administrators at the hospital to let her leave, but he said it was out of his hands. So I got hold of one of my attorneys and he managed to get her out after she'd only been there about a day and a half.

As usual, I hadn't been there when she really needed me. It was pretty clear to both of us that things were over between us. She hadn't just wanted out of 3-B—she wanted out of the marriage, too. Oh, we'd still live together in that giant house on Panorama Drive for a while longer—but we were two people no longer in love, just going through the motions like so many people do.

Chapter Ninety-Five

WHILE THOSE THIRTEEN EPISODES OF *Hee Haw* were airing from June to September of '69, I went back to my usual routine of being on the road, in the studio, or taping *The Buck Owens Ranch Show.*

About the only thing that was changing was the age of my audience. I was getting older, but a lot of my fans were getting younger. I guess it first started back when "I've Got a Tiger by the Tail" had become a Top Forty hit on the pop charts. Then it picked up a little more steam when the Beatles recorded "Act Naturally." And when I played the Fillmore those two nights in '68, I think everybody in the audience was younger than I was.

But I knew for sure that I was reaching a younger audience when I ended up being in *Rolling Stone* magazine. In those days, *Rolling Stone* was mostly about music, but it was mostly about rock music. The cover photos were usually of people like Jimi Hendrix or Eric Clapton or Joe Cocker or Janis Joplin. It wasn't the kind of magazine where you'd find an article about a country singer who was almost forty years old.

The title of the article that came out in the June 28th issue was "California White Man's Shit-Kickin' Blues." It was a pretty long piece about a bunch of us who had become successful in country music out of LA and Bakersfield, but the writer—a guy named John Grissim Jr.— focused mainly on me. I wasn't too crazy about some of the things he wrote, and I wasn't too crazy about the title, either. But you know what they say—any press is good press as long as they spell your name right.

That same month, Capitol put out my third live album, *Buck Owens in London.* Believe it or not, just as I was getting ready to do a series of shows at the Bonanza Hotel in Las Vegas that July, Ken Nelson told me they wanted to record one of those shows, too, so they could release *another* live album.

By then my package shows included my son Buddy, Susan Raye, the Hagers, and some other performers. So, I had Ken record the show just the way we did it every night at the Bonanza Hotel. I didn't think my fans were dying to hear another live album of just me and the Buckaroos.

While we were in Vegas, "Johnny B. Goode" went to number one on the country charts. I guess Johnny really was a country boy, after all.

Chapter Ninety-Six

MY MOTHER'S MOTHER USED TO TELL ME to "always beware of tall, dark strangers." That saying just kind of stuck with me over the years, so when I wrote the song "Sweet Rosie Jones," I had a tall, dark stranger come and steal her away.

I liked the image of that mysterious character so much, I went back to him again when I wrote "Tall Dark Stranger." The song wasn't like anything I'd ever written before, but I thought it was one of my better ones—at least it was a lot more dramatic than those "freight train" kind of songs that I could write in my sleep by then. So, when we recorded it in early '69, I decided it needed to sound more dramatic, too. I admit I was going against my usual way of thinking, but I felt like it was the kind of song that needed strings and background vocals. Ninety-nine percent of the time I didn't think that sort of thing was right for the kind of records I was making, but this was that other one percent.

"Tall Dark Stranger" came out in July and went to number one a couple of months later. Meanwhile, I'd gone back to Capitol Studios and finally finished up my second gospel album. I also recorded the studio version of a song called "Big in Vegas."

When we'd recorded that live album at the Bonanza Hotel, I'd opened the show with "Big in Vegas," but I'd decided to go in the studio to record it again because I wanted to do a bigger production of the song than we'd been able to do at the Bonanza.

"Big in Vegas" actually started out as "Big in Dallas." "Big in Dallas" was written by a guy named Terry Stafford. Terry was a recording artist in the '60s. He had a big hit called "Suspicion" in '64, and about a decade later he'd co-write a song called "Amarillo by Morning" that would become a big hit for George Strait. Well, "Big in Dallas" didn't become a big hit for anybody. But when I heard the song, I knew it had potential, so I went to Terry and asked him if I could do a little re-writing, including changing the location from Dallas to Vegas. He said it was fine with him, so I made the changes and started doing the song every time I had a gig in Las Vegas.

Once the single of that studio version of "Big in Vegas" came out in October, I started doing it everywhere I performed. I was disappointed that it kind of stalled out at number five on the charts, but even though it didn't become my twentieth number one record, it became one of my most requested songs. It didn't matter if I was in Las Vegas or not—I didn't have a choice anymore. If I was doing a show, I was going to be doing "Big in Vegas" because my fans demanded it.

Now, speaking of studio recordings—like I said earlier, one of the things that I had to pay for as a Capitol recording artist was the cost of renting time there at Capitol's own recording studio in LA. So, when this old movie theatre in Bakersfield became available in '69, I acquired the building and started having it turned into my own state-of-the-art recording facility. I'd been making records for Capitol for over a decade at that point, always under that pressure to get four songs recorded in three hours. With my own studio, I knew I wouldn't have to deal with those time constraints anymore. And I knew if I wouldn't be using it to make my own records, or for the Buckaroos to make their records, I could always rent it out to other artists to use.

Around the time I started having my recording studio built, JayDee Maness left the Buckaroos and Doyle Curtsinger came on board. For the first time in over a decade, I didn't have a steel guitar player in the band. Instead, I had two bass players named Doyle. Doyle Holly switched to acoustic guitar, and Doyle Curtsinger played bass for me both live and in the studio.

* * *

Before the summer was out, Jack McFadden told me the producers of *Hee Haw* wanted me back in Nashville to tape more shows in November. They'd already said there weren't any slots available for the show in the fall, but I guess the folks at CBS knew something was bound to get cancelled, so they wanted us to have more shows ready for 'em when the first of the year rolled around.

So, on November 2nd, me and the Buckaroos did "Big in Vegas" and "Tall Dark Stranger" on *The Ed Sullivan Show*, and the next day we were on our way to Nashville to tape those new episodes of *Hee Haw*.

Chapter Ninety-Seven

N OW, FOR *The Buck Owens Ranch Show*—even though we'd eventually do things in a more modern fashion—we were still shooting the entire half-hour show live to tape in 1969. *Hee Haw*, though, was a completely different kind of situation.

I'd go down to Nashville, and for the first couple of weeks we'd tape all of the musical segments for the next batch of shows. I'd perform a bunch of songs with the Buckaroos; the musical guests would come in and perform with the Buckaroos backing them up; and then the whole cast would get together and we'd tape all of the sing-alongs that were part of every show, and all of the segments where Roy and me would do the "Pickin' and Grinnin'" jokes.

After all of the music segments were done, we'd tape half a season's-worth of comedy material where we'd be standing in the cornfield doing one-liners and all that other silly stuff. If you saw the show, you know what I'm talking about. The point is, the whole time we were in Nashville, we'd be shooting everything out of order. All of the different parts of the show would be taped back-to-back, and then after we'd all finished the particular sections we were in, we'd be done. I might already be back in Bakersfield or out on the road while Archie Campbell was still on the set, taping all of his comedy bits in the barbershop. None of us who were in the cast knew what the finished show was going to look like until we saw how it'd been edited together when it aired on TV.

So, on November 3rd, me and the Buckaroos flew to Nashville to tape our section of the shows that would start airing as soon as one of CBS's fall shows bit the dust. In those days, we taped everything at WLAC, which was Nashville's CBS-affiliated TV station. Sure enough,

CBS cancelled *The Leslie Uggams Show* after it'd been on the air for only about three months, so *Hee Haw* took its place that December.

* * *

Just like they'd done with my albums *Open Up Your Heart* in '66 and *I've Got You on My Mind Again* in '68, Capitol waited until right after Christmas of '69 to put out my last album of the year, *The Buck Owens Show: Big in Vegas.*

It was my fourth live album in as many years, but to tell you the truth, it was as much a showcase for other acts as it was a Buck Owens album. I opened the show with the song "Big in Vegas," and then turned things over to my son Buddy. He was followed by a group called the Sanland Brothers, then Susan Raye, and then the Hagers. The second half of the album I sang a few songs, but so did Doyle Holly and Don Rich and a guy named Ira Allen.

The Buck Owens Show: Big in Vegas barely made it into the Top Ten on the album charts, which was a hint of things to come. The more popular *Hee Haw* got, the less my records sold. It was the beginning of a pattern that I'd suspected might happen—but I just couldn't turn down that *Hee Haw* paycheck.

Chapter Ninety-Eight

SOME PEOPLE HAVE CRITICIZED ME because I've blamed overexposure on television for damaging my record sales so badly. To tell you the truth, I had a pretty good idea of what I was walking into at the time, but I did *Hee Haw* anyway, hoping I'd be the *one guy* who wouldn't be affected by it.

I'd done an interview—over a year before *Hee Haw* even started—for *Country Song Roundup*. The interviewer asked me if I felt that radio was more important than television when it came to promoting country music. I told him, "I think you'll find that too much exposure on TV destroys the mystery of an artist. I think that once you become a household name, it removes that necessary mystery."

I already knew back then what a gamble it would be to do a weekly network TV show. I was predicting my own future when I told that interviewer, "Of course, you can do quite well financially with TV." I mentioned Jimmy Dean and Perry Como as a couple of examples of artists whose popularity on records had plummeted after they started doing TV, and then I said, "Perhaps they don't need the income from the records. It is a calculated risk, I suppose."

So, I was willing to take that calculated risk. The big difference in my case was that, with *Hee Haw*, my whole image changed practically overnight. If you were one of the thousands of people who saw me onstage live somewhere, you saw a man playing a Fender Telecaster, wearing a suit designed by Nudie Cohn or Nathan Turk, standing in front of a big row of amps and speakers. But if you were one of the tens of millions of people watching me on TV, you saw a guy who looked like a country bumpkin, wearing his overalls backwards and standing in front of a bail of hay. I mean, how do you take that guy seriously?

* * *

In early February of 1970, I did my final sessions at Capitol's studio in LA. On the 2nd and 3rd, I recorded my next single, "The Kansas City Song," and some more duets with Susan Raye. We'd already recorded "We're Gonna Get Together" back in December of '68, and a couple of others in late '69, so Capitol started putting out a series of singles and albums by me and Susan.

"We're Gonna Get Together" became our first hit. It reached number thirteen on the country charts. People got to know about Susan through our duet records, and that caused her to start having a pretty successful solo career, too.

Meanwhile, *my* solo career wasn't getting off to a great start in the new decade. Back in '66, my first gospel album had gone to number one on the country albums chart. My second gospel album, *Your Mother's Prayer*, didn't chart at all. It came out in March and went absolutely nowhere. It looked like that overexposure from being on network television every week was already starting to take its toll.

Chapter Ninety-Nine

ONE OF THE GOOD THINGS THAT HAPPENED in 1970 was that I finally had my studio up and running in Bakersfield. If I was in the mood to record, I'd just call the guys and tell 'em when to be there. I didn't have to deal with having to find out when Capitol's studio would be available anymore, or go to the trouble of driving down to LA every time we were going to record, or knowing that every minute I was recording at Capitol it was costing me money. It was still costing me money to record at my own studio, of course, but at least I wasn't billing myself at an hourly rate that would be charged against my record royalties like Capitol had done to me all those years. I needed somebody to look after the studio, so I put my old friend, Bob Morris—the guy who wrote "Buckaroo" and played bass on so many of my sessions—in charge of running it.

One of the other good things that happened in 1970—one of the great things, really—was having Jim Shaw join the band. Jim was a keyboard player from up in Fresno who was a friend of Doyle Curtsinger's.

Now, Doyle had been a Buckaroo for about four or five months by March of 1970, but he was still living up in Fresno. I guess he'd decided not to move to Bakersfield right away because he knew how many bass players I'd been through. Anyway, I'd called a session for March 7th, so Jim Shaw came down to Bakersfield with Doyle because Jim wanted to check out the studio. When me and the Buckaroos weren't recording there, we'd rent it out to other acts from the area who didn't want to go down to LA. Jim was the bandleader at a club in Fresno called Nashville West, and he was thinking about having his band record an album at my place. Of course, I didn't know any of that at the time. All I knew was that we were in the studio trying to cut a song called "Down in New Orleans," and that the keyboard player on the session just flat could not play the song. Since we didn't have a keyboard player in the Buckaroos, I'd hired David Frizzell—Lefty's younger brother—because I'd been told he was a pretty good piano player. In the '80s, David would have a bunch of hits as a singer, but that day in 1970, he was driving me crazy because he couldn't get the piano part right on "Down in New Orleans."

After we'd tried it several times, I decided to take a break. That's when Doyle came over and told me this piano player from Fresno was there, checking out the studio. So I went out and found the guy and asked him if he could play the song we'd been trying to cut. He said yes, he could, so I brought him into the studio and he nailed it the first time through. I asked him if he'd stay and play on the rest of the session, and he said yes, he could do that, too.

So, I took David Frizzell aside and told him I'd pay him for the session, but that I wouldn't be needing his services any more that day. I was real happy for him a few years later when he had that string of hits with "I'm Gonna Hire a Wino to Decorate Our Home" and "You're the Reason God Made Oklahoma" and a bunch of others. He might not have been able to play piano on "Down in New Orleans," but he turned out to be a real good singer. And it was thanks to David Frizzell's bad piano playing that I ended up having Jim Shaw in my band.

*   *   *

By April of 1970, Richard Nixon had been President for a couple of years. Jack McFadden told me that President Nixon wanted me to do another command performance at the White House on April 17th, but I had a European tour that started on April 13th, so we had to turn him down. A couple of years earlier I might've rearranged my tour of Europe to be able to play at the White House—but I'd done that gig already, so I said we'd have to schedule a performance for President Nixon at another time. Unfortunately, President Nixon's stay in the White House turned out to be shorter than he'd planned, so we never did get to play for him—although he was the inspiration for a song of mine that I'll tell you about a little later.

"The Kansas City Song" was released in May. *Billboard* raved about the single, saying, "It's sure to keep him at the top of the country charts." It came close, reaching number two for a couple of weeks, which was a little better than "Big in Vegas" had done.

About the same time "The Kansas City Song" came out, me and the Buckaroos went back to Nashville to tape thirteen more episodes of *Hee*

Haw. The show was doing great in the ratings, and the producers told us to keep October clear because we'd need to tape enough episodes to get us through spring of '71.

*   *   *

I got on this jag where I started writing and recording a whole bunch of songs that had the names of places in the titles. When my album, *The Kansas City Song*, came out in July, it had songs on it like "It's a Long Way to London Town" and "Amsterdam" and "Black Texas Dirt" and "Scandinavian Polka."

Now, speaking of songs with places in the title, I'll tell you about an experience I had in New York that inspired me to write one about that place. In March of 1970, we'd gone to New York City to do *The Ed Sullivan Show* again. That whole trip, me and Don were getting hassled and hustled. It made me think back to my very first trip there in the winter of '64.

That first time I went to New York, from the time I got off the plane it seemed like everybody in town was looking for a tip. There was a guy at the airport who hailed a cab for me, so I had to tip him. Then the cab driver went out of his way to drive me out of my way, going all through Central Park just to jack up the fare. When I got out at the hotel, he complained that I hadn't tipped him enough.

Then there was a bellboy who took my bags from the cab to the lobby, so I had to tip him. Then there was a different bellboy who took my bags from the lobby to my room, so I had to tip him. It just never stopped. You had to tip the maid, the valet, the doorman—even the desk clerk was looking for a tip because he'd gotten me a corner room. Before it was over, I think I'd given out more tips than what it cost to stay in that corner room for the night.

So, six years later, it was the same shakedown all over again. Between me and the band, it took two cabs to get us from the airport to the hotel, and the guy driving the cab that Don was in was so rude, he somehow managed to piss Don off. I mean to tell you, it took a hell of a lot to piss off Don Rich. He was the one always in charge of calming me down when I'd get upset, but I had to calm him down that day. I told him, "I wouldn't live here if they gave me the whole damn town." And as soon as I said it, I knew I had a song to write. So, I wrote "I Wouldn't Live in New York City (If They Gave Me the Whole Damn Town.)" At least that was the original title. The folks at Capitol said country radio wouldn't play a song with the word "damn" in it—especially one with "damn" right there in the title—so they begged me to change it to something else. That's how it became "I Wouldn't Live in New York City (If They Gave Me the Whole *Dang* Town)."

We recorded the song in Bakersfield, but then I got an idea about a way to make it more authentic. The next time I was in New York, me and Jack McFadden went to Capitol's offices there and Jack had 'em set up their remote equipment on the sidewalk. So, I re-recorded my lead vocal right there on West 46th Street. Thanks to *Hee Haw*, even people in Manhattan recognized who I was, so a crowd started to gather around me while I was singing the song. Pretty soon a cop driving by saw the commotion, turned on his siren, and pulled over to find out what was going on. We'd already recorded some street sounds to put at the beginning and end of the record, but that siren wasn't part of the plan. I thought it had messed up the take, but when I listened back to it, I decided to leave it in. I just wish I'd left the word "damn" in, too.

Chapter One Hundred

SINCE ME AND SUSAN RAYE WERE RECORDING TOGETHER, Capitol was releasing our duet singles and my solo singles right around the same time every few months. I was already beginning to deal with overexposure on TV, so the last thing I thought I needed was to be overexposed on radio, too. But Capitol saw things different than I did. The one advantage I knew I had over the label was that my contract was going to be expiring in 1971, and I'd already begun to formulate a new plan with my lawyer, Al Schlesinger.

But in 1970, Capitol still ran the show. So, they put out "Togetherness"—my second single with Susan—and it did a little better than our first one had. Our next one, "The Great White Horse," became the biggest hit we'd have together. It reached number eight on the country singles chart.

Right after "The Great White Horse" came out, I received one of the honors that I'm most proud of. By September of 1970, I'd had nineteen number one singles, and another dozen that had hit the Top Ten—all on Capitol Records. I'd also had all those duet hits with Rose Maddox and my son Buddy and Susan Raye on Capitol. So, on September 1st, Capitol Records declared it "Buck Owens Day" at the Capitol Tower there in Hollywood, and they gave me a plaque naming me "Country Artist of the Decade." Even though I had plenty to complain about when it came to a lot of the things Capitol had done over the years, I really appreciated the recognition they gave me. And if they considered me worthy of being named "Country Artist of the Decade," I felt like it gave me even more leverage when it came to negotiating my next contract.

That same month, *Billboard* devoted over twenty pages of their magazine to me in a big feature they called "The Many Worlds of Buck Owens." A lot of folks took out ads in the magazine to congratulate me, including the Buckaroos—Don Rich, Doyle Holly, Jerry Wiggins, Doyle Curtsinger, and Jim Shaw. It would turn out to be "Dashing" Doyle Holly's last official act as a member of the Buckaroos. He'd been in the band off and on since 1963, but the time had finally come for us to part ways for good.

Having so much attention paid to me by my label and by *Billboard*, I got to thinking that maybe I really *was* going to be that one guy who could get away with being a network TV star and still manage to keep selling records and getting a ton of radio airplay.

Then "I Wouldn't Live in New York City (If They Gave Me the Whole Dang Town)" came out and only made it to number nine on the charts. I hadn't had the A-side of a single do that poorly since "You're for Me" had topped out at number ten back in 1963.

Like Perry Como and Jimmy Dean and Eddy Arnold and so many others, I'd taken that calculated risk of starring in a network television show. You had to sell a hell of a lot of records to make the kind of money I was getting paid to be on *Hee Haw* every week, so I took the TV money and decided to shift gears as far as my music was concerned. If every single I put out wasn't going to be a number one hit for me anymore, I decided it was time to go into the studio—my studio—and have some fun.

Chapter
One Hundred and One

THE FIRST THING I DID WAS TO FINISH UP the album that would become *I Wouldn't Live in New York City*. On the album before that one, *The Kansas City Song*, most of the songs had names of places in their titles. For the *I Wouldn't Live in New York City* album, all of the songs had the names of cities in 'em. And just like I'd already done with the single, "I Wouldn't Live in New York City (If They Gave Me the Whole Dang Town)," I put in sound effects to go with every song on the album. For "Reno Lament" I included sound effects from a casino. For "(It's a Long Way to) Londontown," I put those famous Big Ben chimes on it. For "Houston-Town," I used some sounds from one of the Apollo missions. Like I said, I'd decided the time had come to have some fun, so I did.

In October, we all headed back down to Nashville to tape those episodes of *Hee Haw* that would get us through the spring. The producers were excited because the ratings had just kept getting better. We had one of the hottest shows on CBS despite the fact that the critics still hated us.

Just as we were wrapping the *Hee Haw* taping, Capitol put out *I Wouldn't Live in New York City*. But right before that, they decided to take advantage of the whole *Hee Haw* thing by taking twenty of the songs from my two Christmas albums and putting out a two-record set called *A Merry "Hee Haw" Christmas from Buck Owens and His Buckaroos*. That was just about the last straw for me. I couldn't wait for 1971 to arrive so I could either negotiate a new deal with Capitol that gave me control over my own music, or go to another label that would give me the kind of control I wanted.

But when '71 rolled around, I still had albums to record under my old deal until it expired that May. I might not be able to stop Capitol from repackaging my Christmas albums or constantly putting out "Best Of" packages, but having my own studio in Bakersfield, I could record whatever I wanted to without having a bunch of label honchos breathing down my neck.

So, I shifted gears again and recorded an album that included half songs written by me, and half songs written by guys like Paul Simon and Bob Dylan. Ken Nelson thought I'd lost my mind. I didn't care. I felt like I needed to stretch—to make the kind of music that appealed to me at that point in my life.

Along with the songs I wrote, we did Paul Simon's "Homeward Bound" and "I Am a Rock" and "Bridge Over Troubled Water." We did Donovan's "Catch the Wind," and a song by Terry Clements and John English called "(I'm Goin') Home."

I knew I'd get another backlash from certain fans saying, "That ain't country," so I went with a preemptive strike. On the back of the album, I wrote that these were songs that had a country heart because they were mostly songs of longing. I also said we'd given 'em all country arrangements—which we had. I nearly drove Jim Shaw nuts when I wouldn't let him play all of those diminished chords on "Bridge Over Troubled Water." I wanted to do the song—all of the songs—with as much of a country feel as possible. And I'll tell you the truth—a lot of people over the years have told me that *Bridge Over Troubled Water* is their favorite Buck Owens album. So, even though Ken Nelson didn't like me doing an album with no steel guitar on it, I've never regretted making that record because so many folks have told me how much they enjoyed it.

When the single, "Bridge Over Troubled Water," came out in February of '71, radio jumped on it right away. As the record started going up the charts, I knew I'd made the right move with my music. Times were changing, my audience was changing, and I was changing, too. I hadn't had a number one single since "Tall Dark Stranger" in '69, but this one was clearly on its way toward the top of the charts. And then out came this publication called "The Mindszenty Report."

Cardinal Mindszenty was based in St. Louis, Missouri—I guess that made him a "St. Louis Cardinal." But even though he was based in Missouri, apparently his publication really got around. On the front page was a piece called "'Rock' and Revolution." The article started by quoting the first ten lines of "Bridge Over Troubled Water." Then the writer said that two words in the song—"silver girl"—were about a hypodermic needle filled with heroin.

Oh man, you should've seen the letters I got. I didn't just get letters from angry fans—I got letters from upset disc jockeys, too. Luckily, none of those deejays sent me pictures of people throwing copies of "Bridge Over Troubled Water" into a bonfire, but their letters were still pretty painful. Every one of 'em seemed to say the same thing: "I'm a big fan of yours and I've been playing your records for years, but I'm going to have to stop playing this one because our radio station doesn't play songs that promote drugs."

One week the record was sitting at number nine, and the next week it started flying down the charts so fast, it was like the thing had an anchor tied to it. I wrote letters to program directors at the major market country stations, but all I could say was I didn't know if Paul Simon was talking about heroin in his song or not, but that I certainly didn't intentionally record a song about drugs, and that I'd never heard anybody even suggest it was about drugs until that piece in "The Mindszenty Report" came out.

Looking back on it now, that whole article was pretty silly. It didn't just accuse "Bridge Over Troubled Water" of being about heroin. It said the Beatles' "Hey Jude" was about heroin, too. It also said Ford Motor Company was sending subliminal drug messages in an ad that said one of their cars would "blow your mind," and that the airline TWA was promoting drugs by using the phrase, "Up, up and away." I'm not kidding! But I guess people didn't read the whole article. They saw that first paragraph that said "silver girl" was a syringe filled with heroin and that's all it took. They say heroin kills. Well, it sure killed my single.

Chapter
One Hundred and Two

AROUND THE SAME TIME MY SINGLE of "Bridge Over Troubled Water" died, *Hee Haw* died, too. I'd been watching the TV ratings for *Hee Haw* just like I'd always watched the *Billboard* charts to see how my singles and albums were doing.

The show had just kept moving up over the course of the two seasons it had been on. It had gone from being somewhere near the bottom to being in the twenties to being in the teens to being as high as number twelve one week. If you're familiar with TV shows from the '70s, let me put this in perspective for you. At the end of the '69-'70 TV season, *Hee Haw* was ranked as the number twenty-one network show on television—higher than *Mod Squad*; higher than *Bewitched*; even higher than *The Ed Sullivan Show*. *Hee Haw*'s average weekly viewing audience was just over 12,000,000.

At the end of the '70-'71 season, it came in at number sixteen—above *My Three Sons*, the *Mary Tyler Moore Show*, the *Dean Martin Show*, the *Carol Burnett Show*, the *Partridge Family*, and every other network TV show from number seventeen on down. That year, *Hee Haw* had an average audience of almost 13,000,000—but by the time the annual ratings came out, it had already been cancelled by Fred Silverman, the guy who was the head of programming at CBS.

Mr. Silverman had decided that it was time to change CBS's image. He wanted his network to reach younger viewers who lived in cities like New York and Chicago and LA. He didn't want people to think of CBS as the network that appealed to an older audience, or to a rural audience. So, *Hee Haw* wasn't the only rural-type show to get the axe in the spring of '71. Fred Silverman also cancelled shows like *Green Acres*, the *Beverly Hillbillies*, and *Mayberry R.F.D.* My old friend Pat Buttram, who had been one of the stars of *Green Acres*, said later that it was the year CBS cancelled everything with a tree—including *Lassie*.

Everybody had their own reasons to be disappointed. For me, I knew it meant I'd have to go back out on the road a lot more to be able to make the kind of money I'd been making on *Hee Haw*. But I also knew it was a chance for me to get out of those backwards overalls and try to reclaim the image and status I had before *Hee Haw* had come along in the first place.

Before it starts to sound like I'm complaining too much about the show that made me a household name, let me tell you that I had a lot of fun during those early days of *Hee Haw*. They were a great group of people to be around, and I never laughed so much in my life as I did when we'd all get together to tape the shows. Plus, it was thanks to *Hee Haw* that millions of people got to see my red, white, and blue guitar. Like I told you earlier, Semie Moseley helped me create the original version. A lot of people had asked me about it at concerts over the years, but when folks saw it on *Hee Haw*, it seems like everybody wanted to know where they could get one. In fact, guitar manufacturers were lining up to try to get the rights to put out a Buck Owens red, white, and blue acoustic guitar.

I listened to what the various manufacturers had in mind, but what I had in mind was to find the company that could make a good, quality guitar that everybody could afford. I decided to go with Chicago Musical Instruments—the same company that made Gibson Guitars—because they said they could make 'em and sell 'em for $82.95 apiece. And the great thing was they were able to strike a deal with Sears. When I was a kid, my folks had ordered things for me out of the old Sears & Roebuck catalog. Now folks could order my guitar—the "Buck Owens American"—from the Sears catalog, and they could also buy 'em in Sears's retail stores. And for every guitar Sears sold, I got paid $2.50. I had no idea how many folks would want to buy a red, white, and blue guitar, but I found out fast when the very first check Chicago Musical Instruments sent me was for $15,000.

Naturally, when I got the word that *Hee Haw* had been cancelled, I figured that was pretty much it for my guitar sales and everything else that had to do with the show. What I didn't know was that John Aylesworth and Frank Peppiatt had other plans in mind. They'd decided to see if they could get the show syndicated, just like *The Buck Owens Ranch*

Show was syndicated. Of course, my show was small potatoes compared to a show that had been on a major network. John and Frank felt like they could get a whole lot of the local CBS affiliates around the country interested in keeping *Hee Haw* on the air. They knew a lot of those TV stations had been real disappointed that the show had been cancelled since it had clearly been one of the top shows in the country before Fred Silverman decided to ignore everybody that wasn't living in a big city. So, they went out there and worked their magic, and by the time they'd finished negotiating with everybody, they had well over two hundred TV stations signed on to carry the show. Mr. Silverman had killed *Hee Haw*, but John and Frank and their crew had brought it back to life. And since over a hundred and fifty of the stations that agreed to carry it were CBS affiliates, most folks never knew the show had been cancelled in the first place.

LEFT: Buck with his star on the Hollywood Walk of Fame. Hollywood, California.

BELOW: On the set of *Hee Haw*. (*Left to right*) Don Rich, Lulu Roman, Doyle Curtsinger, Jerry Wiggins, Jim Hager, Susan Raye, Jeannine Riley, Buck, Jon Hager, and Doyle Holly. "As much as I hated the name, I still thought the idea of having a weekly network TV show that featured country music was a great idea."

(*Clockwise from upper left*) Buck with Liberace, John Wayne, Evel Knievel, Ronald Reagan, Johnny Carson, and Ed Sullivan.

(*Clockwise from upper left*) Buck with Jackie Gleason; Dean Martin; Johnny Cash; Ray Charles; Roy Rogers, Dale Evans, and Roy Clark; and Garth Brooks.

ABOVE: Latter-day lineup of the Buckaroos on the set of *The Buck Owens Ranch Show*. Back row (*left to right*): Ronnie Jackson, Jerry Wiggins, and Jim Shaw. Front row (*left to right*): Don Rich and Doyle Curtsinger.

RIGHT: Buck with his fourth wife, Jennifer Joyce Owens. "Jennifer Joyce is not only my companion—she's the absolute love of my life."

Ringo Starr and Buck on the set of the video shoot for their duet of "Act Naturally." "I think the video might've been more popular than the record was.... Ringo told me he'd always been a big country music fan, so he was happy to have his first single to hit the country charts, even though it wasn't a huge hit."

Dwight Yoakam and Buck on the "Streets of Delano." "I did have a little problem with the 'Streets of Bakersfield' video, . . . because we didn't shoot it in Bakersfield. Can you believe that? It was shot up there in Delano, California, about thirty miles north of where the streets of Bakersfield actually are."

ABOVE: The Owens family, "Together Again." (*Left to right*) Michael, Bonnie, Buck, and Buddy.

LEFT: Buck with his Academy of Country Music Pioneer Award, April 10, 1989.

FACING, BOTTOM: The famous Bakersfield sign after it was moved to Sillect Avenue, with Buck's Crystal Palace in the background. "That sign was like a beacon to me in the old days. I can't tell you how many times I used to make that drive from Bakersfield to LA to Bakersfield— but I always knew I was almost home when I'd see that sign with those big blue capital letters coming into view."

Upper photo: (*Left to right*) Buck, Jim Shaw, and Dwight Yoakam. Lower photo: Buck's nephew Mel Owens, Buddy, Buck, and Michael. Photo on right: Buck with his long-time secretary, Lee Ann Enns.

ABOVE: Brad Paisley with Buck, onstage at the Crystal Palace.

RIGHT: Buck with his original "Buck Owens American" red, white, and blue guitar, sitting at the Crystal Palace bar. Bakersfield, California, 2005.

PART V

"There's Gotta Be Some Changes Made"

Chapter
One Hundred and Three

EVEN THOUGH "THE MINDSZENTY REPORT" HAD KILLED my
last single, I decided I'd stick with my plan to have fun by making
the kind of records I wanted to make. And the one thing I knew for sure
was that nobody would be able to say any of the songs I was about to do
for my next record had any drug references in 'em—unless they considered corn liquor to be a drug.

Remember how I said I used to listen to the Monroe Brothers on the
radio when I was a kid in Texas? Well, when the act broke up and Bill
formed his own band—Bill Monroe and the Bluegrass Boys—he created a type of music nobody had ever heard before. And Bill's type of music got even more exciting when Earl Scruggs joined the band in 1945
and started playing his amazing three-finger banjo picking style. Folks
went crazy over the sound of that band. They called it bluegrass music,
after the name of Bill's group.

A lot of what I heard in the labor camps in California was similar
to what Bill and his band were doing. The music in the camps wasn't as
fast, and nobody played the style of banjo that Earl Scruggs played, but
the key elements were there—guitar, mandolin, banjo, fiddle, and high
harmony vocals.

When Don and I started singing our high harmony vocals together
in the late '50s, I wasn't really thinking about the fact that we had some
of those same bluegrass elements in the music that we were making, but
we sure did.

By 1971, I'd been listening to bluegrass music for most of my life,
so I decided the time had come to make my own bluegrass album. The
problem was, I didn't have a banjo player. Then one night I heard this
young man playing banjo on the *Grand Ole Opry*. Roy Acuff introduced
him, and said the guy didn't have any records out, but that he was so
good, Roy wanted everybody to get a chance to hear him anyway. His
name was Ronnie Jackson.

I got Ronnie's phone number and gave him a call. I told him I was going to be in Memphis in a few days, so he came to my hotel room there and we picked a couple of tunes together. I remember we did "Foggy Mountain Breakdown" and "Rollin' in My Sweet Baby's Arms."

When I introduced him to the other guys in the band and told 'em Ronnie was our newest Buckaroo, I'm sure they thought I'd finally gone 'round the bend. Here we were—still with no steel guitar player—and now I'd added a banjo player to the mix. But once I got Ronnie into the studio, it all began to make sense to everybody.

You know, every time I made any kind of change in my music, some of the country purists would complain that I wasn't making country music the right way anymore. Well, let me tell you something—when it comes to purists, nobody's more set in their ways than those bluegrass fans. According to them, when you make bluegrass music, you've got to do it the same way Bill Monroe did it. You've got to have a mandolin, a banjo, a guitar, a fiddle, and an upright bass. Those are the rules! You can't have any electric instruments—and you sure as hell can't have a keyboard player.

So, I knew I was probably going to upset everybody from the casual bluegrass fan to Bill Monroe himself with what we were about to do, but I did it anyway. Me and my latest lineup of Buckaroos—Don Rich, Ronnie Jackson, Jerry Wiggins, Doyle Curtsinger, and Jim Shaw—went into my studio and cut ten tunes in our own "Buckaroo Bluegrass" style. Most of the songs were bluegrass standards; one was a song my son Buddy wrote called "Corn Liquor;" and one was a song I'd written and recorded a few years before called "Heartbreak Mountain." When we originally did it in '67, we'd done it in our usual "freight train" style. It turned out to work as a pretty good bluegrass tune, too.

It's hard to imagine that a bluegrass record would be a big seller these days, but there was just something in the air at the time. The movie *Bonnie and Clyde* had come out in '67, and Flatt & Scruggs's "Foggy Mountain Breakdown" had been used all through it. A year after my bluegrass album was released, the movie *Deliverance* came out, and it featured a bluegrass instrumental called "Dueling Banjos." That thing was so catchy, it turned out to be a big hit on the pop charts.

So, my timing had been exactly right. In April, we put out our first bluegrass single, "Ruby (Are You Mad)," and it shot all the way up to number three on the country charts. And it was just when "Ruby (Are You Mad)" started its run up the charts that I got a call from the producers of *Hee Haw*, telling me to come on down to Nashville at the end of May because we were back in business.

Chapter
One Hundred and Four

RIGHT BEFORE I WENT BACK TO BEGIN TAPING that third season of *Hee Haw*, the time had come for me to renegotiate my contract with Capitol. I had my lawyer, Al Schlesinger, tell 'em their "Country Artist of the Decade" wasn't interested in signing another deal like the ones I'd been signing since 1957. Of course, the royalty rates on my contracts had improved a little since that first one, but I swear, every one of 'em still had that language in there about "breakage" and all sorts of other things that were just no longer acceptable to me.

Al Schlesinger and I had decided it was time for me to take the bull by the horns. First of all, I didn't want an advance. A big advance is one of the things record labels have always dangled in front of artists like a carrot on a stick. They say, "We're gonna give you a lot of money. Don't you want a lot of money?" And, of course, most artists say, "Yeah, I want a lot of money. Where do I sign?" But what ends up happening is the label deducts all of that advance money they've given you from the royalties they owe you until they've gotten back every penny they've advanced to you. They call it an "advance." I call it loaning you your own money. The only way they don't get to recoup all of your advance money is if you don't sell enough records for 'em to be able to get it all back. Of course, if you don't sell enough records for 'em to get their money back, they drop you from the label. So, you either sell a lot of records and let 'em get back all of your own money they loaned you, or you're a flop and you get dropped.

On top of that, if you do finally recoup your advance, you only get to keep a tiny percentage of the money your records generate. The label gets to keep the vast majority of that income. Back when my daddy was a sharecropper, we got to keep half of the profits on the crops we grew. Record labels would just laugh if you told 'em you wanted half of the money they collected from your record sales. So, record contracts are worse than the deals landlords used to offer Texas sharecroppers in the 1930s.

Now, as bad as all that sounds, the thing I hated most—the most egregious thing in all of my previous record contracts—was that Capitol got to keep the rights to everything I recorded for 'em in perpetuity. It didn't matter when I recorded it—they got to keep the rights to my recordings forever.

And it wasn't just me they did that to. That's what all of their contracts said—even Frank Sinatra's. Here he was, probably the biggest singing star of the twentieth century, but everything he recorded for Capitol in the '50s and '60s is still owned by Capitol.

So, Al and I told 'em we didn't want their advance money, and we didn't want their single digit royalty rate. What we wanted was what's called a "P & D" deal. That stands for "production and distribution." I'd produce all of my records, and Capitol would do the manufacturing and distributing. In fact, we told 'em we didn't want the agreement to be with me as an artist. We wanted the agreement to be with my company, Buck Owens Enterprises. That way I could produce recordings by me or any of the artists signed to my company, and Capitol's job would be to create the physical product and get it out to the radio stations and stores.

In exchange for me giving them to right to manufacture and distribute the recordings I provided to 'em, instead of paying me that single digit royalty rate, they'd pay Buck Owens Enterprises twenty percent. It was still a long way from "farming on the halves," but it was over double what I'd gotten in the past.

But more than anything, I wanted to get the rights to all of my masters back—not just the stuff I was going to be recording for 'em under my new deal. I wanted everything going all the way back to my first record on Capitol.

So, we put in the contract that the agreement with Buck Owens Enterprises would begin as of June 1st, 1971, and that it would end on May 31st, 1976. It said that Capitol would have the right to manufacture and distribute everything recorded during those five years, and they'd have that right all the way through to May 31st, 1980—but come June 1st, 1980, all of those masters would belong to Buck Owens Enterprises.

But the best part was that it went on to say I wouldn't just get back those masters recorded between 1971 and 1976—come June 1st, 1980, I'd get back *everything* I'd ever recorded for Capitol.

No country artist had ever entered into a deal like that before. It was just unheard of. You didn't get your masters back from your label. Once you made a record, it was just understood that the record company would own it forever.

Of course, Capitol could've said they weren't interested. They could've said, "No thanks, Buck. We'll just keep everything we've got and let you make your new records for some other label."

But they knew that my older records weren't selling all that much anymore. To them it was just old product taking up warehouse space. What they were interested in most was having me deliver new records to 'em. They were all about the immediate future. They didn't stop to think that the day might come when somebody would want to use my recordings in major motion pictures, or in national commercials. They also didn't stop to think that the day might come when record buyers would be interested in reissues of older records. And they sure didn't stop to think that the day might come when a new format like the compact disc would be invented and just about everything that had ever been released on vinyl would be rereleased on CD.

Of course, I didn't know the CD was coming either. I just knew that I wanted all of my masters back—and when Elliot Chaum of Capitol Records put his signature on that contract, I knew it was official that the day would come when they'd all finally belong to me.

Chapter
One Hundred and Five

WHEN ME AND THE BUCKAROOS FLEW DOWN to Nashville in late May to tape thirteen more episodes of *Hee Haw*, my brother Melvin was already very sick. He had cancer—a disease that would eventually strike every member of my family, including me.

Like I told you earlier, when that big ol' red-headed boy made the mistake of messing with my brother's cap in the peach orchard when we were kids, Mel had shown just how scrappy he could be. Even when I sat next to him there in the hospital on his last day, he held my hand incredibly tight. He still had that strength he'd always had, but he needed more than strength to win his battle with cancer. I sat there with him for his last few hours, wondering what was going on in his head. He wasn't conscious, but he just kept squeezing my hand—and then he let go. My brother passed away on June 14th, 1971. He was only thirty-nine years old.

It was a sad summer for all of us. To have a member of our family die at such a young age was really hard. But, you know, they say the saddest thing is when parents outlive one of their own children—so it was a particularly difficult time for my mom and dad.

They also say the show must go on, and I really had no choice. I had concerts to play, two different TV shows to tape, and records to make under my new contract. Exactly a week after Mel passed away, Capitol put out my bluegrass album. We called it *Ruby and Other Bluegrass Specials*. It went to number nine on the country albums chart—my highest-charting album in a couple of years. And unlike my last several albums, we released a second single from it. "Rollin' in My Sweet Baby's Arms" came out in August and ended up being an even bigger hit than "Ruby (Are You Mad)." It hit number two for a couple of weeks, but that's as high as it went because Lynn Anderson's "How Can I Unlove You" just wouldn't fall out of that top spot.

Since my son Buddy and Susan Raye were both signed to Buck Owens Enterprises, I spent a lot of time in the studio with them that summer, making records that fell under my new deal with Capitol. Me and Susan recorded a Christmas album together, and me and Buddy finally recorded an album's-worth of duet material together. Right at the end of the year, one of the duets I did with him, "Too Old to Cut the Mustard," reached the Top Thirty on the country charts.

*   *   *

I want to tell you about one other thing that happened in '71. One of the acts that signed with my publishing and management companies in the late '60s was a singer/songwriter named Freddie Hart. Freddie had been around since the early '50s, writing and recording one minor hit after another. He was on Capitol even before I was. Then he moved to Columbia for a while, and then Kapp Records for a while, and then he signed with Capitol again around 1969. I thought he was a really good songwriter, which is why I signed him to Blue Book Music. One of the songs he wrote was "Togetherness," which was a minor hit for him before it became a major hit for me and Susan Raye.

Well, after he got signed to Capitol that second time, he made an album called *California Grapevine*. Capitol put out the title song as the single off the album. It floundered around at the bottom of the charts, and then it fell off. After that single died, a disk jockey heard another song on the album called "Easy Loving." When the deejay started playing that album cut, other radio stations started picking up on it, too. In July of '71, Capitol finally got around to putting it out as a single, and it became a huge, huge hit. It didn't just go to the top of the charts and stay there—it sold over a million copies, which was really rare for a country single in those days. It went to number seventeen on the pop chart, and even made it onto the easy listening chart. Then it won the CMA "Song of the Year" for 1971. And then a year later, it won the CMA "Song of the Year" award again. So, I never won a CMA award as a performer, but Freddie and my publishing company won two of 'em—and we won 'em both for the same song.

Chapter
One Hundred and Six

WHEN I DID MY DEAL WITH CAPITOL IN '71, it called for me to provide material for the label to release on a pretty steady basis. Even though me and Ken Nelson had been working together for years, he didn't like my new deal at all. He was used to controlling everything that had to do with the country records that were going to be released by Capitol, and now here I was up in Bakersfield, sending the label tapes that they were required to press onto vinyl and distribute. Now remember, this was the same label that had put out six Buck Owens albums in '68, four Buck Owens albums in '69, and five more in 1970.

I already told you about Buddy and Susan Raye. I also had other acts signed to Buck Owens Enterprises like Tony Booth, Mayf Nutter, and the Bakersfield Brass. And then, of course, there was me. So, I kept things busy at my studio, recording all these various artists and sending the tapes to Capitol—and then Capitol started complaining that I was sending them too much product. That's right—the same Capitol Records that put out fifteen Buck Owens albums in three years thought I should cut down on the amount of material I was sending to 'em.

They could complain all they wanted as far as I was concerned because Susan and Buddy and Tony all had hit records during those years. And I had a few more myself.

Even though I didn't have enough songs cut for a new album, I sent Capitol the tapes for my next single. I'd written a ballad called "I'll Still Be Waiting for You" that I felt real good about. The recording featured some beautiful piano playing by Jim, and it also had the latest Buckaroo on it—my new steel guitar player, Jerry Brightman. The single came out in January of '72, and ended up reaching the Top Ten.

It had been so long since I'd had a number one hit, I'd begun to think there just weren't going to be any more until I heard a song Bob Morris and his wife Faye had written called "Made in Japan." Things have sure changed now, but years ago you used to see all this cheap stuff that had "Made In Japan" stamped on the back. It was a phrase that everybody was familiar with. Well, Bob played the song for Don Rich and Jim Shaw, and the two of 'em worked up a demo of it for me to hear—and what I heard was the chance to have a huge hit. The song was about an American man and a Japanese woman, so the man in the song is singing about being in love with this little lady who was "made in Japan."

We went in the studio and cut it, with Jim playing Farfisa organ and Don overdubbing his fiddle parts to give the whole arrangement a Far East kind of sound. The single came out in April. Two months later, on July 15th, "Made in Japan" hit the top of the country charts.

It had been almost three years since I'd had a number one record, and when I saw that issue of *Billboard* with my single sitting there at number one, I thought, "My twentieth number one hit! I guess I was all wrong about television hurting my record sales."

Well, it turned out I was all wrong about being all wrong. It would be seventeen years before my next chart-topping single—and sure enough, that next number one wouldn't come until my days on *Hee Haw* were long over.

Chapter
One Hundred and Seven

IN 1972, THE TIME HAD FINALLY COME—well, it was way past time, really—for me and Phyllis to officially end our marriage that had unofficially ended years earlier. When my next single came out— "You Ain't Gonna Have Ol' Buck to Kick Around No More"—a lot of folks who knew about the divorce probably thought I was singing about Phyllis. But the inspiration behind that song was actually something Richard Nixon had said.

Way back in '62, Nixon had run for governor of California against Pat Brown. When he lost the election, he called a press conference the next day and told 'em, "You won't have Nixon to kick around anymore because, gentlemen, this is my last press conference."

Well, I got to thinking about that line and how funny it was because he'd told those reporters that he was done with politics. And now, ten years later, he was President of the United States.

Once I'd written the song, it turned out that I was so busy doing *Hee Haw*, *The Buck Owens Ranch Show*, and tours in both the US and Europe that I couldn't seem to find the time to go into my own studio and record it. On top of that, the studio had gotten so popular that folks were coming up from LA to record there. And when outside acts weren't using it, the artists signed to Buck Owens Enterprises were. I finally told Bob Morris to book me some time in my own damn studio. I got in there long enough to cut "You Ain't Gonna Have Ol' Buck to Kick Around No More," but I didn't have nearly enough time to record a whole album.

Luckily, we already had plenty of material that we'd recorded live, including a show we'd done at John Ascuaga's Nugget in Reno. It was a package show that featured Susan Raye, my son Buddy, Kenni Huskey, the Bakersfield Brass, and the Ray Sisters. At the Nugget, we'd played some of my recent hits like "Ruby (Are You Mad)," "Rollin' in My Sweet Baby's Arms," and "I'll Still Be Waiting for You." Susan had performed two of her biggest hits, "L.A. International Airport" and "Pitty, Pitty, Patter." And, of course, me and Susan had done "We're Gonna Get Together." When *Live at the Nugget* came out, it had so many hits on it that it became my biggest-selling live album since the one we'd done in Japan in '67.

Then I remembered we'd recorded the show I'd done at the White House in '68. At the time, I'd wanted to have it on tape just for the sake of posterity. So, we'd recorded the show that night using just two microphones. It wasn't the finest-quality live recording anybody ever made, but it was actually pretty good, considering the circumstances. So, I decided to have Capitol put it out next. I told 'em the album should have my studio recording of "You Ain't Gonna Have Ol' Buck to Kick Around No More," followed by the White House show. I even recorded a little introduction to go at the beginning of the album, explaining where I got the idea to write the opening song, and that the rest of the album had been recorded live at the White House under less than ideal recording conditions.

Well, I found out pretty quickly that my fans weren't too keen on me putting out two live albums in a row. *"Live" at the White House* didn't do all that great. To make matters even worse, my single of "You Ain't Gonna Have Ol' Buck to Kick Around No More" didn't even reach the Top Ten.

My fans might not have wanted to buy my live albums anymore, but they sure still wanted to see me perform live. My schedule was way too busy for me to be able to do the number of live dates I'd done in years past, but when I played, folks showed up. That year, when we performed at the Cheyenne Frontier Days Rodeo in Wyoming, me and the Buckaroos broke their 76-year attendance record.

But I didn't want to break records as much as I wanted to sell records, so I got my ass into the studio and finally recorded enough material for a new album, including a song called "In the Palm of Your Hand" that I'd recorded once before back in '65. I thought it had real potential to be a hit the first time I'd cut it, but Capitol had put it on the flipside of "Waitin' in Your Welfare Line."

By the time Capitol was able to work my new version of "In the Palm of Your Hand" into its schedule, it was early December—not the ideal time of year for a new single. But it probably wouldn't have mattered what time of year they released it. It did even worse than "You Ain't Gonna Have Ol' Buck to Kick Around No More."

Chapter
One Hundred and Eight

MY RECORD SALES WERE TANKING BUT my love life was going great. Since I was on the road so much, Jennifer Joyce ended up traveling with me a lot, which made me a much happier man. I'd also gotten us a place in Bear Valley Springs—about an hour outside of Bakersfield—so we spent a lot of good times there.

By 1973, *Hee Haw* had become the most successful show in the history of syndicated television, so folks kept seeing me there every week in their living rooms, still wearing my overalls backwards—still "pickin' and grinnin'" with Roy Clark and the gang.

I had a couple of minor hits in the spring and fall of that year. One was a cute song called "Ain't It Amazing, Gracie," and the other was a sort of mid-tempo "freight train" song I'd written called "Arms Full of Empty." Me and Susan Raye put out another duet called "The Good Old Days (Are Here Again)," but apparently they weren't, judging from the sales figures.

Between January and September, I put out three solo studio albums—*In the Palm of Your Hand, Ain't It Amazing, Gracie,* and *Arms Full of Empty*—and a duet album with Susan. I don't even want to talk about how badly they sold, but there was one song on the *Ain't It Amazing, Gracie* album that eventually turned out to be one of my all-time favorites. It was called "Streets of Bakersfield."

There was a young man named Homer Joy who was signed to Buck Owens Enterprises and Blue Book Music. He was a good singer and a good songwriter, so we flew him down to Bakersfield to do an album. But we didn't want him to do an album of his own songs. We wanted him to do an album of songs by Hank Williams—sort of like I'd done those albums of Tommy Collins and Harlan Howard songs early in my career. Well, Homer reminded me of myself because he was pretty good at negotiating a deal. He said he'd do the album of Hank Williams songs if we'd let him record some of the songs he wrote, using the Buckaroos to back him up.

Like I told you, Bob Morris was running the studio, so Bob told him that would be fine. Well, we flew Homer down from his home there near Spokane and he came in and recorded the Hank songs—but when he finished, it turned out the Buckaroos were all of a sudden busy doing other things. So, Bob had to keep putting him off. One night while Homer was stuck there in his motel, getting madder by the minute, he sat down and wrote "Streets of Bakersfield."

The next morning he came back to the studio to see if the Buckaroos were available yet, and Bob told him they had the day off. But I guess ol' Bob was starting to feel pretty bad about Homer's situation, so he asked Homer to sing him one of the songs he wanted to record. Homer grabbed a guitar off the wall and played him the song he'd just written the night before—and that's when Bob called me and told me I needed to come to the studio. I listened to the song, and I told Bob to call Don Rich and the guys and get 'em to the studio because I wanted Homer to record the song that day. Well, Homer recorded it and it got released as a single, but it didn't hit the charts or anything, so I decided to record it myself as an album cut. And that's how my first recording of "Streets of Bakersfield" came to be.

Chapter
One Hundred and Nine

FROM 1959 TO 1972, I was on the charts several times each year—and every one of those years I had hit records. In 1973, for the first time in fourteen years, none of my singles even reached the Top Ten. So, I switched gears again. If I couldn't make 'em cry with my sad songs, I'd make 'em laugh with my funny ones. After all, people were seeing me cracking corny jokes on *Hee Haw* every week, so why not be funny on my records, too?

I started by writing and recording "Big Game Hunter"—a song about a guy who won't do any work around the house that his wife wants him to do because he's too busy looking for football games on TV. The single came out at the end of '73, and it got into the Top Ten early the next year.

Then, one day, I heard this really funny song on the radio that was a big pop hit for a group called Dr. Hook and the Medicine Show. Hell, even the name of the band was funny. The song was called "The Cover of the *Rolling Stone*," and it was written by a guy named Shel Silverstein. The song was about this rock band that knew they'd get real famous if they could just get *Rolling Stone* to put their picture on the cover of the magazine.

Shel Silverstein was one interesting cat. He'd done everything from drawing cartoons for *Playboy* magazine to writing children's books.

Well, anyway, when I heard Dr. Hook singing that song, I knew I had to do it with some changes to the lyrics. So, we called the song's publisher to get permission to re-write the song and they said, "Oh, Shel's actually already written a country version." So, I had 'em send it to me, and it wasn't what I had in mind at all. So, I called Shel and asked him if I could take a shot at it, and he said, "Sure." Then I called Jim Shaw and told him that we were going to work on the new lyrics together. What we ended up with was "On the Cover of the *Music City News*." The *Music City News* was that Nashville trade magazine where I'd published my "Pledge to Country Music."

And speaking of Nashville, in early 1974 the producers of *Hee Haw* let me know that they wanted me to stop making new episodes of *The Buck Owens Ranch Show*. During the years that *Hee Haw* had been airing in syndication, my own show—the one that let everybody see who the real Buck Owens was—had actually been picked up by more and more stations. To tell you the truth, in a lot of markets my show would come on right before *Hee Haw*—and sometimes folks would see me doing the same songs on my show that I'd be doing again a half-hour later on *Hee Haw*. So, I agreed to bring *The Buck Owens Ranch Show* to an end as long as they'd let me continue to re-edit segments from old shows and send 'em to the stations that had my show under contract through 1976. Oh, and I also made the *Hee Haw* folks pay me a little more money for making me stop doing my own show.

So, "On the Cover of the *Music City News*" hit the charts in March of '74 and eventually went to number eight. At the time it came out, me and the Buckaroos were on a long, long overseas tour. We were on the road for over a month, playing in places like Japan, Hong Kong, Australia, and New Zealand. In fact, we recorded three live albums specifically for those markets. We did one at the Nakano Sun Plaza in Tokyo; one at the beautiful Sydney Opera House in Australia; and one at Christchurch Town Hall in New Zealand.

Then, one night while we were on that tour, Don Rich forgot the words to "Diggy Liggy Lo." Now remember, this was a song that he'd taught me back in the early '60s—and when I say he forgot the words, I don't mean he flubbed a line. I mean he literally forgot the words to the damn song. When I heard him struggling to get through "Diggy

Liggy Lo," I just kind of turned sideways and looked at him. I thought to myself, "Well, has this ever happened to you?" And the truth is, I couldn't remember a time I'd ever forgotten the words to a song onstage before. But more to the point, I couldn't remember Don ever forgetting the words to a song onstage either.

Don was the leader of the band, and he'd done an incredible job of running the band for me for many years—but I'd noticed that he'd begun to drink more and more. He'd drink scotch on ice, and he didn't make any pretense about it. By that I mean he wasn't trying to hide the fact that he drank from me or the band or anybody else.

I went to check up on him after the show. He was propped up in bed, reading a book, trying to act perfectly normal. We talked for a while, and I thought, "There's something wrong here, and I'm pretty sure it's the booze."

So I went back to my room and called his wife. I told her I wanted her to get on a plane and come to New Zealand. When she landed, I sent Don to the airport. I'd told Don that my son Michael had flown over and I needed him to be picked up. Of course, Don was happy to see that it was actually Marlane who'd arrived, but I'm sure he knew something was going on.

When they got back to the hotel, we had a talk. He admitted that, yes, he had a problem, but that he couldn't just stop drinking cold turkey. I said I understood—even though I didn't—and that he could cut back gradually, but that I needed him to stop. Even with Marlane there, though, he didn't really cut back all that much.

*   *   *

Don and I were so close, but there were some things he did that I just couldn't understand. Maybe he'd started drinking because he was still carrying around the pain of having been abandoned as a child. I wondered for years after I met him if he even knew he'd been adopted. I knew about it because his Aunt Tootsie had told me, but I didn't know Don knew until we were sitting in my office one day in the '60s, listening to songwriter demos.

I had one of those desk chairs that would spin all the way around. I had my chair facing the speakers, and Don was sitting behind me on the other side of my desk. I put this demo on and sat there just sort of staring at the speakers, listening to a song by a writer named Gene Price. The guy in the song was asking his mother if she even stopped to kiss him when she left him at a stranger's door.

As I was turning my chair around to face Don, I was saying, "Man that really gets to your heart"—and that's when I realized Don was crying. It was the only time I ever saw him cry. Big ol' tears were just running down his cheeks. I knew right then and there that Don knew he'd been adopted.

Chapter
One Hundred and Ten

A LOT OF THE GUYS IN THE BAND HAD MOTORCYCLES. Jim Shaw and Don Rich both had Harleys. I absolutely hated motorcycles. The guy that built our recording studio—the very *day* he finished the job—he bought himself a new motorcycle and killed himself on it. After that, Jim sold his bike—and the kid he sold it to died on it less than a week later.

God, I detested those things. I'd cut out newspaper articles about people getting killed on motorcycles and tape 'em up on the wall in the studio so everybody could see 'em.

But no matter what I said, Don just wouldn't get rid of his. One day I finally told him, "Don, you're going to have to sell your motorcycle or you and me are going to have a fist fight. You've got to get rid of that thing and that's all there is to it."

Don said, "Chief, I'll make you a deal. I promise that I'll only ride it on dirt. I won't ride it on the street anymore."

Well, like a fool, I agreed to the deal because I figured it was the best I was going to get from him. I knew if he rode it on dirt trails, at least I wouldn't have to worry about him getting hit by a car or a truck. But of course he was still riding it on the street. He just didn't do it when I was around to see him. I didn't know enough about motorcycles to know you don't ride a Harley on a dirt trail. I just knew they were dangerous and deadly.

On July 17th, Don and Jim were in the studio, working on a Tony Booth album. Tony was one of the guys signed to Buck Owens Enterprises who we'd been having a little bit of success with on the country charts for a couple of years at that point. When I stopped by the studio to see how things were progressing, Don told me he was going to join his family at Morro Bay to go deep-sea fishing the next day. I thought he meant he was going to *leave* the next day—and I thought he meant he was going to be driving one of his cars since he'd already agreed that he wouldn't take his motorcycle on the road anymore.

The phone rang at 6:30 the next morning. It was my son, Michael, informing me of the accident. Don had been riding his motorcycle on Highway 1, and he was just a couple of miles away from Morro Bay when his bike hit the center divider.

Don Rich—my partner, my brother, my best friend—was dead.

PART VI

Cryin' Time Again

Chapter
One Hundred and Eleven

DON'S FUNERAL TOOK PLACE ON JULY 22ND at Hillcrest Memorial Chapel in Bakersfield. Even though I went to his funeral and saw him there in the casket, I couldn't accept the fact that he was gone.

I was in such bad shape that I was convinced he'd just show up one day like nothing had happened. I kept waiting, but he didn't come back. Years later, Jim Shaw told me he thought I'd had a nervous breakdown when Don died. To tell you the truth, it was a lot worse than that. Everything just seemed to close in all around me. I felt trapped inside this bubble I couldn't escape from.

A lot of times when someone dies, folks will say, "I can't believe so-and-so is gone." Well, in my case, I literally couldn't believe Don was gone. I just wasn't able to cope with it. I honestly thought I wasn't going to be able to survive, and there were days when I didn't really care if I survived or not.

I was an emotional and mental wreck. As hard as I've tried to explain it to people, there's no way I can properly express how it felt to have Don ripped away from me like that. I fell into a deep depression that I didn't think I would ever come out of—and there are still days when that depression hits me hard. It doesn't matter how many years pass. On the day Don died, something permanently changed inside me.

I've said it many times, but I'll say it again: Don Rich was as much a part of the Buck Owens Sound as I was. I was already signed to Capitol when I met Don, so I might've become a success on my own—but when Don came into the picture, he changed everything for the better. I don't think there's any way I can articulate how important he was to me, or to my music, because I don't think the words exist.

Chapter
One Hundred and Twelve

AFTER DON'S DEATH, weeks went by before I started thinking about performing again. I couldn't imagine being onstage without Don beside me. But Jack McFadden told me he thought the best thing for me to do would be to get back to work, so even though I dreaded the thought, we started auditioning guitar players.

I ended up hiring a guy from Fresno who was friends with Jim and Doyle. His name was Don Lee. When we went back out on the road, I'd look to my right and see Don, but it wasn't the Don I was expecting.

Just before Don Rich died, Capitol had released my next single— another of my humorous songs called "(It's a) Monster's Holiday." It was terrible timing. First of all, it was nowhere near Halloween—and secondly, I sure as hell didn't feel like laughing. But it became a Top Ten hit, and so did the next one.

"Great Expectations" came out in November, and made it to number eight on the charts in February of '75. It was the last single that had Don Rich on it, and it was the last Top Ten hit of my career on Capitol Records.

* * *

Right around the time "Great Expectations" came out, we went in to do our first recording session without Don. By then I'd added a fiddle player to the band. Her name was Jana Greif, but onstage she went by Jana Jae. I'd met her at a show we were doing in Redding, not long before Don died. She was a really unique musician because she played in orchestras and things like that, but she also played fiddle in a bluegrass group.

Anyway, she came backstage during intermission and introduced herself to me. When she told me she played the fiddle, I asked her if she had it with her. She said it was out in the car, so I told her to go grab it and come back and play something for me. When she came back, she played "Orange Blossom Special"—and she was *good*. I told her to stay close by when we went onstage because I wanted to have her come out and do "Orange Blossom Special" with Don. Well, she came out and she and Don just blew everybody away. They had real chemistry together.

After that night in Redding, Jana kept in touch with Jack McFadden. Of course, now that Don Rich was gone, we didn't have a fiddle player in the band anymore, so Jack suggested that it might be a good idea to add Jana to the lineup. She had showmanship, and she was pretty, and she could really play.

So, we went into my studio in late '74 and recorded a song that Jim Shaw had written with Dennis Knutson. It was called "41st Street Lonely Hearts' Club," and it was a fun one to do because the beginning of the song sounded a lot like "Act Naturally." We also had a fun ad campaign to promote the single, telling everybody that ol' Buck was looking for a wife.

The single scraped into the Top Twenty. Radio liked the B-side, too, which was a song called "Weekend Daddy" that I'd written with Danny Shatswell and Dennis—but that was pretty much the end of the line. Capitol put out two last singles. "Battle of New Orleans" didn't even reach number fifty, and "Country Singer's Prayer" didn't chart at all.

My contract was originally supposed to expire on May 31st, 1976, but me and the label mutually agreed to terminate it a few months early. In 1970, Capitol had named me the "Country Artist of the Decade." Thanks to being on *Hee Haw* every week, I was the most recognizable country singer in the world. But, as far as I'm concerned, it was also thanks to being on *Hee Haw* every week that I was no longer wanted by the label I'd provided with twenty number one hits.

Chapter
One Hundred and Thirteen

A S SOON AS THE WORD GOT OUT that my deal with Capitol was ending early, I got a call from Andy Wickham of Warner Bros. Records. Andy was a British chap based in LA who was a fan of mine. He said he wanted to sign me to Warner's, and that he thought Norro Wilson would be the perfect person to produce my records.

Now, Norro was a really good songwriter with a lot of hits under his belt, and he'd eventually become a very successful record producer. But, at that point, he was just starting his record-producing career. I know he'd produced an album by Asleep At The Wheel, which was a modern-day Western Swing band, but I don't think he'd produced much else yet. Hell, I wouldn't have minded doing a Western Swing album myself. That would've actually been fun. But that's not what Andy and Norro had in mind. They said they wanted me to go down to Nashville and make a country-pop record. If it had been two or three years earlier, I would've fought 'em tooth and nail. I did put up a little bit of a struggle at the beginning because I wanted to record things my own way and at my own studio in Bakersfield. But, to tell you the truth, I didn't have much fight left in me as far as my music was concerned.

So, I went to Nashville and recorded an album using Nashville studio musicians. That should pretty much tell you all you need to know about how much I cared. But Andy really believed it would work, and Norro believed it would, too.

Well, it didn't.

The only good thing about that album was the title—*Buck 'Em*. A few years earlier, Capitol wouldn't even let me say "damn" in one of my songs. Now I had an album out on Warner Bros. that was probably the most suggestive title in the history of country music up to that point. But it wasn't the title that caused the record to do so poorly. It was the music on it.

264

Well, the label started putting out singles right and left. The first one, "Hollywood Waltz," made it to the mid-forties on the charts. The next one, "California Okie," also made it to the mid-forties on the charts. The next one, "World Famous Holiday Inn," made it to number ninety on the charts. The next one, "It's Been a Long, Long Time" entered the charts at the lowest possible spot—one hundred—and that's as high as it got. And the album? It didn't touch the album charts at all.

But it was really every bit as much my fault as it was Norro's. I sang the songs the way he said he wanted me to, but my heart just wasn't in it. Part of the problem was being in Nashville. Part of the problem was using musicians I wasn't familiar with. Part of problem was not writing most of the songs myself like I'd always done before. But most of the problem was that I just couldn't do it without Don Rich.

Chapter
One Hundred and Fourteen

RIGHT IN THE MIDDLE OF MY STRING of flops for Warner Bros.—just when I was thinking things couldn't get any worse—my dad passed away. He died of leukemia on August 26th, 1976, at the age of sixty-seven.

I guess not many people from his generation were comfortable with showing affection in an outgoing way. It just wasn't done—especially not by the menfolk. My mother and I could say, "I love you" to each other, but it was really hard for my dad to say those words. Well, I loved my daddy and I wanted him to know it, so during his last few years, every once in a while I'd tell him that I loved him. Let me tell you boy, it made him uncomfortable as hell because he wouldn't even respond—just stony silence. The only time he ever told me he loved me was when we were talking on the phone once. As we were getting ready to hang up, I told him, "I love you, dad." Before he had a chance to think about it, he said, "I love you, too." And that's the only time he ever said those words to me.

*　*　*

By 1977, Jennifer Joyce had been living with me for quite a while—first at the place we had in Bear Valley Springs, and then at the ranch I'd bought north of Bakersfield in '74. Our house sat on a hundred and sixty acres of land, with the nearest neighbor not near at all.

We were happy and I was very much in love with her. But like I've said so many times already, my biggest problem in life has always been having too many women at the same time. Jennifer had horses and all sorts of animals she loved tending to at the ranch, so she didn't go on the road with me anymore. So, Jennifer was back at home, and right there on the road with me was Jana Jae.

Jana Jae was a lovely lady with two children. She was very intelligent, pretty, talented—all of those things, and, well, Jana and I got involved. In fact, we got a lot more than involved. On May 2nd, 1977, we got married at one of those wedding chapels in Las Vegas.

I'll tell you right now, if the good Lord was to say to me, "Buck, I'll let you take back one thing you did in your whole life," that one thing would be to take back what happened with me and Jana Jae. Not only did I pierce Jennifer's heart, but before it was over, I'd pierced Jana's heart, too. I caused everybody so much pain.

It was madness—my madness. I was in love with one woman, and now I was married to another one. Me and Jana Jae got married on a Monday, and when I woke up on Tuesday morning in the honeymoon suite at the Landmark Hotel in Las Vegas, I realized what a mistake I'd made.

Years later, I concocted a story about how I'd taken diet pills and drunk a bottle and a half of wine—and the next thing I knew, I was married to somebody I didn't mean to marry. But the truth is, I wasn't drunk on wine—I was drunk on Jana Jae. Even though I was so happy living with Jennifer, I kept proposing to Jana when we were on the road. I know it sounds crazy, but Jana made me feel like I'd never felt before. When I was with her, it was like she put me in a trance. It wasn't exactly love—it was more like hypnosis. I knew marrying Jana Jae was going to hurt Jennifer, but I wasn't capable of sound thinking. And then—just like that—I'd proposed again, this time she'd accepted, and now we were married.

When we got back to Bakersfield, I didn't know what to do. The first thing I did was to tell my sister Dorothy to let Jennifer know what had happened before she learned about it on the national news. Dorothy told me later that Jennifer had fallen to her knees, just wailing and sobbing. She couldn't understand why I'd do such a thing. Of course, there was no way I could explain it to her because I didn't understand why I'd done it either.

I couldn't face Jennifer, and I couldn't face Jana Jae, so I just disappeared. A day or two later I filed for an annulment. Then a couple of weeks after that, I filed to retract the annulment papers and tried to get Jana to come back. I took out ads in newspapers, apologizing to Jana Jae for being such a fool. So, a couple of months after we got married, she came back and lived at the ranch for a while. But there was no way it was going to last. By August I'd filed for divorce.

Meanwhile, I'd had Dorothy move Jennifer up to the place in Bear Valley Springs. So, even while Jana Jae was still living with me and her kids at the ranch, I was making trips up to Bear Valley Springs, begging Jennifer to forgive me.

Over the course of just a few months, I'd managed to create total chaos in my personal life. My professional life was getting pretty chaotic, too.

Chapter
One Hundred and Fifteen

MY FIRST ALBUM FOR WARNER BROS. had been such a monumental failure that we decided to all get together and do it again. The second album—which, just like the first one, never touched the charts—was called *Our Old Mansion*. When the title song was released as a single, it did a lot better than my last single had—it went all the way to number ninety-one before it fell off the charts. The next one—a song I wrote called "Texas Tornado"—might as well have not come out at all.

In 1976, England Dan & John Ford Coley had a lot of success on the pop charts with "Nights Are Forever Without You." A couple of years later, when my version of the song came out and went to number twenty-seven on the country charts, everybody at Warner Bros. was celebrating my "big hit." Hell, over a half-dozen of the B-sides of some of my Capitol singles had done better than that.

Since my cover of a pop hit had done so well, Norro Wilson decided we should try that same formula again. So, I covered the Top Forty song "Do You Wanna Make Love"—but it turned out that formula of me covering a pop hit only worked once.

Then, finally, we did something right. I recorded a duet with the beautiful Emmylou Harris.

I've always loved Emmylou. She told me once that when people would ask her to define country music, she'd tell 'em to just listen to my recording of "Second Fiddle," and they'd learn all they needed to know. But I don't love her just because of that. I love her voice, and I love the fact that she's a sweet person, and such a big proponent of country music and country music history.

This story's a little complicated, but I'll do my best to explain what happened. There were these two guys named Charles Stewart and Jerry Abbott who had written a song called "Play 'Together Again' Again." It was a song about my song, and since my song was in their song, I got a co-writer credit, which was nice. But more important than that, since Emmylou was also on Warner Bros. Records, Norro came up with the idea of me and Emmylou doing the song as a duet.

It really made a lot of sense, too, because I'd had a number one hit with "Together Again" back in '63, and Emmylou had had her first number one country hit with her version of "Together Again" in '76. Got all that?

OK, so in March of '79, I went to Emmylou's house and we recorded "Play 'Together Again' Again" at her place, using this remote recording studio called the Enactron Truck that was built by Brian Ahern—the fellow who was her husband at the time.

Warner Bros. put the single out the next month, and country radio just ate it up. Those program directors and deejays knew that I'd written "Together Again" and had a hit with it—and, of course, they knew Emmylou had had a big hit with the song, too—so they thought it was really cool that me and Emmylou had recorded a new song that was about this old song that had been a hit for both of us.

Chapter
One Hundred and Sixteen

M Y SINGLE WITH EMMYLOU CAME OUT IN APRIL, and while it was on its way up the charts, me and Jennifer Joyce Smith got married. That's right. We were finally together, again.

By 1979, Jennifer had forgiven me for all the grief I'd put her through with the whole Jana Jae thing. That year we were spending part of the winter up at Bear Valley Springs. We'd taken a couple of her horses up there, and we had our new Rottweiler puppy with us. The puppy was just a couple of months old. Well, it snowed one day, and there was five or six inches of snow on the ground. Jennifer had gone out to feed her horses, so I was sitting there by the big picture window, watching a football game on TV.

When I looked out the window, I saw her coming back toward the house—and there was that little black puppy, jumping high in the snow, trying to stay close to Jennifer.

I sat there and thought, "I'm just like that puppy. How in the world would I ever get along without Jennifer?"

When she came in, I said, "You wanna get married?"

Jennifer looked at me and said, "Oh, I don't know. I guess I haven't thought about it in a long time."

Well, it took some convincing on my part, but on June 21st, 1979, we got married in my office, with just a small number of our family members present.

A few years later, we re-did our wedding vows, and that time we did the whole thing with the big wedding dress and the photos and hundreds of people.

Jennifer Joyce is not only my companion—she's the absolute love of my life.

Chapter
One Hundred and Seventeen

MY DUET WITH EMMYLOU ENDED UP being the biggest hit I'd have while I was under contract to Warner Bros. "Play 'Together Again' Again" went to number eleven on the charts. But just like what happened with me and Rose Maddox back in my Capitol days, nobody at Warner's was interested in rushing us back into the studio to see if we could score another hit together while we were hot.

But I have to give Warner Bros. credit. After two albums that went nowhere, and after more than half a dozen solo singles that didn't go very far, they stuck with me. So, I began recording the tracks for what was supposed to be my third album for the label. I'd go in the studio and cut some songs, and then every few months Warner's would release a new single. One single after another failed to get much traction on the charts, so it was becoming pretty clear to all of us that my days of having hits was probably behind me.

Warner Bros. decided not to even bother putting out that third album, and I couldn't blame 'em. When Warner Bros. walked away, I walked away, too—and not just from the business of making records.

In August of '79 I'd turned 50 years old. With the Warner Bros. debacle behind me, at the beginning of 1980 I called the Buckaroos together and told 'em my touring days were over. If I decided to play a gig every once in a while, I'd let 'em know—but there'd be no more tours, no more package shows, no more days in the recording studio trying to come up with that next hit. I had so many businesses going that I gave jobs to all the Buckaroos that wanted to stay with me—and most of 'em did.

Of course, they were disappointed about my decision not to tour or record anymore. Nobody wants the music to end. But, to tell you the truth, the music had already ended for me the day Don Rich died.

Like I've said many, many times about that whole "being famous" thing, Lady Limelight can be pretty goddamn fickle about how long she's going to let her light shine on you. I could've kept touring. I could've found another record deal. I could've kept writing songs. But before Lady Limelight could get her finger on that switch, I just reached out and turned her light off myself.

Chapter
One Hundred and Eighteen

IN EARLY 1980, I was asked to play a part in one of those made-for-TV movies that used to be on all the time. I jokingly told everybody the director wanted me because he'd been real impressed with my work in *From Nashville with Music*.

The movie was on ABC and it was called *Murder Can Hurt You!* It was a comedy that poked fun at cop shows and detective shows. Back in the '70s and early '80s, those kinds of shows were the big thing on TV: Raymond Burr was in one about a detective named Robert T. Ironside. He went around in a wheelchair solving crimes. Paul Michael Glaser and David Soul starred in a show called *Starsky and Hutch*. Robert Blake was a private detective in *Baretta*. Peter Falk was a police lieutenant in *Columbo*. The beautiful Angie Dickinson played Pepper Anderson in *Police Woman*. Telly Savalas was the star of *Kojak*. And Dennis Weaver starred in *Mc-Cloud* as this marshal from Taos, New Mexico who'd become a cop in New York City for some reason. His character's name was Sam McCloud.

So, like I said, this movie I was in was making fun of all of those characters. *In Murder Can Hurt You!*, Victor Buono played Ironbottom. John Byner and Jamie Farr were Studsky and Hatch. Tony Danza was Lambretta. Burt Young was Lieutenant Palumbo. Connie Stevens played Salty Sanderson. Gavin McLeod was Nojack. And then there was me. Since I'm an old country boy like Dennis Weaver, they had me play Sheriff Tim MacSkye.

Well, once again, I didn't win any awards for my acting skills—and the names of the characters was probably the funniest thing about that whole movie—but at least I wasn't standing in a cornfield or getting hit in the ass by a fencepost.

Yes, even though I'd decided to stop touring and making records, I was still hanging onto *Hee Haw*. By 1980, I'd spent the last eleven years of my life going down to Nashville twice a year to tape my segments of the show.

I could write a whole book just about my years with Junior Samples, Grandpa Jones, Minnie Pearl, Archie Campbell, Gordie Tapp, Don Harron, Stringbean, Lulu Roman, Cathy Baker, Victoria Hallman, Linda Thompson, Misty Rowe, Barbi Benton, Gunilla Hutton, George "Goober" Lindsay, Lisa Todd, Roni Stoneman, Sandy Lyle, Bill Davis, Bob Boatman, and all the rest. Every time we'd get together to tape new episodes of the show, it was always like old home week.

Well, in case I don't get around to writing a whole book about *Hee Haw*, I'll just tell you a couple of quick stories. One has to do with Lulu Roman. Lulu was from Dallas, but I met her in Oklahoma City in the mid-'60s. We were taping *The Buck Owens Ranch Show*, and I saw her performing at a big hotel there while I was in town. I told her that night that I was going to make her a big star. I meant it, too. I always thought she had that special something that would appeal to a mass audience. Now, she tells the story a lot funnier than I do, so I'll tell her version. When folks ask her how she ended up on *Hee Haw*, she tells 'em that John and Frank had a list of the type of people they wanted on the show—a beautiful blonde; a beautiful brunette; a girl-next-door type; a boy-next-door type; one fat, dumb guy; and one fat, dumb woman. Then she says, "When Buck saw that list, he said, 'I've got your woman.

She lives in Dallas.'" And she always ends the story by saying, "I was the beautiful blonde."

Now if you ever saw Lulu Roman on *Hee Haw*, you know which one she really was. But I've always been real proud of her and all of her success—and I'm especially proud that I was the one who was responsible for getting her on the show.

The other thing I'm proud of is what Miss Minnie Pearl used to say about me. She used to tell the other cast members that I was the "Cary Grant of Country Music." When I found out she'd been saying that, I didn't know what she meant because me and Cary Grant sure don't look alike—and he's a slightly better actor. So, when I got the opportunity, I finally asked her, "Minnie, what's this I hear about you calling me the 'Cary Grant of Country Music?'"

She told me, "I had the opportunity to work with Cary Grant many years ago. He was always on time, he always looked so nice, and he always knew all of his lines." Then she paid me a real compliment. She said, "I admire you so much because you're a real professional—just like Cary Grant."

Well, it was one of the nicest things anybody ever said to ol' Buck—and coming from someone who had been in the business as long as Minnie Pearl had, it meant an awful lot to me.

Eventually though, as the years wore on, my part on the show seemed to become less and less important. Now, I loved Miss Minnie and all of the other comedians who were in the cast, but I'd joined the show because I thought it would be a great thing to have a national TV show that featured a lot of country music. But over time, *Hee Haw* went from being about half country music and about half comedy to being a comedy show with some country music in it. And since Roy was the musician in the cast getting all the comedy spots, there just wasn't a whole lot left for me to do. But I stuck around anyway.

Starting around the late '70s, at the beginning of every season I'd say to myself, "Okay, Buck, this is gonna be your last year. As soon as we finish taping this season's shows, you're gonna tell 'em you're gettin' the hell out of Kornfield Kounty for good." But I couldn't bring myself to do it because I couldn't justify turning down that big paycheck for just a few week's work twice a year. So, I kept whoring myself out to that cartoon donkey.

Then, in '86, the producers decided to cut back expenses by getting rid of some of the cast, including the Hagers and Don Harron and the beautiful, voluptuous Lisa Todd. When they said they were going to have to start cutting salaries on some of the other folks—including me—I decided the time had come to make my escape. I resigned that March, and ended my seventeen-year run as cohost of the show.

A few years later, Roy Clark wrote a book about his life—and, of course, he included some stories about our years together on *Hee Haw*. He called me a country music legend in one paragraph, but a couple of paragraphs later he called me a prima donna when he related his version of an incident that took place on the set one day—an incident that I recall a whole lot different than he did in his book.

One of the guys who was an important part of the show was Sam Lovullo. While John Aylesworth and Frank Peppiatt were called the creators and executive producers in the credits, Sam was the one who did the real on-the-scene producing of the show.

Well, one day I had a flight booked that I had to catch. I told Sam about it the day before, and I even told Roy about it because he was notorious for showing up late. I told Roy I really needed him to be on time the next day because I was throwing a big party for the governor of California at my ranch in Bakersfield, and I couldn't be late to my own party. Roy said not to worry, he'd be there by nine o'clock. Well, he didn't show up at nine, and he didn't show up at ten, and he didn't show up at eleven.

In his book, Roy didn't say anything about being late. He said the delay was caused when one of the cameramen missed a shot and we had to do a retake. He said that I got mad about having to do the scene over again—and then he said that I called Sam Lovullo out of the control room and started yelling at him because I wanted to leave. It wasn't a case of me wanting to leave. I *had* to leave and Sam knew it, and Roy knew it, too. But instead of yelling at my cohost for causing us to be so far behind, I yelled at Sam. The way I saw it, Sam was in charge, so he was responsible for getting Roy there on time and for getting things wrapped up in time for me to catch my flight. At that point, though, I guess it had pretty much become Roy's show, and the producer didn't want to do anything to upset Roy.

I was pretty surprised that Roy would tell the story the way he did in his book. I really thought it was uncalled for. But I have to tell you this: I might've yelled at Sam Lovullo because I thought I was going to miss my flight, but me and Roy never had a harsh word between us in all those years we were doing *Hee Haw*—and seventeen years is a mighty long time to go without getting into a single argument with somebody.

*   *   *

A couple of years before I left *Hee Haw*, I sold my music publishing company. Blue Book Music had brought in a lot of money since the days me and Harlan Howard first formed the company back in 1957, and it brought in a whole lot all at once when I sold it.

There was a company in Nashville called Tree Music Publishing that a man named Jack Stapp owned for many years. In fact, that's the same company Harlan Howard was getting ready to sign with when he sold me his half of Blue Book Music. Anyway, after Jack died, one of the executives there at Tree—a guy named Buddy Killen—bought the company. And once Buddy had bought Tree Music, he started looking for other publishing catalogs to buy. Blue Book was one of the biggest independent country music publishing companies around in those days, thanks to songs of mine and Merle Haggard's and Red Simpson's and Don Rich's and a lot of other songwriters. Well, Buddy kept raising his price, and when he got to $1,600,000, I finally said, "The price is right!"

Chapter
One Hundred and Nineteen

ONE OF THE SADDEST DAYS OF MY LIFE was May 27th, 1986. That was the day my mother passed away. She died of congestive heart failure, but just like my dad and my brother Melvin, she'd had her own bout with cancer in her later years.

She always talked to me a lot more openly than my dad ever did. Of course, like I said before, a lot of the men from his generation just weren't very good at expressing their emotions. But my mom told me many times how proud she was of the things I'd accomplished. She told me my dad was proud of me, too. I guess it was easier for him to tell my mom how he felt about me than it was for him to tell me himself.

Not long before she died, my mom told me her dreams were complete because she'd been living vicariously through me. Those were her exact words. She'd been a musician all her life, but she was never once in the spotlight. She told me I'd done all the things she'd ever wanted to do, and that was good enough for her. I was just happy that I'd been able to help make the last half of her life so much easier than the first half had been.

Since I'd quit touring—and even quit *Hee Haw* by then—I'm sure during her last few years that my mom thought my professional career was pretty much over. I did, too. I had developed other interests, and I was enjoying spending time with Jennifer at the ranch. The music business was about the last thing on my mind.

Well, not long after my mom passed on, I started hearing about this country singer named Dwight Yoakam. Some of the guys from my radio stations started telling me they'd seen a report here and heard an interview there where Dwight was saying that he was a big supporter of the music of Buck Owens. He said he thought it was a shame that country disc jockeys and other folks in the business had forgotten about me. Evan Bridwell, my program director at KUZZ, told me he thought a Buck Owens revival was coming soon. I told him, "It's fine with me if there's a Buck Owens revival as long as I don't have to attend."

Then, one day in September of 1987, my secretary, Lee Ann Enns, came into my office and said, "There's a guy out here that says he's Dwight Yoakam and he wants to see you."

I said, "Lee Ann, is it Dwight Yoakam or not?"

She said, "It *looks* like him. He's sure skinny!"

I said, "Well, send him in here and let's find out."

So the guy came in and, sure enough, it was Dwight. He was a big ol' tall boy, at least six feet when he had his boots on. He was just matchstick thin, and the knees of his jeans were worn away. I liked him from the moment I met him. We hit it off right away, and I could tell from that very first meeting that me and him were going to be good friends.

He told me he was appearing at our fair, the Kern County Fair, and he asked me to come out to his show. I had only been to one other person's show out there. I had gone to see George Strait one year and he'd asked me to sing a few songs with him. But I knew that the folks around Bakersfield had seen me a jillion times, and I knew they paid good money to see George Strait, so I declined. But, with Dwight, for some reason, when he asked me if I would perform at the fair with him, I said, "Hell, yeah! Let's do it."

So that night, I was there at the fair, standing just offstage while Dwight did a few of his songs. And as soon as he said, "Please join me in welcoming Bakersfield's favorite son, Buck Owens," the place turned absolutely electric.

When he and I started singing together, the response from the crowd was overwhelming. In all my years, I'd never experienced anything like that. I think we did about five of my songs, and then I sang with him on "Little Ways," which had been a big hit for him that summer.

It was a great night, and I'd be lying if I said it didn't get my juices flowing a little bit—but I figured it was just a one-and-done deal. Once again, I was wrong.

PART VII

"Streets of Bakersfield"

Chapter
One Hundred and Twenty

A FEW WEEKS AFTER ME AND DWIGHT had our big night at the Kern County Fair, I got a call from some guy at CBS who said that the network was going to be doing a special on country music. He said Merle had been asked to be on the show, so he wanted to know if I'd come, too. That way, the guy said, me and Merle could represent the West Coast Sound. I remember I told him, "I'll do your show, and Merle can represent the West Coast Sound if he wants to, but I'll be representing the Bakersfield Sound."

The guy said, "Fine. Whatever. And can you please bring a song that the two of you can sing together on the show?"

Well, I started going through all of my old records, trying to find a song that would work. I figured Merle wouldn't want to sing one of my hits, and I'd feel a little funny singing one of his, so it took me quite a while to come up with something that seemed right—until I dug out that old Capitol album, *Ain't It Amazing, Gracie*. I saw that title, "Streets of Bakersfield," and listened to the song for probably the first time since the album came out in 1974. I thought, "This is the one!"

Then—wouldn't you know it—the guy from CBS called about a week before the show and said Merle wasn't going to be on it after all. I don't know if Merle cancelled on 'em, or if they ever really asked him to be on the show in the first place, but after breaking that bit of news to me, the guy said, "Is there somebody else based on the West Coast that you can bring with you?"

I didn't even have to think about it. I said, "How about Dwight Yoakam?"

The guy said, "Fine. Just remember to bring a song with you that the two of you can sing together."

Dwight was flying from LA and I was flying from Bakersfield, so we met in the Dallas airport, on our way to tape the show back East. I gave him a cassette of "Streets of Bakersfield," and I said, "Dwight, learn this. This is the song we're gonna be doing together."

So, Dwight learned the song, we sang it together on the TV special, and all of a sudden there was a big hullaballoo about it. Disc jockeys called me from all over the country—even from Canada. They had taped the TV show and wanted to know if they could play the audio portion of me and Dwight singing "Streets of Bakersfield" on their radio stations. I said, "Well, I reckon you could. It's all right as far as I'm concerned, and I'm sure Dwight wouldn't care."

Now, I'd thought my recording days were long over by then, but I could tell from the reaction we were getting—without even having a record out—that "Streets of Bakersfield" could be a hit if I could just convince Dwight that we should get into a studio and cut the thing. Hell, I figured it was the least he could do since it was all his fault that I'd been bit by the music bug again in the first place.

Well, he finally agreed that we should record it, so we did. In fact, we cut it at Capitol Studios. After we finished the vocals and everything else, Flaco Jimenez came into the studio and added his Tex-Mex accordion part, which turned the record into something really special. To my ears, the track was so good that I felt like it should be more than just a cut on Dwight's next album. I thought it should be his next single. But Dwight seemed pretty nervous about that idea. He'd already had a half-dozen Top Ten singles as a solo artist over the course of just a couple of years, so I'm sure he thought it was awfully early in his career to start putting out duets—especially when, in this case, his duet partner was fifty-nine years old.

Even though he'd had a lot of hits in a pretty short time, the one thing he didn't have yet was a number one record. So, I said, "Dwight, I guarantee if you release that song as a single, it will go to the top of the charts. You'll finally have your first number one."

Well, he hemmed and hawed about it for a while, but finally he agreed. Of course, we had to do a video, too. The director thought that might be something new to me, but I told him I damn near invented the idea when we filmed "Sweet Rosie Jones" twenty years earlier. I did have a little problem with the "Streets of Bakersfield" video, though, because we didn't shoot it in Bakersfield. Can you believe that? It was shot up there in Delano, California, about thirty miles north of where the streets of Bakersfield actually are. The only scene in the video that took place in Bakersfield was a shot of the famous Bakersfield sign that went across the old Highway 99. Now, I thought the video came out great, but I still feel like it was downright sacrilegious to shoot the damn thing in Delano.

The single and the video came out in June of '88, and that record slowly started heading up the charts. Man, I'm telling you, it took its time—but on October 15th, "Streets of Bakersfield" finally claimed that number one spot. It was Dwight's first number one of his career, and it was my twenty-first. It was also the first number one single I'd had in sixteen years—and it felt great.

Chapter
One Hundred and Twenty-One

YOU KNOW, I've achieved a lot of things during my years in the music business, but one of the things I managed to do that nobody had ever done before in country music, or in any other style of music for that matter—and I'd put money on it never happening again—was to be the first artist to ever record a number one single without having a record deal.

Hell, I wasn't looking for one, either. But before all of the excitement over "Streets of Bakersfield" died down, I got a call from Jim Foglesong at Capitol Records, asking me to come back to my old label. Having so much fun singing with Dwight was what caused me to want to record again, but I hadn't really thought about going back into the studio and making a whole album on my own. I have to admit, though, I was happy to see a major record label was still interested in me—a man of my age who'd been away from the whole music scene for so long. But I guess ol' Jim just couldn't have me sitting out there unsigned while I had a hit single on the charts. So, at an age when most country artists are getting dropped from their labels for being too old, I signed with Capitol and went into the studio to cut my first new album in eleven years.

It wasn't like recording for Warner Bros. either, thank God. I got to record it on the West Coast, and I got to use my own band. My own recording studio wasn't active anymore, so we recorded the album in Fresno—a town even farther away from Nashville than Bakersfield, which was fine with me. Jim Shaw produced the album and played keyboards. My bass player, Doyle Curtsinger was still with me. So was Terry Christofferson, who'd been my guitarist and steel player since April of '75. My brand new drummer was Jim McCarty. And then there was Ralph Mooney. Ralph had played steel on some of my earliest Capitol records, so it was great to have him back with me after all those years. I also got Dwight to come help me re-do "Under Your Spell Again" as a duet.

In fact, a lot of the songs were ones I'd recorded before, including "Don't Let Her Know," "Second Fiddle," and "Hot Dog." By 1988, I wasn't worried anymore about offending anybody by recording a rockabilly song. So, when "Hot Dog" came out as a single, I used my real name this time around.

Since we knew "Hot Dog" was going to be the first single, we decided that would be the title of the album, too. I went down to LA and did the cover shot at this famous old hot dog stand—the one that's shaped like a hot dog—called Tail o' the Pup.

It was a good time again for country music in the late '80s. There were a bunch of artists having hits doing country music the way I'd done it in the '60s. The press called 'em the "new traditionalists." So, on the back of the album, I dedicated *Hot Dog!* to those guys—Dwight, of course, and Randy Travis, Ricky Skaggs, Rodney Crowell, Keith Whitley, and several others.

Well, it turned out that their new records sold a lot more copies than my new one did. But I was happy that my album and single both hit the charts, which was more than I could say for some of my singles and both of my albums on Warner Bros.

Hot Dog! had come out in November, and then, in December, the Country Music Foundation in Nashville re-released my old *Carnegie Hall*

Concert album on CD. Remember, I'd gotten the rights to all of my Capitol masters back several years earlier, so I let the CMF release it. And the really great thing about it was that they included the whole concert instead of using the shorter version that Capitol had put out in '66. So, for the first time, folks got to hear several more songs from the show, and all of our comedy routines. I thought it was interesting that the Nashville-based Country Music Foundation—which is part of the Country Music Association—was finally showing some interest in this ol' boy from Bakersfield. It seemed like things might be changing a little bit down there.

Of course, some things never change. Me and Dwight got a CMA nomination for our duet of "Streets of Bakersfield," but we didn't win.

Chapter
One Hundred and Twenty-Two

BETWEEN RECORDING *Hot Dog!* and everything else I was doing that year, I began touring a little bit with Dwight Yoakam and his band. He'd do these really long tours, so I'd mainly just fly in on the weekends to wherever he was playing, and I'd do the Friday and Saturday night shows with him. It was great fun for me. Every night, when he'd introduce me, the audience was so receptive. Hell, I was just thrilled they remembered who I was. Every single night I'd get a big standing "O," and it seemed like the cheers and applause was never going to stop.

So, I'd go out there and sing a bunch of my hits, and then Dwight would come out and sing some songs. Then, right in the middle of his set, he'd have me come back out and sing "Streets of Bakersfield" with him. After our song was over, I'd leave the stage, and then that would be it for me for the evening.

And every night, after we'd finish doing "Streets of Bakersfield," I'd stand backstage and watch. It seemed to me that it was extremely hard for Dwight to get the audience to stay enthusiastic for the rest of his show after we'd done our duet. Every single night, it was the same problem.

Now, I'm just an ol' country boy from Texas, but I've got to tell you, one thing I know about—and I don't think very many people would disagree with me on this—is show business. I know how to entertain a crowd. Back in the late '80s I'd been performing longer than Dwight had been alive. So, I decided to try to be helpful.

I went to Dwight's manager, R.C. Bradley, and I said, "Look, why don't we do this? Instead of me coming back in the middle of Dwight's set to do "Streets of Bakersfield," why don't we just save it and do it as the encore? That way, Dwight won't have to spend the rest of the night trying to win the crowd back after we do the song."

I mean, I thought Dwight was suffering needlessly. It had to be painful to hit that same lull in the show every night I was on tour with him, and then spend so much of the rest of the show trying to get his momentum back. But R.C. finally said to me, "Look, Buck. Dwight thinks it's best for people to leave the venue thinking they've been to a Dwight Yoakam concert—not a Dwight and Buck concert—and I think that's what's best for him, too."

Naturally, I disagreed with that line of thinking, but I didn't put up a fight. It was Dwight's show, and I was just along for the ride. So, he could do whatever he wanted to, of course. I was just trying to help him because he had been so helpful to me.

A lot of the press at that time was talking about how Dwight Yoakam was responsible for my comeback, and they were absolutely right. The only problem I had with the whole thing was that some of the stories weren't exactly accurate. By then I was already a pretty successful businessman with radio stations and quite a few other interests keeping me busy. But some of those reporters made it sound like I was spending my days sitting on my front porch in a rocking chair, counting cars as they drove by, drinking iced tea and swatting flies. According to some of those articles, Dwight showed up, pulled me out of my rocker, and got me going again. Well, he didn't exactly pull me out of my rocker, but he definitely got me going again.

Me and Dwight have been wonderful friends ever since that day he first came to my office. He's an incredible talent, both as a singer and an actor. And if it hadn't been for Dwight, I wouldn't have toured any more. I wouldn't have had my twenty-first number one record. I wouldn't have signed a new record deal. I wouldn't have made a bunch of new fans. He changed my life for the better.

If people still thought of me at all before "Streets of Bakersfield" came out, they were probably thinking of that character from *Hee Haw*. Dwight is the one who made people think of Buck Owens as a serious country artist again—and I'll always be grateful to him for that.

Chapter
One Hundred and Twenty-Three

I HAVE TO HAND IT TO THE FOLKS AT CAPITOL RECORDS. They did everything they could to promote the hell out of *Hot Dog!* Even though the first single had only made it into the forties on the charts, they put out a second single in January, and then a third one in March. Unfortunately for Capitol and me both, each record did a little worse than the one before.

But, I didn't want to look like I wasn't holding up my end of the bargain—and I sure didn't want folks to think I'd gone back to counting cars in my rocking chair, so I went back out on the road with my latest gang of Buckaroos. And I don't mean just a couple of gigs here and there. In late March of '89, we headed back overseas for the first time in several years.

Before we left, though, I got an idea. So, I picked up the phone and called Ringo Starr. I said, "Me and the Buckaroos are doing a European tour in March. Do you wanna have some fun?"

He didn't even ask what I had in mind. He just said, "Sure!"

I told him I was back with Capitol Records again, and that I thought it might be a blast if the two of us went to Abbey Road Studios and recorded "Act Naturally" together. Remember, Ringo's the one who sang the lead vocal on the Beatles' version back in '65.

He said, "Let's do it. Just say when."

We met him there at Abbey Road on March 27th. I figured since this was Ringo Starr we're talking about, he'd come with a big entourage—or at least an assistant or two. But he just came walking in by himself, said "hi" to everybody, and we went to work.

Now, as exciting as it was to get to record with Ringo, I have to tell you that just walking up those steps that lead into Abbey Road Studios caused me to get chilly bumps all over. Being right there, doing that song in the same studio where the Beatles had recorded so many of their hits was an indescribable experience. For an old Beatles fan like me, it was just about as excited as I've ever been—standing up, anyway.

On the session there at Abbey Road, me and Ringo just sang. I didn't play guitar and he didn't play drums. We let the Buckaroos just do their thing. Lord knows they'd played the song enough times to have it down pretty well by then. The only extra guy we brought in was Reggie Young to play lead guitar. If you don't already know who Reggie is, he's the guy who played on all those great records they made down at American Sound Studios in Memphis. He played on sessions with Elvis, Dusty Springfield, Willie Nelson, Johnny Cash, Merle—just a bunch of great artists. And he did a fine job on our record, too.

Of course, I knew it would have to be the first single off my next album, so that meant we'd need to make a video. All I can tell you is, if you've never seen the video me and Ringo made for "Act Naturally," you need to. We shot it on this set of an old Western town, and we had a blast.

If you remember the TV show, *Alice*, then you remember Mel from Mel's Diner. The guy who played Mel was Vic Tayback. Well, Vic played the bartender in the saloon me and Ringo strolled into at the beginning of the video. We were both dressed in our cowboy outfits, and we were both wearing those long western coats called dusters. So, at that point in the video, we turned to each other and started knocking the dust off of each other's dusters—and we did that for several seconds, until the whole saloon was just filled with this fake dust stuff. We could barely see each other by the time we finished the scene. It was so funny that ol' Vic had a really hard time trying to keep a straight face when the camera was on him.

The single and the video came out that June, and it made a lot of noise. I think the video might've been more popular than the record was. But, the single managed to reach number twenty-seven on the charts. Ringo told me he'd always been a big country music fan, so he was happy to have his first single to hit the country charts, even though it wasn't a huge hit.

Lo and behold, just like had happened with me and Dwight the year before, me and Ringo got a CMA nomination for "Vocal Event of the Year." And just like what happened with me and Dwight, we lost. We got nominated for a Grammy, too, for "Best Country Vocal Collaboration," but we lost again.

We lost both times to a duet of "Tears in My Beer" by Hank Williams Sr. and Hank Jr. Hey, nobody wants to lose, but it's really hard to beat the guy who's probably the most revered figure in the history of country music—especially when he makes a new record after he's been dead for thirty-six years.

*   *   *

My next album, *Act Naturally*, came out in late '89. Even though it had the duet with Ringo on it, and a new duet with Emmylou Harris, it didn't make the charts. The album had some new songs I'd written on it, including one I really believed in called "I Was There"—but Capitol thought the re-make of my old hit "Gonna Have Love" should be the next single. I don't know if "I Was There" would've been a hit or not, but "Gonna Have Love" sure wasn't—at least not this time around.

Chapter
One Hundred and Twenty-Four

NINETEEN NINETY GOT OFF TO A TERRIBLE START. On January 3rd, my older sister passed away. Mary Ethel was just sixty-two years old. She died of arteriosclerosis—hardening of the arteries—but she'd also had cancer, just like my mom and dad and Melvin. Mary Ethel—well, she loved me the way a sister loves a brother—but she was also just the biggest fan of Buck Owens, the country singer. Going all the way back to when I was on Pep Records, I remember her taking my singles around to all the radio stations in the area that played country music. She'd drop my latest single off at a station and tell 'em, "You need to play this record because this guy Buck Owens is gonna be big!" Bless her heart, she believed in me from the very beginning.

* * *

That same year, I recorded my last album for Capitol. It was called *Kickin' In*. On the other two albums, I'd gotten to record with my own band, and I'd gotten to do those duets with Dwight and Ringo and Emmylou. But, since neither one of those albums did what Capitol had expected 'em to, the label decided to try something different for the third one.

So, I headed back to Nashville without any of the Buckaroos. Jimmy Bowen—who was a top-flight producer in those days—was put in charge of the album. It was sort of like my Warner Bros. days again. Nashville producer, Nashville musicians, and about half new songs written by the current hot Nashville songwriters. At that point—knowing where this one was heading—I just kinda went through the motions, but then so did the label. They put out a couple of what's called promo-only singles. What that means is they made just enough copies to send out to radio stations to see if one of 'em would catch on. The idea was that there was no need to waste money pressing up singles for the fans to buy if radio didn't put the single in heavy rotation. Well, no money was wasted.

And that's all she wrote. My second round with Capitol didn't pan out the way I'd hoped. I'm sure the folks at Capitol had hoped for more, too, but like they say, lightning seldom strikes in the same place twice.

*   *   *

I know I'm repeating myself when I say this, but no matter how hard I'd tried, making music just wasn't the same for me after Don Rich died. The joy just wasn't there anymore. I've tried to explain it to folks, but it's just about impossible to explain because I don't know if very many other people have had the kind of partnership I had with Don.

We were very different people in a lot of ways. He was always calm. I've always been kind of high-strung. He loved his scotch. I've always been a teetotaler. I worked my ass of to become a country star. He was perfectly happy to be the guy singing harmony vocals with the country star rather than becoming a big star himself. There was also that twelve-year age gap between us. So, outside of the music, we really didn't have a lot in common.

The older I've gotten, the more I've started to wonder if there really is such a thing as reincarnation—because, if there is, there's no doubt in my mind that me and Don were brothers in another lifetime. And we weren't just brothers—we were twins. You've heard about how some twins seem to have a sort of telepathy with each other. Well, that's how it was with me and Don—musical telepathy. And no matter how I searched for another person who could read my musical mind the way he could read mine and I could read his, I couldn't find anybody else like him.

So, even though the Buckaroos were incredible musicians—and still are—without Don, the fire was gone. A kind of depression had set in after his death, and I kept trying to push it away. I thought if I kept making music, everything would be all right. Then, when that third Capitol album died without so much as a whimper, I decided to hang it up.

On August 23rd, 1991, I played a show at Billy Bob's in Fort Worth. I told everybody it was my last concert. At the time, I really thought it was. My plan was to do this one last show, and then go home to Bakersfield and Jennifer, and live as happily ever after as possible.

Chapter
One Hundred and Twenty-Five

JUST WHEN I THOUGHT I was out of the business for good, I got a call from James Austin at Rhino Records in LA, telling me about how he wanted to put together a box set of a bunch of my old recordings. To my mind, Rhino was, without a doubt, the best reissue label in the business, so I told him I was interested. When I got off the phone with James, I thought, "Well, my future might not look too bright, but my past has a lot of potential."

Outside of letting the Country Music Foundation reissue my Carnegie Hall album on CD, I really hadn't done a whole lot with my old Capitol masters at that point. So, I made a deal with Rhino Records, and then me and Jim Shaw and James Austin got together and went to work. We ended up with a three-CD box set with sixty-two songs on it. The first song on the first CD was my first hit, "Second Fiddle," and the last song on the third CD was the duet of "Act Naturally" that I'd done with Ringo.

One of the real nice things that James Austin did was to get a bunch of country artists to say something about me in the booklet that came as part of the box set. Now bear with me because I don't want to leave anybody out. James got quotes from Rose Maddox, Chris Hillman, Loretta Lynn, Harlan Howard, Keith Whitley, George Jones, Ken Nelson, Hank Williams Jr, George Strait, Rodney Crowell, Marty Stuart, Ricky Van Shelton, Jerry Garcia of the Grateful Dead, Elvis Costello, Emmylou Harris, Dwight Yoakam, Randy Travis, Garth Brooks, and John Fogerty—and not one of 'em said a word about *Hee Haw*. They all talked about me and my music—and the things they said meant an awful lot to me.

The box set was called *The Buck Owens Collection (1959–1990)*. It came out in '92 and it got a lot of press and a lot of real good reviews. I felt like it was kind of the icing on the cake as far as my music career was concerned.

*   *   *

Over the years, I've made a lot of friends in the music business—everybody from Loretta Lynn to Brad Paisley, and a whole lot in between. One of my favorite artists that I came to be friends with was Roger Miller. He didn't just write and sing country songs, he also had hits on the pop charts—and before he was done, he went and wrote an award-winning Broadway musical called *Big River*.

I always enjoyed being around Roger. He had a fertile mind and he was hilarious. He was one of those guys who managed to find something funny to say about everything and everybody. He wasn't hurtful. He was just plain funny.

In 1991, word got out that he'd developed lung and throat cancer. Even in the face of that kind of adversity, Roger was still funny as hell. He'd had surgery at a hospital in LA, and when they wheeled him into his room, he asked one of the nurses to open the shades. When she pulled those shades back, there was the Pacific Ocean right outside the window. Roger looked out the window and said, "Well, I see they finally put the pool in."

I was sitting with him at one of those awards shows in '92, and I said to him, "Roger, how's your health?"

He said, "Well, Buck, they tell me they got it all."

I said, "That's just wonderful. I'm glad to hear it."

So, it was a real shock to me when I woke up a few months later, turned on the TV, and there was a newsman on, saying that Roger Miller had died.

Roger died on October 25th, 1992. I was sad and angry at the same time because I'd grown so tired of losing so many people to that terrible disease.

*   *   *

Since I considered my music career officially over in '92, I began to focus on my other businesses. By then, I'd moved everything—including my Bakersfield radio stations—into a beautiful, two-story, 32,000 square foot building on Sillect Avenue. In addition to having my radio stations, I'd also started producing three weekly publications—the *Kern*

Shopper, which is a local shopping guide that goes out to just about everybody in town. Another one is a real estate publication called *Home Preview*. Then I have a third one called *Camera Ads*. When somebody has a car or a truck or a boat for sale, they take out an ad with a photo of what they're selling. Then, every week, we distribute thousands of copies of *Camera Ads* all over the county.

It may not sound as exciting as being in the music business, but my various operations require a pretty big staff, which I believe is a good thing for this town. I wasn't born here, but Bakersfield will always be home to me, so I'm happy and proud to keep a lot of local folks employed.

Oh, I also ended up with a TV station that I hadn't really planned on owning. My sister Dorothy worked for me for decades, and when I formed Buck Owens Enterprises, I made her the vice president and general manager. Since I was on the road so much during the '60s and '70s, she was always there to take care of my businesses—and she was a real hard worker. To tell you the truth, I couldn't have done everything I did, businesswise, without her.

In 1987, she'd come to me and told me she was getting an FCC license to develop a new TV station in Bakersfield. Being her brother, before she went too far with the idea, I tried to give her some advice on how I thought she should run it. In those days, it was against FCC regulations for me to give her advice *after* the station started broadcasting because I already owned radio stations in town. Well, just like happens with brothers and sisters from time to time, she chose not to listen to me. To make a long story short, the station went bankrupt in less than two years, and I ended up having to buy it out of bankruptcy.

By 1993, then, I owned radio stations, a television station, and my three weekly publications. My businesses were all going good, and everything was running smoothly in my personal life, too.

Then, one day, I was driving along in my car. When I swallowed, something felt really, really strange in my throat—and the first thing that flashed through my mind was my old friend Roger Miller saying, "Well, Buck, they tell me they got it all."

Chapter
One Hundred and Twenty-Six

I IMMEDIATELY WENT TO SEE BOB MARSHALL, the best ear, nose, and throat doctor in Bakersfield. He looked down my throat and said, "Well, you've got something growing there, but I'm not sure what it is. We need to get a little piece of it and have it analyzed."

A couple of days later, they put me under and the doctor got a little slice of the growth and sent it to a lab. It took the first lab a week to say they couldn't tell for sure if it was cancerous or not. So, they sent it to another lab, and the second lab came back with the same answer. Now two weeks had passed. Finally, it went to a laboratory in Virginia, and after another week went by, the lab in Virginia said the tests they ran had come back positive.

If you've never had to wait three weeks for lab results, let me tell you, it was one nerve-wracking ordeal to have to go through. And when I found out—after waiting all that time—that the growth was cancerous, I ended up in a real bad frame of mind.

Since they didn't do throat cancer surgery in Bakersfield, me and Jennifer went down to UCLA. The doctor who saw me there was about six foot four and looked like a military man. He stood straight as a rod.

When we walked in and sat down, he had his back to us, looking at the lab report. Then he spun around to face me. Here he was, this really tall guy standing up over me while I'm sitting down. I was at least ten years older than him, but when he finally started talking to me, he said, "Young man, here's what I have to tell you. We're definitely going to have to get that growth out of there."

I thought, "Well, this one's got an interesting bedside manner"— but then he just started making things worse. See, the growth wasn't attached to my throat. It was attached to my tongue, way down there right where my tongue is attached to my throat. So, without warning me or anything, he said, "Sometimes in these situations we have to start by splitting your lower lip."

I thought, "Splitting my lower lip! I've got a really big lower lip. George Jones has been making fun of my lower lip for decades. What if it doesn't grow back right and one side ends up a lot lower than the other side? George will laugh his ass off."

But the doctor didn't stop there. Next he said, "And then there are occasions where we have to split the tongue."

I said, "Split the tongue!"

He said, "Yes, young man. Sometimes we have to open the tongue up so we can get down to where the growth is."

I said, "Let me get this straight. First you split the lip and then you split the tongue."

He said, "That's right, young man. Sometimes we have to do both."

I was sitting there, looking up at this guy, feeling nauseous and about ready to faint when he said, "And on rare occasions, we've also had to split the chin."

Well, when he said that, I thanked him for his time, and then me and Jennifer got the hell out of there.

I went back to Dr. Marshall and said, "Do you know somebody else who can do the surgery without splitting open my lip and my tongue and my chin?"

So, he sent me to Dr. Willard Fee at Stanford Medical Center. Dr. Fee looked in my throat and said, "This kind of surgery isn't easy, but I'm sure we won't have to split your lip or your tongue or anything else."

I said, "Well, I'm mighty glad to hear that."

He said, "We can do it by just slitting your throat."

I guess he could see from the look on my face that having my throat slit wasn't exactly the answer I'd been expecting. So, he tried to make me feel better by showing me this diagram. He said, "See, we just cut your throat along this line here, and then we'll be able to pull your tongue out through the hole in your throat, and that way we'll be able to get to the growth we need to remove."

I sat there wishing he hadn't told me anything about the procedure. As far as I was concerned, he could've just said, "We can do it without splitting open your lip and your tongue and your chin" and I would've been perfectly happy.

The surgery took place on August 17th, 1993. When they were done, I got wheeled into the first recovery room—the one they put you in before they move you on to the recovery room where you can have visitors. I was still in a fog at that point—just starting to come to. I had all sorts of tubes going in me and coming out of me. Then I looked down and saw they had my feet tied down to the bed. And then, when I tried to move my arms, I realized they had my hands bound to the bed, too.

I was lying there, sort of fading in and out of consciousness, when all of a sudden I heard somebody start yelling and screaming. I couldn't tell how close the guy was, but I knew he was in the same recovery room as me. I thought, "What on earth is going on here? For Pete's sake, can't they get that guy under control?"

I remember hearing an orderly saying, "Somebody go out and get this guy's wife so we can see if she can do anything with him."

I thought, "Yeah, would somebody please go get the guy's wife? His screaming and yelling is bugging the hell out of everybody in here."

Lo and behold, in walks Jennifer. When she came over to me, I said, "Did you hear that guy yelling and screaming?"

Jennifer just patted me on the arm as she said, "Daddy, that was you."

Chapter
One Hundred and Twenty-Seven

IN THE MONTHS AFTER MY SURGERY, I decided it was a good thing I'd retired from singing because I've never been able to speak as clearly as I could before the operation. But then, in March of '94, I got a phone call about a benefit show for my old friend, Billy Mize. Billy's the guy who'd loaned me one of his guitars after I lost mine to the pawnshop when I first moved to town.

Not long after he loaned me his guitar, Billy became a regular on just about every country music TV show there was in Bakersfield and LA. He came off so good on camera that the Academy of Country Music named him "TV Personality of the Year" three years in a row back in the '60s. Billy's a damn good songwriter, too. In fact, he wrote a big hit for Charlie Walker called "Who Will Buy the Wine" that's been recorded many, many times over the years.

Well, when they told me that Billy was recovering from a stroke and they wanted me to perform, I couldn't possibly turn 'em down, even though I didn't really know if I could still sing or not. So I played and sang at his benefit show for about a half-hour—and I found out I could sing better than I could talk.

* * *

As happy as I was with the box set that Rhino Records had put out, I was still sitting on hundreds of masters from my Capitol Records days that hadn't been released on CD yet. So, when a young man named Bob Irwin called to let me know he wanted to start putting out all of my old Capitol albums, he got my attention real fast. I asked him if he was the same Bob Irwin who had produced that great compilation of Bob Wills material for Sony. He told me that, indeed, he was, but that he also had his own label called Sundazed Music based out of Coxsackie, New York. He told me he was a big fan of mine and Don Rich's. Well, I was a big fan of that Bob Wills package he produced, so we worked out a deal. Since 1995, Bob and Sundazed have been putting out all of my old albums on CDs, with a lot of extra tracks on 'em that weren't on the original vinyl records. He even released a wonderful collection of Don's work with the Buckaroos called *Country Pickin': The Don Rich Anthology*.

* * *

On November 20th, 1995, my younger sister Dorothy passed away. She and I had always been close. Since she'd gone to work for me in 1962, I'd spent a lot more time with her than I had with any other member of my family. She'd always been there for me. Things have never been the same around the office since she's been gone. And the reason she was gone, as unbelievable as this is going to sound, is because cancer had gotten her, too. She was sixty-one years old. And once Dorothy was gone, that meant I'd lost my whole family—my dad, my mother, my brother, and both of my sisters.

I've always wondered if we might have gotten hold of something during those farming years. A lot of new chemicals came along in the early 1940s, and Lord knows we were out there breathing that stuff in all day long for years. I'll never know for sure if that's what got us, but it does seem rather odd that my daddy, my brother, and my sister all three died of cancer—and my mother, my older sister, and I had it, too.

Chapter
One Hundred and Twenty-Eight

I'VE HAD A LOT OF THINGS TO SAY ABOUT NASHVILLE in this book, and a lot of what I've said hasn't been particularly kind. Well, we've reached the part where I'm going to be nice to 'em for a little bit because in 1996, they finally decided to be nice to me.

One of the nice things they did was to induct me into the Nashville Songwriters Hall of Fame. Like I told you earlier, there was a time at the beginning of my career when nobody was much interested in buying my records, but quite a few big stars were interested in the songs I was writing. The first money I made in the music business—outside of playing live—was from writing songs that got cut by other artists. And I guess anybody in the business will tell you, about the biggest honor a country songwriter can receive is to get inducted into the Nashville Songwriters Hall of Fame.

So, on the night of September 29th, 1996, I was one of the inductees, along with Jerry Chestnut, Kenny O'Dell, my old friend Mel Tillis, and Norro Wilson. That's right—the same Norro Wilson who produced all my records when I was signed to Warner Bros. Now, Norro might not have had much luck trying to record hits with me Nashville-style, but there's no denying he's a hit songwriter. He wrote big ones for Charlie Rich, George Jones, Tammy Wynette, and a bunch of others.

As big a thrill as that night was, I had an even bigger one three nights later. That's the night I got inducted into the Country Music Hall of Fame. The other two inductees that evening were Ray Price and "The Cowboy's Sweetheart," Patsy Montana. Patsy had passed away just a few months earlier. Backstage, I told Ray Price that the Country Music Association must've finally decided to induct the two of us because they probably figured we'd be the next to go. Then I made the mistake of telling Ray I was going to go out there and say that—after being passed over for so many years—I was starting to feel like Susan Lucci. If you don't know the name, she's a soap opera actress who'd had sixteen Emmy nominations by 1996, and she hadn't won a single time in all those years.

The show was on network television, and it took place like it does every year at the Opry House in Nashville. Well, they went and inducted Ray before they inducted me, and that ol' S.O.B. went out there and used my line about Susan Lucci.

When it finally came time for me to be inducted, Dwight was there to do the honors. He told the audience the story about how he'd come to my office in '87, and how I went out and did the show with him at the fair. Then he said, "At one time he'd played Carnegie Hall, but it had been over a decade since any of us had seen him play live. He was the king of country music and the baron of Bakersfield's honky-tonk sound, but in the '70s and '80s, people were more aware of him as the cohost of *Hee Haw*. That man was Buck Owens."

Dwight might've been pouring it on a little thick, but it meant a lot to me when he said, "I'll be forever grateful to Buck Owens. His music is what inspired me to be who I am today."

Then Dwight introduced me, and when I came out, that room full of Nashville folks at the Opry House gave me a standing ovation. Me and Dwight sang a verse of "Act Naturally," and when we finished, everybody in the room stood up and applauded again. They stood and cheered for so long that I finally had to tell 'em to sit down because I knew I was only going to have a minute or so to say my piece.

I thanked Don Rich, my sister Dorothy, Ken Nelson, Harlan Howard, my sons Mike and Buddy, my nephew Mel, and Jack McFadden—and

God help me, I forgot to thank Jennifer. I still haven't forgiven myself for that.

But even though Loretta Lynn, Merle Haggard, and so many other folks who came on the scene after me had all been inducted years before I was, I was finally in. They never gave me a single CMA award while I was writing and singing all of those hits, but I guess I hung around long enough that I finally outlived Nashville's "old guard"—the ones that had refused to recognize me because I'd refused to play the game their way.

Chapter
One Hundred and Twenty-Nine

I'M GOING TO TAKE YOU BACK A FEW YEARS NOW—starting with my early days here in Bakersfield. Like I told you, back then there was a handful of taverns and honky-tonks—the Round-Up, the Lucky Spot, the Clover Club, the Blackboard, and a few others that came and went. The Blackboard—where I played for so many years—was the fanciest joint in town—and believe me, it wasn't much to look at.

As the years went by and I began to have success as a studio musician, as a songwriter, and then as a recording artist, from time to time I'd think, "This town really needs a *respectable* place for people to go to." And being a musician, I thought about how nice it'd be for the performers to have a chance to work in a place that had good lighting and a quality sound system. Like I told you before, at the Blackboard our "lighting" was two big yellow spotlights, and our "sound system" didn't even include monitors that would've let us hear ourselves on stage— and *that* was at the best club in town.

When I started having a lot of hits, I got to thinking that I should seriously consider building my own place for me and other musicians to play. I wanted to create something for the people in Bakersfield who'd been so faithful and supportive—the ones who, in those early days, had come out to any old spot I played. But I spent so much time on the road and in the studio and doing TV shows that I knew I wouldn't be able to give a place like that the kind of attention it would need. If I was going to create a venue like that, I wanted to be able to play there myself. And, of course, I'd need to be around to oversee everything—and in those days, that would've been impossible.

Since I knew it wasn't a realistic venture for me to try to develop back then, I decided the best way I could help my community was to organize charity events like the annual Toys for Tots campaign that we did for many years. I also raised money for cancer research by putting on the Buck Owens Pro-Celebrity Invitational Golf Tournament, and an event we called the Buck Owens Rodeo & Frontier Days Celebration. I'd always make time to work those events into my schedule because I knew they were important things to do. But I just wasn't home nearly enough to get serious about building and running a nightclub.

Then, when I cut back on my touring in 1980, I began to seriously formulate a plan to create this place I had in my head. I even got as far as having some preliminary plans drawn up. But when I realized what a big undertaking it would be to build what I had in mind, I started thinking I might be biting off more than I wanted to chew. I was still waffling about whether I wanted to build a venue or not when Dwight came along and kick-started my music career—so, during the '80s, I never got any further than those preliminary blueprints.

Then one morning in the early '90s, I was standing in front of the mirror shaving. All of a sudden I felt this really severe pain in my back. I looked at myself in the mirror and said, "Buck, if you're gonna build that place you've been dreaming of for half your life, you'd better get started on it pretty damn quick."

So, I got it rolling. I already knew I wanted my venue to be kind of a mixture of three of my favorite places to play—Rockefeller's in Houston; the Birchmere in Virginia; and the Crazy Horse Saloon in Santa Ana. But the other thing I wanted was to display a lot of keepsakes I had collected over the course of my career—guitars, stage outfits, photos, awards, gold records, and a lot of other memorabilia having to do with me and the music that came from Bakersfield. I wanted my place to be like a museum—but not feel like a museum. And I wanted to call it Buck Owens' Crystal Palace.

Well, of course, as happens with anything you design from the ground up, it took a lot longer than I thought it'd take, and it cost a hell of a lot more than I thought it'd cost, but it came out even better than I had imagined.

The Crystal Palace has the best of everything—from the stage lighting to the sound system to the food and drinks. On the outside it looks like an old Western town, and on the inside it's got the most beautiful bar in Bakersfield. Hanging over that bar is a Pontiac designed by Nudie Cohen. That's right—Nudie didn't just design clothes. He designed cars, too. Well, he didn't design their shape or their engine. He'd just take a regular car and turn it into a spectacle.

The Nudie car that's hanging over the bar at the Crystal Palace is one that he'd planned on presenting to Elvis Presley. It even says "ELVIS" on the spare tire cover. Nudie never got a chance to present it to Elvis, so I took it off his hands. The car has these real long steer horns on the grill, and a decorated saddle between the front and back seats. It's got pistols and rifles and chrome-plated horseshoes, and the interior has more than five hundred silver dollars worked into the design. But the way you can tell it's mine and not Elvis's is because the personalized license plates say "BUCK U2."

The Crystal Palace has got enough memorabilia in it to make a museum curator pretty jealous. It's got things like the prototype of my red, white, and blue guitar, and several of my stage outfits, including the one I wore at Carnegie Hall. It's got that first Fender Telecaster I bought used for thirty dollars—the one that still has a little piece of my comb in the nut to hold that E string in place. There are photos of me with big entertainers like John Wayne and Jackie Gleason and Dean Martin. There's stuff from my *Hee Haw* days, including a *Hee Haw* lunchbox. I always liked that lunchbox, mainly because—on the front of it—I'm wearing a jacket and tie, and Roy's wearing an old floppy hat and overalls.

The museum portion of the Crystal Palace also has items that belonged to other artists. There's one of those colorful dresses that Rose Maddox used to wear on stage, and there are several items that belonged to Don Rich—from his silver meta-flake Telecaster to his red, white, and blue fiddle. We even have that blunderbuss on display that he used to fire at the Beatle wig during our concerts in the '60s. All the display cases along the walls are filled with wonderful artifacts—just the way I'd imagined it.

I'm proud to say that the Crystal Palace turned out to be what I'd always wanted it to be—the classiest place in town. In fact, some people think it's the best country music nightclub anywhere. We had the official grand opening on October 23rd, 1996—and in 1997 it won the Academy of Country Music's award for "Nightclub of the Year."

Chapter
One Hundred and Thirty

WHEN WE OPENED THE CRYSTAL PALACE, it was like old times for me and the Buckaroos. The lineup was Jim Shaw, Doyle Curtsinger, Terry Christofferson, and Jim McCarty—the same lineup I'd had for several years by '96. In fact, those four guys have been with me longer than any other group of Buckaroos I've ever had.

Getting inducted into the Country Music Hall of Fame reminded a lot of folks that I was still around. The CMT network came to the Crystal Palace in February of '97 and shot a documentary about me called *The Life and Times of Buck Owens*. They didn't just interview me—the show included Dwight and Emmylou and Vince Gill and Joe Diffie and a whole bunch of other young stars saying nice things about me.

They also interviewed my old songwriting partner, Harlan Howard. Now, Harlan is a guy who always speaks his mind. In the documentary, he said he watched me on *Hee Haw* and thought to himself that the guy they were calling Buck Owens on TV wasn't the Buck Owens he knew. He said he knew that I was just doing my job, but that there was a lot more to me than being an emcee on what he called a "lightweight" TV show. People who don't know me very well might think I'd get upset that he'd say something like that, but he was speaking the truth.

I guess I'll always have mixed emotions about *Hee Haw*. I have too many good memories from those days to say I shouldn't have done it at all, but I know that a lot of younger people only know me from that "lightweight" TV show.

If I'm going to be remembered after I'm gone, I'd like to be remembered for my music first—and if *Hee Haw* was something folks enjoyed, then it's okay with me to be remembered for that, too. I just hope they'll keep in mind that the reason the producers asked me to be on that TV show in the first place was because they knew the viewers would want to hear my music.

*   *   *

On June 16th, 1998, Jack McFadden—the only manager I ever had—passed away from cirrhosis of the liver. He had been my manager for thirty-five years. Like I told you before, when he first became my manager he said our motto was going to be "whatever it takes." He was determined that the two of us were going to be successful in every venture we got ourselves into together—and I'm here to tell you, that's exactly what happened.

About three years after I decided to end the constant touring, Jack felt like he didn't have enough to do to keep him busy in Bakersfield anymore. So, he moved down to Nashville and opened his own company called McFadden Artists Corporation. He still managed me, but he also managed Lorrie Morgan and her husband, Keith Whitley, and several others.

One of the biggest things he did after he moved to Nashville was to discover Billy Ray Cyrus. He signed Billy Ray to his management company, and then he got Billy Ray signed to a record deal—and the first thing Billy Ray did was to go out and have one of the biggest-selling country hits of all time with "Achy Breaky Heart."

Before he left to go to Nashville, Jack said to me, "I don't know if they're gonna let me in there or not"—meaning he didn't know if Nashville would accept him after he'd spent so many years on the West Coast with me. But, he went down there and bought himself an office building right on Eighteenth Avenue, in the heart of the Nashville music scene, so the folks down there knew he meant business. They accepted him, and he was very successful down there.

And I have to tell you this: It was Jack who always used to tell me that one day he was going to see me in the Country Music Hall of Fame. I know that he was one of the voices down there who kept bringing my name up year after year, so a good part of the reason I got in was thanks to Jack McFadden. I used to tell folks that the reason they finally picked me was because they wanted to get me inducted while I was still alive. Well, after he'd campaigned so hard for it, I'm glad they went and inducted me when they did—while Jack McFadden still with us to see it happen.

Chapter
One Hundred and Thirty-One

FOR A GUY WHO WAS SUPPOSED to have stopped performing, I did a pretty bad job of staying retired in the late 1990s. Along with playing at the Crystal Palace every Friday and Saturday night, me and the Buckaroos still got out and did shows at other venues from time to time. Mostly we stayed in the state of California, but we played in Washington and Michigan and Minnesota, too.

In the old days, we would've played all those states in the same week. This time around, we didn't even play 'em in the same month. But if I felt like playing, I'd accept one of the gigs being offered to me, and we'd hit the road. We just wouldn't hit it nearly as hard as we did in the old days.

We even played at an outdoor thing called Hootenanny '98 in Orange County. Now, if you don't know anything about the annual Hootenanny event, you might think that sounds like something a bunch of folk singers should be performing at. Well, let me tell you, all the other acts on the bill that day were punk rock bands. I'm not kidding. One was called Social Distortion; one was called the Cramps; and the other one was just called X. I knew I'd been around a mighty long time when we played the Hootenanny because the audience that day was kids who could've been the kids of the kids who came to see me at the Fillmore West back in '68.

The *Los Angeles Times* wrote a review of the show, calling me "the most anticipated performer of the day." When I got a look at that crowd, I was just anticipating getting the hell out of there. But it turned out that while I'd been off the road for most of the decade, another whole new generation of fans had come along without me realizing it.

From the looks of that Hootenanny crowd, a lot of my new fans had spiked hair and more piercings than a pincushion, but they cheered after every song just as long and loud as any audience I've ever had. I'd been pretty nervous about how they might respond, but when they showed me they were really enjoying what they were hearing, I was mighty happy—happy to see that my music has continued to mean something to people, generation after generation.

In September of '98, I went down to Texas to do a show at the Cattle Barons' Ball with Dwight Yoakam. Then, the very next month, me and the Buckaroos performed a concert at the Bakersfield Convention Center. My opening acts were the Bakersfield Masterworks Chorale and the Bakersfield Symphony Orchestra. Not bad for an ol' country boy from Texas. The Bakersfield Symphony Orchestra performed works mostly by Leonard Bernstein and Aaron Copland, and then me and the Buckaroos came out and performed works mostly by Buck Owens, with that great big orchestra backing us up. I was real proud to have the opportunity to work with such great musicians right here in Bakersfield.

Speaking of Bakersfield, when I built the Crystal Palace here, the address was 2800 Pierce Road. Well, in November of '98, the city changed the name of the street from Pierce Road to Buck Owens Boulevard. These days, when folks ask me how to get to the Crystal Palace, I just tell 'em to take Highway 99 and get off at Me Boulevard. Seriously, though, I felt really honored that my adopted hometown would do something that special for me.

Chapter
One Hundred and Thirty-Two

I STILL HAVE MY RADIO STATIONS IN BAKERSFIELD, but in 1999, I sold the two I had in Phoenix. For many years, right up until the stations were sold, my son Buddy was the music director, and my son Michael was the general manager.

One of the many reasons I'm so proud of Michael and Buddy is because they took those radio stations in Phoenix and made 'em very, very popular. They also made 'em very, very profitable.

When I first started investing in radio stations, my tax advisor used to give me a hard time, complaining that none of my stations were making much money. I remember he said it was "pure folly" for me to have so much of my capital tied up in radio. I'd always say to him, "Well, at least they ain't *losin'* any money, so I'll just keep hangin' onto 'em for a while longer."

When we finally sold the two Phoenix stations in March of '99, the price tag was $142,000,000—and I'm here to tell you, my tax advisor has never uttered the phrase "pure folly" around me again.

A couple of years before I sold those radio stations, I sold my TV station—the one Dorothy had started that I ended up having to buy. Now, I wouldn't have minded if my tax advisor had called my TV station pure folly because it definitely wasn't a money-maker. It took years just to get it to the break-even point. Then one day I happened to be standing by my secretary Lee Ann's desk when she answered the phone. She looked at me and said, "This man on the telephone says he'll give you ten million dollars for your television station."

I'd put four million into the thing, and now here was somebody offering to pay me more than twice that much for a business that was barely in the black. I said, "Hang up. It's a prank call."

So, she hung up, and he called right back. Lee Ann said to me, "He says he's not kidding. He said, 'Will you please tell Mr. Owens that I'll give him ten million dollars for the television station?'"

I told her to hang up again, and I left the office for the day.

The next morning, the guy called back. I told Lee Ann to have the guy talk to Mel. Mel is my nephew—Melvin's son—who's the general manager of my radio stations here in Bakersfield. Mel talked to the guy on the phone and then came into my office and said, "This guy's for real. He's with Univision."

Well, I knew that Univision was this huge multi-billion dollar conglomeration in Mexico, so I just couldn't imagine why they'd want to pay so much for this little UHF station in Bakersfield.

Then Mel said, "By the way, now he's offering to pay eleven million."

I was sitting there thinking, "Eleven million dollars? Hell, I would've taken the ten million."

But, like I told you, going all the way back to when Bill Woods forced me to be the singer at the Blackboard, I've always been the kind of person to see if there's a little more money on the table. I hadn't been able to get a raise in pay to be both the guitar player *and* the singer at the Blackboard, but this time around I didn't have to worry about losing my job. This time around, it was just a matter of seeing how high this guy was willing to go.

Well, a few days later Mel told me the guy was now offering twelve million, but that the guy said he didn't think he could go any higher. I told Mel to tell the guy that if there was an offer on Mel's desk for fourteen million the next morning, the station was his.

Meanwhile, to tell you the truth, I'd been dying to get out of the television business. There were so many cable channels coming along by that time that I knew local stations like mine would be making less and less money in the coming years.

So, when that fourteen million dollar offer came in the next morning, I didn't just say yes—I said, "Hell, yes!"

Now I didn't tell you about me selling my radio stations and selling my television station to brag about what a great businessman I am. I told you those stories to show you that it's possible to be a musician and still have a head for business. I've heard so many country artists say they can't focus on the business aspects of their careers because it would take time away from them focusing on their art. Well, I'm here to tell you, I don't know if I'll ever make another record or not, but I still focus on my art by writing songs, and I still focus on my art every Friday and Saturday night at a place called Buck Owens' Crystal Palace.

Chapter
One Hundred and Thirty-Three

I'VE SAID IT MANY TIMES, and I'll say it here again for the record—Merle Haggard just might be the greatest all-around talent in the history of country music.

There was a time when me and Merle both lived here in Bakersfield. I tried hard—at least I feel like I did—to be friends with him, but it didn't seem like he wanted to be friends with me. The funny thing is, if you were to ask Merle, he just might say the exact same thing.

The one way we're real different is that I've always paid attention to the business end of the entertainment business, and Merle's always been more of a free spirit—but there's no doubt about his talent.

In June of '99, Merle asked me and Dwight to do a concert with him at the Kern County Fairgrounds. Now, that might sound like a natural thing to you, but Merle and I hadn't played together in over thirty years. I hadn't really thought about it until we were being interviewed by a reporter the night of the show. When the guy asked us when was the last we'd performed together, we both had to think about it—and after we ruminated over it a while, we realized we hadn't played on the same stage since the '60s.

And then that reporter went and asked the same old question people have asked me a million times. When he asked me to define the Bakersfield Sound, I said, "It's what Merle and I do."

Merle just nodded his head and said, "Good answer."

Until I sold Blue Book Music in 1984, Merle and I had a business relationship because my company published a lot of his songs. Like a lot of songwriters, Merle would ask for an advance from time to time.

Now, what a publisher will do when a songwriter comes asking for an advance is to look and see how much the writer's going to be due on his next statement. If the writer's not asking for more—or at least not too much more—than he's going to be due on his next statement, a fair publisher will give the writer the advance he's looking for, or maybe something close to what he's looking to get.

Merle was prone to asking for advances to the point that sometimes there wouldn't be hardly anything left to be paid to him when his statement was due. He wasn't the only writer I had who was that way, but it happened a lot with him.

Well, Jack McFadden came into my office one day and said, "Merle wants to sell you half of 'Sing Me Back Home.'"

Since I was Merle's publisher and already owned half of it, what Jack meant was that Merle wanted to sell me half of the songwriter's share of the song. When Jack told me what Merle wanted to do, I said, "You're kidding."

Jack said, "No, I'm not. He wants the money that bad. So, he wanted me to ask you if you'd do it."

I said, "Well, if that's really what he wants."

I was so used to Merle getting just about everything he was due in advance money that I didn't even look to see if he was owed anything on his next statement. I figured he'd already drawn up anything he had coming to him for the next pay period, so I just asked Jack how much Merle wanted. When Jack said, "He wants $16,000," I wrote the check.

Years went by, and then one day I got a letter from this attorney. It said something like, "We don't think you acted properly in buying half of 'Sing Me Back Home' from Mr. Haggard because you were his publisher and you knew how much income the song was generating."

The letter used a bunch of legal language to say that I hadn't been fair to Merle, and it went on to say that Merle wanted his song back or he was going to sue me. Well, I didn't argue with 'em. I could've put up a fight, but even though I knew what Merle and I had agreed to, I sold him back the other half of his song.

Just like Roy Clark, Merle wrote a book, too. In his book, Merle told the same story I just told you, but he told it a little different. I'm not denying I bought half of his song and sold it back to him years later. But there's one thing he said that just wasn't so. He said in his book that he found out later I had a royalty check for him on my desk for $35,000 that would've totally covered more than the amount he was asking for, but that I bought half of the song from him anyway. I don't know where on earth he got that idea from. I guess it made for a better story than just saying he sold me half of one of his songs one time and bought it back from me a few years later.

But like I said, Merle's right there at the very top when it comes to country music's greatest talents—and now every time anybody asks me to define the Bakersfield Sound, I just tell 'em the same thing I told that TV reporter back in June of '99—"It's what Merle and I do."

Chapter
One Hundred and Thirty-Four

I GUESS MY FAVORITE LANDMARK in this town has to be the famous Bakersfield sign. That old sign has been in all sorts of movies and TV shows over the years. When it was built in the '40s, it stretched all the way across what's now old Highway 99. There was a big hotel here at the time called the Bakersfield Inn. One wing of the hotel was on one side of the highway, and the other wing was on the other side. So, the owners of the hotel built this walkway over the highway, and then they put the Bakersfield sign up on both sides of that walkway so you could see it from either direction.

That sign was like a beacon to me in the old days. I can't tell you how many times I used to make that drive from Bakersfield to LA to Bakersfield—but I always knew I was almost home when I'd see that sign with those big blue capital letters coming into view.

Well, times change. When the new Highway 99 was finished, that part of Bakersfield where the sign was became a less desirable part of town. Before long, there was nobody around to do any upkeep on the sign, and it fell into disrepair. By the mid-'90s, there was talk of tearing it down because some of those state transportation bigwigs said it could be a hazard.

That sign really meant something to an awful lot of folks in Bakersfield, and I couldn't stand the thought of it not being here anymore. So, when I heard there was a campaign to try to save it, I knew I had to do what I could to help.

Well, we couldn't save the sign at its old location, but we did save a lot of the original structure, and we were able to save those beautiful blue capital letters that spell out "BAKERSFIELD." I paid to have it all moved to Sillect Avenue—where my office and our radio stations are located—and in July of '99, we had a big party to celebrate the fact that the sign had survived.

Before we did the big dedication that day, I snuck out of my office to go take a look at the folks beginning to gather for the ceremony. I was just dressed in my normal clothes—no cowboy hat or boots or any of the rest of my entertainment rig. I stood out there watching as thousands of people were arriving, and then I overheard these two elderly ladies standing near me talking to each other.

One lady said to the other one, "Now, dearie, why is it you said we should come here?"

The other old lady said, "Well, to see the sign, and to get to see Buck Owens in person."

The first old lady said, "Buck Owens?"

The second old lady said, "Yes, we're gonna see Buck Owens!"

Then the first old lady said, "Oh, I thought he was dead."

I didn't know whether to laugh or cry. I just went back to the office and put on my cowboy hat and boots and the rest of my outfit and went back out there to show that old lady and everybody else that I was still alive and well.

Chapter
One Hundred and Thirty-Five

O N AUGUST 12TH, 1999, I TURNED SEVENTY YEARS OLD. Well, you only turn seventy once—if you get there at all—so three nights later we had ourselves a hell of a party at the Crystal Palace. For the first time in many, many years, Doyle Holly, Tom Brumley, and Willie Cantu were onstage with me again. Bonnie was there, too, and so were Susan Raye and Red Simpson and JayDee Maness. We also had a lot of youngsters like Brad Paisley, Chris Hillman and Herb Pedersen, Lee Roy Parnell, Jim Lauderdale, Rick Trevino, and a whole lot of other performers, including my current lineup of Buckaroos.

I loved having all those people there to celebrate my birthday, but I would've given anything to have just one more person there with me that night. Even with all those wonderful people onstage, I still missed Don Rich.

*   *   *

We closed out the old millennium at the Crystal Palace with a big New Year's Eve celebration. Dwight Yoakam was there to usher in the year 2000 with me. Needless to say, it was the hottest ticket in town.

And speaking of Dwight, he was one of the artists they interviewed a few months later when the folks from A&E came to see us. I'm a big fan of A&E's *Biography*, so it was fun to sit down with 'em and be the subject of a show I'd always enjoyed watching.

When they interviewed Dwight, he talked about how "Streets of Bakersfield" had been his first number one song. Then, when he was describing what "Streets of Bakersfield" was about, he expressed something that I thought was real eloquent. He said, "It deals with the itinerate nature of country music—the itinerate nature of the population that came from Arkansas, Oklahoma, North Central Texas where Buck's family came from, to the West Coast—across the Continental Divide into that blindingly golden light that was the end of the rainbow."

Those folks in *The Grapes of Wrath* called their destination "the land of milk and honey," but I think Dwight described it even better. A lot of people might see Bakersfield as just another town they have to drive through on their way from Fresno to LA. But for me, it'll always be that blindingly golden light at the end of the rainbow.

Afterword

The Final Years and Continuing Legacy of Buck Owens

To PARAPHRASE DYLAN THOMAS, Buck Owens did not go gentle into that good night. According to Jim Shaw, "Jack McFadden always told us Buck wasn't going to age gracefully, and boy was he right."

Around the same time Buck was finishing the cassette recordings of his life story, his health began to deteriorate. He had developed a serious problem in his right knee while still in his late sixties, but he chose not to go under the knife again—primarily because his tongue cancer surgery had been such an unpleasant and life-altering experience.

"So," says Jim Shaw, "He started taking Vicodin—*lots* of Vicodin."

In addition to Buck's knee issues, he suffered from clinical depression—a condition he initially refused to admit because, in his own words, "I thought if people found out I'd been to a shrink, they'd say, 'Aw, that son of a bitch is crazy. I always knew he was.'"

"In his later years, Buck was terribly depressed," says Shaw. "He'd always been a mountain climber, and all of a sudden he didn't have any more mountains to climb."

Just as he had chosen Vicodin as a substitute for knee surgery, Buck developed his own method for adjusting his depression medication as well. "He was taking all different kinds of antidepressants," says Shaw. "He was taking uppers and downers simultaneously. I don't know how he lasted as long as he did. He must've been made of cast iron."

317

Not surprisingly, Buck's overuse of multiple prescription drugs began to wreak havoc on those around him. "When I tried intervention two or three times," says Shaw, "he'd be mad at me for months afterward. Part of him knew that he'd lost control, and part of him wouldn't admit to it."

Buck's inevitable personality changes brought on by the drugs were more than even Jennifer could cope with. In 2003, their twenty-four-year marriage came to an end.

As the decade rolled on, Owens was in and out of the hospital, being treated for heart arrhythmia, lung problems, and a blood clot, among other ailments. In February of 2004, he had a mild stroke, resulting in a dramatic cutback in his performance schedule.

Despite everything, in May of 2004, Buck told journalist Robert Price that he was feeling better than he had in months. By August, Buck was ready to celebrate another milestone. Over six hundred family members, friends, and fans packed into the Crystal Palace on August 10 to celebrate Buck's seventy-fifth birthday two days early. There were plenty of performers on hand as well, including Brad Paisley, Dwight Yoakam, Jim Lauderdale, Chris Hillman and Herb Pedersen, and Raul Malo of the Mavericks.

Telegrams from Toby Keith and California governor Arnold Schwarzenegger were read. There were also congratulatory phone calls from Garth Brooks and George Jones piped in over the sound system. During the call from Jones, Buck and George joked about which of the two was older. Buck also took the opportunity to remind George about a conversation they'd had in person a few years earlier when Jones was making a slightly impaired appearance at the Palace. "You were so drunk when you were here," Buck said, "You told me that *you* were *my* all-time favorite singer."

* * *

From the day of its grand opening, Buck had planned to play at the Crystal Palace every weekend he was in town. Although he kept that commitment for nearly a decade, his stroke and other health issues prevented him from being able to perform as frequently as he had originally intended. Friday, March 24, 2006, was one of those nights when he didn't feel up to playing.

After telling the Buckaroos he wouldn't be joining them onstage that evening, Buck walked out of the Crystal Palace and headed for his car, ready to drive back to his ranch for some much-needed rest. But as he was walking through the parking lot, a couple from Bend, Oregon, spotted the singer and excitedly told him they had driven over seven hundred miles to see him perform that night.

Buck Owens—a showman to the very end—turned around and went back inside his Crystal Palace, strapped on his Telecaster, and stayed on the bandstand for an hour and a half.

The final song he sang on that final night was "Big in Vegas"—the one about a man who dreams of having his name in lights, a man who dreams of getting standing ovations. For the man in the song, they are only dreams. For Buck, every dream he'd ever dreamed had come true. There were no more mountains to climb.

When the song ended, he received one last standing ovation, said good night to the crowd, and headed home.

Buck Owens passed away in his sleep in the early morning hours of March 25, 2006.

*   *   *

Unlike so many other country acts of his era, the memory and legacy of Buck Owens has not quickly and quietly faded away. Although his name will be forever linked to *Hee Haw*, it is his songs, his voice, his guitar, his *sound* that continues to resonate.

A month after his passing, the Academy of Country Music's nationally broadcast awards show featured a special segment honoring Buck's life and music.

In March of 2007, former Asleep at the Wheel vocalist Jann Browne released an album entitled *Buckin' Around: A Tribute to the Legendary Buck Owens*. Three months later, the Derailers put out *Under the Influence of Buck*. And before the year was out, Buck's most devout of devotees—Dwight Yoakam—contributed his own heartfelt homage with *Dwight Sings Buck*.

The following year, Buck was posthumously inducted into the Texas Country Music Hall of Fame. On August 12, 2008, the Minner Station Post Office in Oildale—a suburb of Bakersfield—was officially renamed the Buck Owens Post Office. That November, the Brad Paisley album *Play* was released, which included a Buck Owens composition entitled "Come On In." Using Buck's original recording of the song, Paisley created a Brad/Buck duet using the same technology Hank Williams Jr. and Natalie Cole had used when creating posthumous duets with their fathers.

One of the finest—if not most unexpected—tributes to the man came in March of 2012 when the Country Music Hall of Fame and Museum in Nashville opened a new exhibit entitled "The Bakersfield Sound: Buck Owens, Merle Haggard, and California Country."

That same year, in cooperation with the Owens estate, Los Angeles–based Omnivore Recordings began putting out previously unreleased Buck Owens material.

One day, while Jim Shaw and record producer Patrick Milligan were searching the vault for more unreleased material, Jim spotted a tape box that had previously gone unnoticed among the hundreds of tape boxes primarily comprised of the masters from Buck's years with Capitol Records. But the box Jim's eyes fell on did not say "Buck Owens" on the spine.

Years earlier, when Buck was recording his life story on his cassette machine, he spoke of his attempts to get Don Rich to make his own solo album: "I'd say, 'Don, let's go into the studio and record something on you.' We managed to get a few songs recorded, but it was like pulling teeth to try to get him to let me record a whole album of him as a solo artist.'"

On the spine of the box that Jim Shaw discovered in Buck's tape vault were the words "Don Rich Sings George Jones." Buck had, indeed, pulled enough teeth to get Don into the studio long enough to cut an entire album. It had been recorded in July of 1970, right before Buck and the band had headed back out on the road for another lengthy tour. Time passed, and Don's album was simply forgotten. As Jim Shaw points out, it's not like Don Rich would have bothered to remind anybody: "Don didn't have a lot of ambition to be a solo artist. He just wanted to read his books about military airplanes and ride his motorcycle."

Over forty years after it was recorded, Don Rich's only solo album was finally released in January of 2013.

* * *

Buck Owens' songs continue to be recorded. Fender Telecasters continue to sell by the thousands each year. When writers, critics, and other pundits discuss the most important country artists of all time, Buck's name is invariably on that list.

His influence on music reached around the world and across generational lines. The sound that he created inspired not only country artists from Merle Haggard to Dwight Yoakam and Marty Stuart to Brad Paisley, but also R&B stars like Ray Charles, as well as rock acts such as the Beatles, the Byrds, Gram Parsons, the Flying Burrito Brothers, the Eagles—even the Grateful Dead.

Because of Buck's entrepreneurial skills and the resultant financial success they afforded him, there were those in the press—and even those among his fellow country artists—who accused Buck of focusing more on his money than on his art. But on the very last night of his life, Buck Owens did not turn around and walk back into the Crystal Palace for financial gain. He went back into the Palace that final night because he wanted to please his fans. As he had said in his "Pledge to Country Music" more than forty years earlier, "Country music and country music fans have made me what I am today. And I shall not forget it."

Buck Owens never forgot.

Acknowledgments

FIRST AND FOREMOST, special thanks to the Big Three: Michael Owens, Mel Owens, and Jim Shaw. Without their guidance and support, this book could not have existed. Also, thanks to Buddy Alan Owens and Lee Ann Enns for all of their help.

Thanks to Dwight Yoakam for his preface and to Brad Paisley for his foreword. Their appreciation for Buck Owens is crystal clear, both in the words they wrote at the front of this book and in the music they make.

Thanks, as always, to my editor, Mike Edison, who once again wrestled my original manuscript into submission. Other Backbeaters who helped the cause were John Cerullo, Bernadette Malavarca, Jessica Burr, Adam Fulrath, and Mark Bergeron.

Bakersfield music expert Scott B. Bomar was kind enough to review the entire manuscript and provide me with much insight into the history of the Bakersfield scene.

Thanks to Dave Kyle for allowing me access to his interview with Buck; to Bob Irwin of Sundazed Music; and to Willie Cantu and Jan Howard for taking the time to reminisce with me about Buck.

Thanks also to Michael Gray, Carolyn Tate, John Rumble, Robert Price, Patrick Milligan, Brad Rosenberger, Cheryl Pawelski, James Austin, and Roger Deitz.

A very special thanks to my wife, Mina, for all of her love and support.

Finally, thanks to the man himself—Buck Owens.

Index